UNITED!
UNITED!

To the two JWs and the Doc's Red Army

UNITED! UNITED!

OLD TRAFFORD IN THE '70s
THE PLAYERS' STORIES

ANDY MITTEN

VSP

Published by Vision Sports Publishing in 2011

Vision Sports Publishing
19–23 High Street
Kingston upon Thames
Surrey
KT1 1LL

www.visionsp.co.uk

ISBN: 978-1-907637-21-6

Copy editing: Alex Morton
Cover design: Doug Cheeseman

Typeset by Palimpsest Book Production Limited,
Falkirk, Stirlingshire

Printed and bound by CPI Group (UK) Ltd, Croydon, CR0 4YY

A CIP Catalogue record for this book is available from the British Library

CONTENTS

INTRODUCTION

manchester United won one major honour in the 1970s. A solitary FA Cup win in 1977 may have stopped Liverpool becoming the first English club to lift the treble, but the Scousers were otherwise unquestionably the top dogs on the pitch. They won the league four times in that decade – and again in '79/80. Derby County won it twice, their neighbours Forest once. Leeds, Arsenal and Everton all became champions too. United didn't come close. Even Queens Park Rangers and Manchester City managed second-place finishes, but the best the Reds could manage was a third-place finish in 1976.

Given the success that United enjoyed before and after the Seventies, the list of final league placings seems unreal. United ended the season eighth for the first three years, then 18th, 21st, first (but in the Second Division), third (back in the top flight), sixth, tenth and ninth during the 1970s. Their average league place finish was 11th.

But the lack of titles and trophies didn't affect how the fans felt about their team, though. Today, trophies are won at Old Trafford most seasons, but United could win the European Cup every year and it still wouldn't compare to the 1970s for those Reds who were there.

That decade was their high point in being a fan, when the atmosphere was loudest, the fandom most extreme and the support most numerous and raucous. I know Reds who feel more strongly about Bobby Stokes being offside in the 1976 FA Cup final than about any issue in the world since. And there are others who retell stories of away trips when they would set off the day before the game, hitching to places like Northampton, Oxford or Ipswich.

They talk of the season in the Second Division as one of the most memorable and, because success was so rare, value that 1977 Cup win more than any other trophy in United's history.

Unlike the Eighties and Nineties, I have virtually no recollections of the events covered in this book. I was born in 1973 and only have a couple of fleeting memories. So, for me, like many Reds of my age and younger, I can only envy the experiences of older supporters and had to research the period extensively.

I was born in Park Hospital, Davyhulme. It's now called Trafford General, and the maternity ward has been shifted to Wythenshawe. Morrissey was born on the same ward, but not at the same time. Like Stephen Patrick, I spent my first formative years in Stretford just off Chester Road and less than a mile from the Stretford End.

My dad was a semi-pro footballer in Manchester. He'd been offered a trial with Leeds United at 14 after going to Elland Road with his cousin – also called Charlie. Cousin Charlie, the son of yet another Charlie, the famous United winger, was a professional footballer himself who'd started out at Old Trafford but never got beyond the reserve team. Still, he made a living as a professional, as did his brother John.

During the writing of this book, I attended the Valencia v United game at the Mestalla. David Meek, the veteran United reporter who still ghost writes Sir Alex Ferguson's programme notes and goes to European games despite being in his 80s, asked for a word. He was with David Pleat, who wanted to know if I was related to John Mitten.

Pleat, a busy man, then regaled me with stories about how the pair of them had been the main men at Exeter City. And how they'd hatched a plan to stop George Best, whose audacious

talents and maverick spirit still loom large in the thoughts of my interviewees here, when they drew Manchester United in the FA Cup in 1969. They were convinced they could do it.

"It failed," smiled Pleat nostalgically. "We lost 3-1 at home."

Dad would go on to play for the long-defunct Urmston Town, managed by the former Manchester United goalkeeper Gordon Clayton. At the time Clayton was still working at Old Trafford, and I'm delighted that his name also popped up several times in interviews for this book.

Clayton joined Manchester United on the same day as his school friend, Duncan Edwards. He was a member of United's outstanding FA Youth Cup team of 1952/53; winners of the trophy by an aggregate score of 9-3 in a two-legged final against his hometown team, Wolverhampton. The benign Midlander had played two games in goal for United but went on to spend far longer working behind the scenes at Old Trafford.

Clayton had access to The Cliff training ground at nights, where Urmston would occasionally train.

I remember going into the changing rooms where the United first team changed and marvelling at a wooden box. Someone told us that it was called a "sauna." My brother and I got in it fully clothed and sat there just like Steve Coppell would have done. We waited for the magic to happen but nothing did – as it wouldn't in a sauna which had been turned off hours before.

Every person I approached to be interviewed for this book was keen to participate, which made a change from the previous two volumes in this series. I did try and get Steve Coppell, but he seems to change his phone number every other Tuesday. Others tried to help me get hold of him, but it still wasn't possible, so any words attributed to him are from past interviews I've done with him.

Tracking down the subjects involved a great deal of travelling. The furthest journey was to McKinney, 30 miles north of Dallas, Texas. I drove 500 miles in one day to get there after watching

United play in Kansas City the previous day. I've never driven anywhere near that distance in one day in my life as I motored through Kansas, Oklahoma and Texas. The radio went from soul to sermons. For one 100-mile stretch across the Bible Belt, there wasn't a radio station without a preaching programme on it. Roadside billboards denounced abortion, while monster trucks slowed the traffic. I passed through oil towns like Tulsa and past signs for Oklahoma City – the site of the notorious bombing by Timothy McVeigh which killed 168 people in 1995.

Oklahoma turned into Texas, and the music began to change. One radio station was obsessed with Radiohead and it made a pleasant change. I stopped three or four times, but I wanted to be at Gordon Hill's house before 6pm. The former United and England winger had invited me to stay.

He was pumping footballs up in his office when I arrived. Claire, his wife of 30 years, welcomed me into their beautiful house. Within half an hour I was out again and on a playing field, Hill's English accent with the tinge of cockney standing out in the lush greenery north of Dallas.

Other players live closer to home. Stuart Pearson had spent six years living on the La Manga golf course in Murcia, Spain.

Despite spending most of his working life in Manchester, Lou Macari lives in Stoke for tragic reasons which he'll explain. Jimmy Greenhoff, the man who claimed the winning goal in the 1977 FA Cup final after Macari's shot deflected off him, lives just north of Stoke in Alsager.

Some players have little contact with their former team-mates and were difficult to track down. A chance comment by a man on a ship on the Suez Canal led me to Gerry Daly. The man, upon discovering that I wrote about United, said, "Ah, Gerry Daly plays in our local golf club most days. You're too young to remember him aren't you?"

Others have stayed in Manchester. Paddy Roche still lives in the same house in Sale that he moved to when he played for United. Sammy McIlroy spent much of his life in Urmston and Flixton

INTRODUCTION

before moving to Lymm. Martin Buchan works in Manchester as
a highly regarded executive at the PFA. Jimmy Nicholl's family
are still in Sale – where United moved the whole family during
the Troubles in Belfast in the early Seventies. Jimmy came back
down to Manchester for the weekend from his home in Scotland,
where he has worked for most of the past two decades in football
management.

Joe Jordan has lived in most British cities and several Italian
ones too. Bristol is where the Jordans have their family home,
but we met in London, where he is still employed by Tottenham
Hotspur as an assistant to Harry Redknapp. Jordan was busy
preparing his team for the visit of Manchester United two days
later, and I waited for four hours at Euston station for details of
where we would meet. Finally, he called and said, "Meet under
the information board at Liverpool Street Station." I got there as
quickly as I could, and he was waiting there for me with the stern
expression of a man with more important things to do than wait
for a journalist in a London rail terminus.

That wasn't how I expected to meet the man whose face had
adorned a poster above my top bunk in 1980. I never told Joe,
but he was my hero when I was eight, and the £1.20 poster of his
gnarled face, which I carefully saved up my pocket money to buy
from the John Menzies store in Stretford Arndale, was the first
piece of Manchester United merchandise I ever purchased.

Some needed more convincing than others. I was told that
Martin Buchan was unlikely to agree to an interview and anxiously
launched a sales pitch to him on the telephone. After eight
minutes, he said, "You've sold it to me. When do you want me
to do it?" Buchan was well worth the effort.

Jimmy Greenhoff claimed that he didn't have enough to say
to fill a three-hour interview. At the end of our extensive chat in
his front room, he smiled and said, "That was just like a lovely
conversation."

I chose a mixture of the biggest names and characters whom I
thought would have the best stories. I heard laughter and saw

tears, witnessed tense emotional moments when the words would not come and many happy reflections. I was slack-mouthed at some of the tales told and felt sympathy for others. And I still can't believe that Gerry Daly arrived to sign for Manchester United nonchalantly puffing on a cigarette.

In keeping with the theme of the Eighties and Nineties books, I only wanted to do one manager and felt that the Doc was the natural choice. Besides, Frank O'Farrell doesn't do media. Or at least I didn't think he did until I got a phone call from an Irish newspaper a few years ago. They asked for a wide-ranging interview with the former United manager. I told them that it would be a pleasure, but that he was unlikely to do it.

"Oh, that won't be a problem," came the reply. "We know his sister, and it is all sorted. Here's his phone number." Some of O'Farrell's thoughtful observations from that interview are included here.

Other important Seventies players like Arthur Albiston and Gordon McQueen featured in the Eighties book, while others not included will fit better in a planned collection about United in the Sixties.

As well as all the former players who made it possible, I had the pleasure of meeting many of their wives. Mary Brown makes great sandwiches and Claire Hill does a fine spaghetti. They've seen football from another angle and know it's not all about the glory – far from it.

My heartfelt gratitude goes out to the copy editor Joyce Woolridge, who often worked through the night at short notice, making sense of stories about things that happened four decades ago. Joyce is a Red with a fine eye for detail, especially where the Seventies are concerned. A Stretford girl who went to the 1976 Cup Final in a pair of platform sandals with red knee socks and stood crying outside afterwards, it's right to dedicate this book to her, and another JW – Jim White. Jim wore flares and stood on the Stretford too. He's been a great help and inspiration in journalism. Both JWs hollered "United! United!" until they were hoarse, just like many of you reading did. In 1974, scientists measured the noise of the Stretford End and compared it to a 747 taking off.

Sincere thanks, too, to Jim Drewett and Toby Trotman at VSP. They're as passionate about their books and authors as they are about their beloved AFC Wimbledon. When we started working together, Wimbledon's rebirth was only just underway and they were playing on pitches surrounded by ropes. Now Wimbledon are a Football League team once again, one of the great modern-day football stories. They were mildly appalled, upon reading the first drafts of this book, that Gordon Hill, who had grown up in nearby Sunbury on Thames, hadn't been spotted by Wimbledon in the Seventies. Thankfully, they employed a Red, Alex Morton, to edit the book. Cheers, ta and all that.

Thanks also to my family in Mancunia. And to my loving wife Ba and our baby daughter Olivia, who learned to crawl in front of my desk as I wrote this book. Olivia also showed her appreciation of my 600-book library – most of them about football – by trying to eat several of them. I wouldn't have been able to complete this book if Ba hadn't taken her away to do something more productive than chew-up some hard-to-find press cuttings of United games from the Seventies.

A lot of effort has gone into this book, but I hope it has been worth the time spent researching, sitting on trains, planes and motorways to meet those tight-shorted heroes of the 1970s. It was written for you, enjoy it.

Andy Mitten, Manchester,
September 2011

1

SAMMY McILROY

SUPER SAM

SAMMY McILROY

S ammy McIlroy could with some justice claim to know more about Manchester United in the 1970s than any other interviewee for this book. After joining the club as a youth player in 1969 as Matt Busby's last signing, the so-called 'Last of the Busby Babes' served under six of United's seven post-war managers. When he left for Stoke 13 years and 419 first-team appearances later in 1982, the 27-year-old midfielder was described as United's 'youngest veteran'. But his extraordinary Old Trafford career was nearly ended before it had had a chance to start.

"I hated it," remembers McIlroy. "For the first 18 months I was always looking to travel back home, hopping on a plane every three weeks or so. More than once I was tempted not to return to Manchester. I told my dad that the standard in the Irish League was good and that I could play there. He would have none of it and told me that I should stick it out in Manchester. That taxi ride back to the airport would be like going to the gallows. The taxi would go through lots of search barriers manned by troops. They would ask where I was going. I would pray for fog or the flight to be cancelled, but invariably I returned to the city where I felt like a stranger.

"I was born in East Belfast in 1954, a stone's throw from the shipyards which built the *Titanic* and Glentoran Football Club," says McIlroy. "I was the only child and I had a great upbringing. My dad – also called Sam – was an amateur footballer. All he was interested in was making me a footballer. I had a ball as a toddler and my dad always encouraged to play with it. The strongest memory that I have from my dad is his love of football. He used to give me a shilling for every goal I scored in the Mersey Street primary school football team. We had a great little side and beat one team 10-0 in a final. I scored nine and he had to give me nine shillings. I was rich at nine!

"Dad worked late hours at a bookmakers in Belfast and my mum worked at the Irish Bonding factory which made drinks."

United's legendary scout, Bob Bishop, had been keeping a close eye on the skinny prospect.

"Bishop was East Belfast as well and saw me at nine and kept watching me until I was 14," explains McIlroy. "I used to see him with his black cap, overcoat and walking boots. He walked everywhere and never took a bus. He always had a cigarette in his mouth and had no teeth. When I was 14, he approached me for the first time and asked for my address. Then he came round and spoke to my mum and dad. He told them stories about George Best and how he had been scrawny like me."

The eccentric scout bought McIlroy his first pair of proper football boots, "the ones with the steel toe caps which used to feel like they were made out of cast-iron".

Despite living in Glentoran territory, McIlroy supported their arch-rivals Linfield.

"My dad had played for their reserve team so he brought me up as a Blue. That got me in a few scrapes where I lived and I used to hide my scarf inside my coat after school. Dad would occasionally take me to Linfield's Windsor Park when he could get time off work. We'd get two buses and travel across the city."

McIlroy continued to impress at football as he moved into secondary school.

"I went to a Protestant school and we'd play against Catholic schools," he explains. "They would want to fight us if we beat them and the teachers would get involved. The kids would wait for us after the game to stone our bus. Sometimes we'd leave the pitch in our kit and get straight on the bus and away as soon as possible without showering. It was frightening."

With United, Everton and Manchester City all showing interest, Bishop asked McIlroy if he would like to travel to Manchester to play some football with United.

"I was excited, but apprehensive at leaving home," he says. "I told myself that it would only be for a week in the Easter holidays. I met George Best on my first day there and he shook my hand. I saw Denis Law too. I was frightened after those encounters, frightened. They looked like gods to me. Then I saw the United apprentices who were all much bigger than me. I felt intimidated and couldn't wait to get home."

He rang his parents on the first night in Manchester and told them that he wanted to come home.

"My dad said, 'Give it a go, you've only been there a day. Give it a go, you're only there a week."

United were impressed, and sent their chief scout, Joe Armstrong, to Belfast armed with apprentice forms. McIlroy signed and took a step closer to his dream of being a footballer, but he'd just turned 15 and his home city was descending into turmoil.

"I left Belfast in '69 when it was kicking off. I was homesick and very worried about my parents. They had no telephone so my mum would go to a neighbour who had one and call me.

"Groups were knocking on the door of my parents trying to get my dad marching. If he didn't do it then there would be consequences."

McIlroy lived "all over Manchester" in digs. "I was really home-sick," he says. "In my first digs, a little bell was rung and that was my instruction to go and eat some sandwiches downstairs. I was a fussy eater and the sandwiches were tuna. I'd never eaten tuna and left them alone."

That wasn't his only problem.

"The landlady also had a cat and I hated cats. She made me kippers for breakfast the next morning and I didn't know what they were. The cat jumped up onto my knee to get closer to them and frightened the life out of me. The landlady was not impressed and reported me to the club. I lasted a week at that house."

McIlroy would play for United's A and B teams at The Cliff.

"We'd play a lot, and my dad wanted me to call him each night to tell him how I'd done. I'd have to call Glentoran's social club where I knew he would be. He would love to hear that I'd scored. Sometimes I would tell him that I'd scored when I hadn't, just so he'd feel good. I was scoring a lot of goals, though."

McIlroy would be the only one of his age group who would make it at Old Trafford.

"I made it because of the determination of my father. I was frightened of letting him down because he would have been so disappointed in me. So after I while I thought, 'I'll give it a real go.'"

In January 1971, United played a friendly against Bohemians in Dublin.

"I was 16 and Matt Busby took me with the first-team squad," recalls McIlroy. "I came on as substitute and played with Charlton, Crerand, Kidd and Willie Morgan. Dalymount Park was absolutely packed. I scored and we won 2-0. At the end, I looked around and half my team-mates were standing by the tunnel. I couldn't work out what was going on. Even Paddy Crerand had run past me, which I'd never seen before! But then the final whistle went and thousands of fans invaded the pitch. The other players were all up the tunnel while fans smothered me and tugged at my shirt."

The United players returned to the Gresham Hotel in Dublin.

"The hotel was besieged by fans. I sat with Carlo Sartori and Tommy O'Neill and we watched the more famous players get swamped. I'd never seen that side of being a footballer before. It was a huge culture shock to me. Nobody knew who I was and I was happy being in the background, but it opened my eyes to how popular Manchester United were."

Matt Busby was impressed and went as far as to say that his latest starlet was showing the class of George Best. "My dad just said that there was only one George Best and there always will be," retorts McIlroy.

United were invited to a five-a-side tournament in London soon after and the emerging star was included with more senior players.

"We beat Chelsea 3-0 and I scored all three," he smiles. "My name was mentioned on *Grandstand*!"

McIlroy signed professional forms in August 1971 and made his debut in November of that year, in a quaint type of fixture which has long since disappeared from professional football, against Manchester City away.

"We usually played a reserve derby on the Friday night before real derbies," he explains. "The reserve coach, Bill Foulkes, told me that I wasn't playing when I got to the ground. I was gutted. I loved playing against City. He told me to report for first-team duty tomorrow and to take a collar and a tie. I thought I was being dropped from the reserves so that I could carry the first-team kit."

McIlroy turned up the next morning, but had no idea that he would be playing until four hours before kick-off.

"Frank O'Farrell, who had taken over from Matt that summer, told me that I was in because Denis Law had failed a fitness test. He told me to enjoy myself and that he'd buy me a bottle of champagne if I scored. I never drank any alcohol, let alone champagne.

"The senior players encouraged me when we all went to Davyhulme Golf Club for our pre-match meal. It was a fantastic game, 3-3," recalls McIlroy, who did score on his debut. "What a feeling that was to score in front of 63,000. Frank brought the champagne into training on Monday morning and I kept it for years."

McIlroy began to feature more in the first team, usually as a substitute.

"I started to be recognised wherever I went," he says. "People would come up to me and say, 'Are you Sammy McIlroy?' Then they would ask me what George Best was really like. I found it all a bit unnerving."

Meeting a girl, Cynthia, had helped McIlroy settle in Manchester and the couple were married in November 1972 when he was 18 and she was 19. The only turbulence in his life came when he went to work.

"United were going through a bad patch and there was a lot of pressure on Frank. We went to Crystal Palace in December 1972 and they beat us 5-0. Denis was on the bench that day and I sat with him. I couldn't believe what I was seeing – it hadn't been that long since United had won the European Cup.

"The result would be the end of Frank. I wasn't playing every week but I noticed the mood change at the club. Players were quiet when previously they had laughed and joked all the time. That journey from south London back to Manchester was the worst ever. Players were talking about a change coming. I didn't say anything."

McIlroy had sympathy for O'Farrell.

"He'd given me my debut so I liked him for that. I don't think he was given a fair crack at the job, but it was an impossible task following Sir Matt. Wilf McGuinness had had a go at managing before him and found it impossible too because players he'd played with didn't respect him being their manager."

O'Farrell's problems were numerous.

"George Best wasn't easy to handle, and Frank disappeared within himself. He should have put his side of the story across through the media, but he blocked everyone out. He was a very good manager but not everybody saw it."

Tommy Docherty took over, but McIlroy had little time to impress as near disaster struck the McIlroys in January 1972.

"We were driving down Cavendish Road in Stretford in my maroon Triumph Herald, my pride and joy," explains McIlroy. "I'd lived there in digs and loved the chippy on that road. John the chip man used to look after me and wouldn't even charge me for fish and chips. Anyway, a car shot out of a side road and smashed into us."

Firemen had to cut the couple from the crash, with Sam hospitalised.

"I was suffering from broken ribs and a collapsed lung," he explains. "I needed stitches to wounds in my head and face too. I would be out for six months. My back was sore and itchy for ages and I had no idea why – until the shards of glass embedded in it started to work their way out."

Tommy Docherty and Paddy Crerand came to see McIlroy, who was drifting in and out of consciousness for days.

"I could see that they were talking to me but I didn't know what they were saying," he explains, "but I do remember Doc saying, 'You'll get your chance, son.'

"Nevertheless, I felt that my career was under threat, although I slowly got better. The youth team used to go to Zurich for a tournament each May and I started to aim for that. Bill Foulkes tried to build me up with weights, which I hated, but he was trying to help me. One day he told me to get in a sauna – I'd never been in one in my life."

McIlroy struggled in the heat.

"I couldn't breathe," he says. "Brian Greenhoff was in there with me and he started laughing and throwing more water on the coals to make it hotter. I kicked the door open and collapsed as I tried to get my breath. It was a set-back and I was really worried about my breathing."

McIlroy went on the Switzerland tour with the rider that "there was no pressure" from Docherty, who also travelled.

"I played a few games and didn't perform well," he says. "I was well off the pace, even with the kids."

Not that the Doc seemed to mind.

"He came into the hotel bar one night and asked me if I wanted a drink. I asked for a lager and he came back from the bar grinning. I was soon all over the place after one pint. He'd slipped a 'mickey finn' [gin] into my drink."

McIlroy got to know Docherty well over the next months.

"I saw him as a flamboyant character who was a law until himself. If he liked you and you got on well together – which usually meant doing things the way the Doc demanded – then all was well and good; if you crossed him, then watch out for trouble."

McIlroy was still uncertain of his future.

"I thought that I was going to be released, though I had a year left on my contract, which ran until the end of '73/74."

The Ulsterman decided that it was his make-or-break season, but he had other worries because of the situation back home.

"Things were getting desperate in Belfast," he sighs, shaking his head. "People I'd gone to school with were dying. One of my mates got shot in the crossfire in trouble on Newtonwards Road. I had to get my mum and dad out of there."

McIlroy returned to Manchester and asked United's secretary, Les Olive, for help in getting his parents over. United paid for a house for McIlroy and his parents behind the Stretford End.

"It took time for them to settle because Manchester and Belfast are very different," he says. "But my dad got really involved in the football. He used to watch United home and away. He would meet up with mates who would drive him to games to see me play. Football helped him settle."

McIlroy was named sub for the first game of the '73/74 season.

"I didn't feel close to 100 per cent, but the Doc told me that nobody would bounce straight back to full fitness after what I'd been through. He was good with me. I didn't know him well but I'd read a lot about him, good and bad. I went from thinking that he was surely going to let me go to thinking that I had a future at United."

McIlroy's worries weren't without foundation.

"I spent a lot of time with Brian Kidd, but the Doc just didn't fancy him and let him go to Arsenal. If Kiddo didn't have a chance then what chance did I have when the turnover of players was so high?"

McIlroy would start 25 games in '73/74, more than twice that of George Best in his final season at the club.

"George was having all sorts of problems – usually of his own making and that upset me," says the fellow Belfast Boy. "He was the main man and United needed him, even though it was one rule for him and one for everyone else. He was concerned with what was happening to the side and United starting going downhill when he stopped playing."

McIlroy knew Best well.

"Because of the Troubles in Northern Ireland, when I got my first international cap the game was switched to Hull in 1971. George saw me a few days before the game and we arranged to catch the train to Hull at 9am the next day. He told me that he'd buy my ticket."

McIlroy got to Victoria Station at 8.45am. Best didn't show. For two days.

"I got off the train in Hull and the Northern Ireland manager, Terry Neill, asked where George was. I didn't want to drop George in it and was deliberately hazy. Next thing, he asked the players' opinions as to whether we should play George, even if he turns up late. I said yes but several players said no. He'd been with a beautiful girl. He played."

1973/74 ended with relegation.

"We lived a Jekyll-and-Hyde existence that season," is McIlroy's assessment of this time. "We had drawn against Liverpool and Leeds at Elland Road, but lost at home to Derby and Coventry. We won 10 games and lost 20. That's relegation form but, looking back, even though it was a tragedy, I think that relegation is the best thing that ever happened to Manchester United."

McIlroy explains why he thought this way as he eats his meal in Rio Ferdinand's Rosso restaurant in Manchester city centre.

"It was easier for the jigsaw to come together in the Second Division. Most of the old players had gone, so the Second Division was perfect for young lads like myself. We came together as a side that year and we had a wonderful team for three years."

McIlroy played 51 matches and scored ten goals.

"The atmosphere was revolutionised in the dressing room. It was a happy place and we couldn't wait for the next game. The fans followed us in huge numbers. We'd go to somewhere like Leyton Orient and there would be thousands of United fans inside and outside the ground. Expectations were high, but we were fine with them. We knew that we had to get promoted at the first attempt."

United had a hooligan problem, especially in the Second Division.

"That was a concern. The grounds were so packed that if there was trouble there was a danger that the games would be held up. The players didn't want that. The support was most intense in London. We had loads of Cockney Reds following us. We'd be sat in the dressing room at somewhere like Fulham and they'd be trying to climb in. They'd get in all kinds of scraps on the terraces. We could see the fighting during the game and then we had to get back to Euston after the match. There would be thousands of young people with red-and-white scarves tied around their arms. They'd see me and shout 'Super Sam! Super Sam!' The noise inside the train station was amplified. It was exciting, but frightening too. People would be drunk and they'd be grabbing at you. You didn't know what was coming next."

It wasn't just the Cockney Reds.

"It was like Beatlemania and the police really earned their wages holding fans back," he says. "We'd get trains back to Manchester and the fans would try and break into the players' carriage."

McIlroy had a decent relationship with the fans.

"I used to care what they thought," he says. "They travelled to support us in all weathers. I knew how much my father travelled. I appreciated their support, but they could be harsh critics. The worst time for me was after the car crash. I had to win the fans over because my performances were not good enough. I think I did that."

Such support could be a double-edged sword.

"After seeing how fanatical the fans were, there was no way that we could let them down. There was a huge buzz about United in the media too. United may have been Second Division, but we got more coverage than any First Division side. The *Manchester Evening News* was all United and you barely heard about City. The Doc helped because he had the journalists in his hand. They always knew that they'd get a headline story and that contrasted totally with Frank."

The McIlroy family moved to Flixton, a little further away from Old Trafford and a more upmarket residential area, and Sam became a father to three children, Sam Jnr, Louise and Faye.

"I lived in a club house where Bobby Charlton and Martin Buchan had lived," he explains. "Players who lived in club houses didn't really do them up. I'm not sure why, but Martin had hammered nails into the window frames. I ended up buying that house, but had to pull all the nails out."

Jimmy Nicholl was a neighbour.

"We once stayed out a bit too late and I knew I would be in trouble if I went home so I went back to Jimmy's. But his wife had disconnected the electric so that we couldn't ring the bell. I had to go home to a very unhappy wife."

McIlroy was confident that United could do well after promotion in 1975.

"We knew it would be harder, but, such was the confidence, we honestly thought we could give the league a crack," he says. "In hindsight we needed a couple of extra players."

McIlroy would enjoy another season in which he played more than 50 games.

"We had a good campaign because we were in contention for the league and the cup. We beat Derby in the semi-final of the FA Cup. We had a big lift before that game hearing that Charlie

George wasn't playing. And another when Leighton James called us a bunch of midgets in the tunnel. Charlie George heard him say that and gave him a rollocking because he thought it would spur us on. It did."

United could also count on superior support.

"We outnumbered Derby in '76 and Leeds in '77, despite both of those teams being closer to Hillsborough. Whenever I looked into the stands I saw red. Whenever I looked between the stands I saw United fans up trees. Despite being underdogs in both series, that support spurred us on to victory."

McIlroy came closest to scoring for United in the '76 final.

"I had a header which hit the underside of the bar," he recalls. "It came from a corner, a move we'd tried many times in training. Lou Macari reckons that if I had left the ball then he would have had a clean header.

"It was a terrible result when we lost the final to Southampton and there were changes at coaching level. Assistant manager Paddy Crerand had lost his job. It saddened me to see the relationship between the Doc and Paddy break down. One month they were fine, the next something was clearly wrong. I liked Paddy. Liked him as a footballer and the way he talked football."

Tommy Cavanagh became United's principal trainer.

"He was a strong-minded Scouser who wasn't for everyone. I remember poor Nicola Jovanovic, United's first foreign player, not understanding a word he said. He hounded Gary Bailey too. We [McIlroy and second wife Linda] went to Cav's funeral in 2007. He'd had Alzheimer's disease for a few years and we drove over to this beautiful church and cemetery in Yorkshire. There was hardly anyone there, which was sad."

Tommy Docherty was present.

"He's well into his 80s and he made the journey to pay his respects too. He was on great form, smiling and joking away and asking me how old my daughter was. I explained that she was my wife!"

The '77 FA Cup final was one of McIlroy's career highlights.

"Not only were we underdogs against Liverpool, but most of the country wanted them to win and become the first club to do the treble.

Comparisons were made between the two teams beforehand.

"I was compared with Ray Kennedy," he recalls. "One newspaper said, 'Kennedy works hard up front, and does a lot of chasing back. And there's the danger of his gifted left foot.'

"About me it said, "He's inconsistent – quick, skilful, capable of anything on his day, but he can also look ordinary.'

"I was the one who had the last laugh about that. There were three quarters of a million people waiting for us to bring the FA Cup to Manchester."

The cup win would be overshadowed by the news that followed as Docherty was dismissed after his affair with Mary Brown became public.

"Lawrie Brown was a pal," says McIlroy. "Should the Doc have been sacked? That's a tough one to call. He's still with Mary to this day, so it was serious. On a football level it was tragic because we were getting better and better. I think there were people in the background who were out for the Doc at Old Trafford. They were after him and they got him out."

Dave Sexton followed.

"Lovely man," says McIlroy. "Loved football and got his point across, but he hated the press, didn't want to speak to them and that backfired on him."

All along, McIlroy was learning from the managers he played under for a future career himself.

McIlroy continued to have an important role in the team. He played 48 games in '77/78 and 51 times in '78/79, the season United again reached the FA Cup final.

"Worst moment of my football life," says McIlroy when asked to talk about that the 1979 final against Arsenal. "I had tears in my eyes when the final whistle blew," he says. "I was choked with disappointment and frustration. I still annoys me to this day, over 30 years later."

He's not blaming his preparation either, despite the unorthodox nature of it.

"Lou and I went to White City dogs in London the Thursday night before the final. Dickie Davies, the suave presenter of ITV's *World of Sport*, was there. We had a curfew at 11pm, which we intended to meet. Dickie Davies told us that he was going to Tramp, a famous London club, and invited us along. I was wearing Puma pumps and jeans but we got in okay. I was worried about paparazzi being there, but we got away with it and sneaked back to the hotel."

And then there was the match.

"People talk about the late comeback, but we could have easily scored a couple of goals before Arsenal scored. Joe Jordan was giving Willie Young a real hard time of it.

"With only four minutes to go, and 2-0 down, Steve Coppell sent a cross in and Big Gordon swept it past Jennings. Two minutes later, Steve chipped a marvellous pass to send me away. I checked inside Sammy Nelson, nutmegged Walford, and slipped the ball past Jennings as he dived at my feet." It was the last minute of the FA Cup Final and McIlroy had levelled the score.

"I was certain that I had scored the goal which would take the game into extra-time. And I could see that Arsenal's players had their heads down.

"We threw it away," sighs McIlroy. "Every professional team knows that they are at their most vulnerable after they have scored. We were still savouring my equaliser, still on cloud nine instead of concentrating on stopping Arsenal. If we'd done our jobs properly we would have made sure the ball went anywhere but to an Arsenal player, and we would have killed them off in extra-time."

McIlroy's memory of those five minutes is photographic.

"I can see Arthur Albiston sitting in the ground, staring at the ball in United's net after the Alan Sunderland had struck the winner."

"We had a banquet that night and right through the meal I kept thinking about the game and going over every move. Mickey

Thomas was worse, it made him ill and he missed most of the night."

McIlroy is keen to stress how talented an outfit United were at that point, and how good dressing room spirit was with a team full of characters.

"Macari used to open Gary Bailey's mail and read out letters he was sending home to his family which mentioned personal things like Bailey complaining about his spots.

"Gordon McQueen would open the hotel room door if a maid knocked on to clean the room," says McIlroy. "He would be wearing nothing but a towel. And he'd have a cigarette in his belly button. He'd ask the maid for a light. He was a good character to have around, Gordon.

"Martin Buchan was very dry. If someone asked him if he had a comb in the dressing room, he'd say, 'Yes, thanks,' and then walk out. A journalist asked him for a quick word and he replied, 'Velocity'."

"We'd be on a train to London and it would go past Gordon Hill's house near Macclesfield," he says. "All of a sudden you would hear imaginary gun shots and see Gordon shooting his fingers against the window. I'd ask him what he was doing and he'd say, 'I've just shot four birds in my garden. I shoot them all the time.'"

McIlroy tried to help Hill.

"I could see that the other lads used to wind him up, but he didn't always help himself. He had to chip back if someone said anything. I told him to laugh things off or ignore them, but he wouldn't listen to me."

Hill was equally infuriating on the pitch.

"He was very, very talented. How many wingers get 20 goals a season? He was a great volleyer and scored unbelievable goals. He could beat a man and cross the ball well. I played inside him and I'd give him the ball and let him go, but sometimes he would frustrate you with his decision making. You'd never asked him to cover defensive duties either, but I have happy memories of him and the fans loved him.

"We had Stevie Coppell on the other wing. He wasn't the first graduate I'd played with because we had Alan Gowling at United until 1972. We called him Bamber [after Bamber Gascoigne, the host of *University Challenge*].

"Stevie got better and better. He became an England international. We were all energy in that midfield and we had fantastic touch players ahead of us like Pancho Pearson. He was hard as nails. He'd play with Jimmy Greenhoff. If you played the ball up to him it would stick. It was a masterstroke to sign him."

McIlroy also rated United's defensive line up.

"Alex Stepney was the second best organised goalkeeper that I ever played with after Pat Jennings. You could hear him in the next county as he told you what to do. He'd shout, 'Head it,' 'Hold it,' or 'Time'. I loved that from my goalkeeper.

"He had Brian Greenhoff in front of him in central defence. I'd come through the ranks with Brian, and we were friends. He had a little bit of weight trouble pre-season but had a great engine and started play from the back. He played alongside Martin Buchan. They weren't the biggest, but they always competed. Martin is one of the best defenders in United's history. His personality wasn't for everyone, but I got on well with him. He liked a pint. The whole team would go to Blackpool for a fitness break. We'd stop at a restaurant owned by one of Tommy Doc's mates on the way home near Chorley. All the players would order a soft drink and Martin would order a pint of lager. The Doc let it go because he knew that Martin always had a pint on a Thursday.

"We had Stewart Houston at left-back and then Arthur Albiston. Stewart was the organiser who got a bit of stick off the fans. He got up and down a lot for a big lad."

McIlroy played 45 games in 1978/79 and 37 a year later, but by 1981 change was underway and relations between United and their number 11 began to deteriorate.

"I had played for Northern Ireland in Sweden and had been away for ten days," explains McIlroy. "We were fog bound in London and late back to Manchester. I was shattered."

Waiting at Manchester was Jack Crompton, who was in temporary charge of United after Sexton had been dismissed. The team were going to go on a three-game post-season tour of Malaysia. It was 4th June 1981.

"I told Jack that I wanted to go home for a few hours to see my family. I told him that I would fly the next day. I couldn't face being on a plane for 11 hours. Jack said that wasn't possible."

McIlroy was checked in for a flight straight back to London for a connection to Kuala Lumpur.

"Norman Davies the kit man gave me an envelope with my spending money, £160. I sat on the plane and I really didn't want to go. I could see that the steps were still there by the plane so I got up and gave Norman the envelope back. The steward asked me where I was going and I told him I was going home. He thought that I was joking but I got off the plane."

McIlroy took a taxi home.

"I got a phone call an hour later off Jimmy Nicholl. He'd left the airport at London and so did Mickey Thomas. They weren't going on the trip. Why? Because Lou Macari dared them to do what I'd done!"

New manager Ron Atkinson, who was appointed that month, fined McIlroy two weeks wages.

"I reacted badly to that and told the club that I'd have to look at my future. That situation festered for a few months."

The £1.5 million signing of Bryan Robson in October 1981 broke the impasse.

"I knew that my place was in jeopardy and so did Ray Wilkins. Bryan signed on the pitch before we played Wolves. It could have been my last game and I just thought that I'd give it my all. We won 5-0 and I scored three. Robbo signed the match ball from, 'The costliest ever substitute'. But, even after that game, I never felt wanted at the club. The writing was on the wall. I wish I could have stayed, and Ron wanted to move me out to left wing, but my stupid pride got in the way."

In order to accommodate his record signing, Atkinson asked

McIlroy to play on the left in the following game, a League Cup match against Tottenham.

"I had words with Ron, which I shouldn't have done," he recalls. "He left Remi Moses out. I should have been happy to be picked, but I wasn't."

McIlroy, who had started seven of United's nine league games that season before Robson signed, started just one of the next six. Other clubs were alerted and Stoke City made a bid for McIlroy.

"Ron told me that Stoke had come in for me," recalls McIlroy. "Foolishly, I said that I'd speak to them. I was headstrong. It hurt my pride. Nobody had ever told me that I wasn't wanted in my career any more and I was only 28.

"Ron said, 'How much do you think you are worth, kid?' Everything was 'kid' with big Ron. I wasn't a kid and told him that."

Atkinson repeated the question and asked McIlroy what he thought he was worth.

'Nothing," replied McIlroy. "I came here as a 15-year-old for nothing and should be allowed to leave for nothing."

"No, no, no, kid," replied Atkinson. "Stoke have offered us £350,000. I can't let you leave for nothing."

A player leaving on a free transfer would be able to negotiate a far better deal for himself at any subsequent club.

"I walked out of his office and went to speak to Stoke. Arsenal and Everton had enquired about me. Shame Ron didn't tell me that at the time."

McIlroy signed for Stoke, a decision he regrets.

"I should have stayed at United and fought for my place. Ron later bought Arthur Graham who played on the left. He was the same age as me. That should have been me fighting for my place."

Stoke paid £350,000 for him in February 1982. The move had been softened by a pay rise.

"I was on more at Stoke than United, who were shocking payers," explains McIlroy, who had been on £900 a week. In contrast, Robson was on £1,900 in 1981.

"Players who came through the ranks were always playing catch up with wages," he said. That is still the case.

"Stoke were a nice little club and I initially enjoyed it there, even though it was such a wrench to leave Old Trafford."

At least he was welcomed by the fans when he returned to Old Trafford.

"I got an unbelievable reception," he says. "Then I went back into the changing room after the game and put my socks on. My feet went straight through. Macari had got in the Stoke dressing room and cut the end off my socks. The little bastard. I went to the players' lounge with no socks on."

Things went well at Stoke initially.

"We only just missed out on European football in my first year there. We had players like Mickey Thomas, Mark Chamberlain, Steve Bould and Paul Bracewell. Our manager, Richie Barker, then went to Lilleshall and then came back having decided that we should play a different way. He told me that he would extend my career by five years. I was to play just in front of the back four. I spent games watching aeroplanes, the ball was in the air so much. It wasn't working and I told him. He ended up getting sacked, which was a shame because he was a nice man."

That was before McIlroy produced a Man of the Match performance for Stoke against United around Christmas 1984. United would have gone top of the table had they won rather than losing 2-1 to McIlroy's side. That was a rare victory as Stoke were relegated later that season with the lowest points total in First Division history.

"The caretaker manager told me that the club couldn't afford to keep me in the Second Division," explains McIlroy. "They gave me a free transfer which was a kind gesture."

In the summer of 1985, the two Albions, Brighton and West Bromwich, came in for McIlroy along with Manchester City.

"I met City manager Billy McNeill in the Bowdon Hotel. He was so enthusiastic and I was really impressed by him that I agreed to join City without speaking to the other two. Staying in Manchester was an advantage but joining City was a big mistake. They didn't have enough quality players to do well in the top flight and I was disappointed with Billy and the way he dealt with me."

The crowd didn't help.

"I was booed by a section of the crowd as I warmed up before I'd even kicked a ball. They were shouting 'Busby this and Busby that' and were giving me flak because I'd played at United for so long. They had some awful songs, damaged my car and it really got to me. I had problems with my Achilles tendon too. Billy's solution was to put me in the reserves."

A brief move to Sweden followed in 1986.

"I went to Gothenburg to play for the then Swedish champions, Orgryte IS. I had the chance to play in the European Cup with them, something I'd always wanted to do with United. We played against Dynamo Dresden and got beat. I stayed in Sweden for six months and would have been happy to stay longer, but my father became poorly and I came home."

McIlroy's parents both passed away within three months of each other in 1986. They'd seen their son play 419 times for Manchester United, which still puts him in the all-time top 20 ahead of Denis Law, Peter Schmeichel, David Beckham and Paddy Crerand. His 71 goals put him 28th in United's all-time goalscorers' chart at the time of writing. He'd also represented his country in two World Cup finals on the way to winning 88 Northern Ireland caps.

"89," he corrects. "It's in all the books that I played 88, but they didn't include a friendly I played against France."

"I made my debut for my country at 17 and loved it. They were an old side when I started and we would get hammered five or six wherever we went until Danny Blanchflower took charge. Later, under Billy Bingham we reached two World Cup finals and won the Home International tournament twice. They were incredible achievements give the size of our country."

McIlroy had loved Spain '82 and Mexico '86.

"Wonderful experiences, both of them," he says. "It gave something back to the people after all the troubles they'd had over there. For a while we matched the great teams. We beat West Germany, Portugal and France. Only Holland beat us at Windsor Park. We always played with great passion for Northern Ireland. You could have nine donkeys playing, but if they displayed the passion we had then it was worth something."

Spain '82 was a highlight.

"Can you imagine beating Spain in Spain?"

Unfortunately, his third World Cup tournament was marred by personal tragedy. "My mum died when I was at Mexico '86," he says. "I was completely heartbroken, totally heartbroken, devastated."

His room-mate Jimmy Nicholl had a solution.

"Let's go to a bar," he said, "you need a drink."

"But we can't leave the hotel," replied McIlroy. "There's security everywhere."

Nicholl knew better. The two soon found themselves ensconced in a Mexican bar along with Norman Whiteside. Pitchers of lager were ordered.

"I couldn't speak by the end of the night," recalls McIlroy, "I had gone. Jimmy, Big Norman and Billy Hamilton were still going strong. I flew home the next morning for the funeral."

McIlroy moved to Bury that summer.

"I had a couple of years with Bury before signing for an Austrian team, Admira Wacker. That was a mistake. They painted a picture that we would be playing class opponents like Austria Vienna and Rapid Vienna. Austrian football was doing well and Rapid had been runners up to Everton in the 1985 Cup Winners' Cup final. We did play against those sides – and got hammered by them. I couldn't believe how bad the standard of the other players or the training was. I knew I had to get out of there one week into a two-year contract. I lasted three months."

He finished his career at Preston North End aged 35 in 1991.

"I could have gone on longer if my Achilles hadn't been so problematic," he says. "It's the type of injury that could be treated routinely now."

McIlroy moved into management after former United goal-keeper Gordon Clayton got him the job at Northwich Victoria.

"Norman Whiteside was my physio and Gordon Clayton my assistant," he says. "Gordon was helping me with management because he had more experience than me. He came in to see me in the clubhouse after one game with the plans for the next match. I tried to buy him a pint and he complained of terrible indigestion and said no. That was the first time he'd refused a drink. He died that night."

After a brief spell at Ashton United, McIlroy took over at Macclesfield Town in 1993. Until then Macclesfield had spent their entire history playing non-league football.

In six short years he took the Silkmen from being within a game of being relegated to a league where the average crowd was 400, to playing a league fixture in front of over 30,000 against neighbours Manchester City.

McIlroy found a club in a mess. With assistant Gil Prescott, he scouted hundreds of semi-professional players. His team finished seventh, before winning the Conference a year later, yet they were denied entry to the Football League because the Moss Rose home didn't make the grade when it had been inspected eight months earlier. Macc were outraged. Their stadium had staged league football with Chester City as residents and was refurbished to the required standard by the time the league was won. Chairman Arthur Jones took the news so badly that he shot himself.

"My chairman had spent an awful lot of his money doing the ground up, and denying us promotion hurt him badly," explains McIlroy.

While Macclesfield's financial position worsened after the death of Jones, their team spirit was indomitable. Refusing offers from Norwich City and Notts County, McIlroy kept his side together. They won the FA Trophy in 1996 and the Conference a year later – by which time their ground had been passed fit.

"It was by some distance the best performance I've ever seen in non-league," buzzed McIlroy.

Macclesfield were promoted again the following season. But, after turning down many offers to go elsewhere, McIlroy moved to take the Northern Ireland job in 2000.

"You can't turn down your country, and the first two years were great, but then important players like Neil Lennon, Jim Magilton and Michael Hughes retired and I was caught in politics of people behind the scenes."

McIlroy resigned and re-entered club management with Stockport County. He then went to Morecambe as assistant manager before taking over as manager. Again, McIlroy led a non-league team into the Football League despite the club's limited resources and the difficulty attracting with players who felt they would be playing in a backwater if they signed. McIlroy defied those odds, established the Shrimps in the Football League and oversaw the move to a new stadium in 2010. His only crime was raising the hopes in a town not renowned for football to a level that became unrealistic. He left after "five great years and one difficult one" by mutual consent in May 2011.

He's stayed living in the North West in Lymm, Cheshire, and married second wife, Linda, in 2003.

"We played a Barry White song at the wedding. He died later that night! Luckily, that's not been a bad omen.

"I've had a great life in football, but United was the best time of my career by a mile," he reminisces. "I still see a lot of the lads through MUTV and get the odd text off Big Norm wanting to go out for a drink. He's great company, but I try and stay clear of that one!"

2

MARTIN BUCHAN

THE CAPTAIN

MARTIN BUCHAN

" **I** twatted one of the players and gave him a bloody nose. He started it! The guy was knocking on my door for a free transfer from the moment I arrived. He'd been stitched up by the previous manager, but that wasn't my fault." Martin Buchan stands up in his office at the PFA headquarters in Manchester where he serves as an executive and re-enacts the fight, miming imaginary punches.

"He made a nuisance of himself – if I asked him to play the ball right in training then he'd play it left. He came into my office one day demanding a free transfer and shouting and swearing in front of the chief scout. The chief scout looked at the player and said, 'The manager has been very honest with you. I've never seen a manager be so honest.'

"The player looked back at him and said, 'What the fuck has it got to do with you?'

"I politely asked him to leave. Twice. He refused so I started steering him to the door, but he threw a punch, which caught me. I punched him straight back in the nose.

"Something in my head said, 'Don't mark him' but I gave him a right good doing. I was hyperventilating, so I went to splash cold water on my face. I went back into my office and the chief scout was pissing himself. It wouldn't have hurt my reputation with the players because they wouldn't have messed with me, as I discovered when I had a meeting with another player a couple of minutes later. He was as white as a ghost. He'd seen the battered player and was worried that I'd do the same to him.

"We had a board meeting a couple of days later. The player had given the chairman a letter complaining. I explained my side of the story, and they agreed to stand by me. A few days later I packed it in. I'd never fought with players when I played football so what was I doing fighting with them as a manager? I didn't need it, so I took a walk after four months. The fight never got in the press."

Buchan's explanation of why he only made a brief foray into football management at Fourth Division Burnley when he finished as a player is at odds with his reputation as one of the United players who always maintained grace under pressure. A flag at Wembley in '77 read: 'The Fonz is cool, but Buchan is cooler'. Not that the cultured Buchan understood it, because he never watched that type of show. But there were rare occasions when his accustomed calm would desert him and he would suddenly explode.

Buchan sits down and starts to talk about growing up in Aberdeen, the city where he was born in 1949.

"I had a very happy childhood. We lived on a council estate on the outskirts of the city. My younger brother, George, was 14 months younger than me and we played together in our primary school team which wore black shirts and black shorts. We won the league one year without conceding a goal."

Buchan senior started out as an inside-forward.

"I'd lost a bit of pace by the time I was 10 and was moved back.

We always played the final of the cup competition at Aberdeen's ground and that was my first experience of the big time."

Aged 12, Buchan began training with Banks o' Dee, an unofficial nursery club for Aberdeen. He later signed schoolboy forms with Aberdeen, but not before passing his 11-plus and winning a place at the prestigious Robert Gordon College – a rugby-playing school.

"It was probably the top school in the north east of Scotland," he explains. "The top achievers in the 11-plus would get a bursary. I was soon mixing with the sons of doctors and lawyers."

Buchan's father had combined playing part-time for Aberdeen with being a riveter in a shipyard.

"My dad played with Dundee United too, before a knee injury meant he ended up at Buckie Thistle in the Highland League. He was top scorer there, a quick player on the lines of Jimmy Greaves."

Buchan could play rugby, but wouldn't turn out for the school team on a Saturday morning because he feared getting injured and missing out on football.

Buchan had little choice but to become an Aberdeen supporter.

"Aberdeen was all we had. After them, the nearest club was 66 miles away in Dundee."

North Sea oil was discovered in 1969, and Aberdeen became a boom town. Not that the Buchans profited from it.

"If my dad ever wanted to take my mum out for a meal he would be paying oilman's prices. The only people who did well in Aberdeen were those who had money to invest in property or commerce. The locals didn't benefit."

Buchan's grades in his Scottish Highers (the equivalent of A levels) were sufficient to get him a place at university. A top grade in Spanish was later boosted by lessons which made him proficient in Castilian, but his plans to go to university were scuppered when the Aberdeen manager asked him to go full-time at 17.

"I sat down with my mum and dad. They didn't want me to give up my education, but left the decision to me. We decided that I would give football a go and if I hadn't made it by the time I was 21 then I'd go and study at university. I would have studied architecture."

Buchan did a full pre-season and made his debut in October 1966.

"It was on 6th October against Dunfermline," he says matter-of-factly. "I played four times in my first season. In those days man marking was in vogue. Scotland was full of clever inside-forwards – play makers. I was asked to man mark several of them. I was good at it. I had a bit of pace and read the game quite well."

Aberdeen went to Washington DC in the close season of 1967.

"America was trying to establish a league, and whole teams were imported to cities and given names. Aberdeen were called the Washington Whips. Hibs played in Toronto, a Brazilian team in Houston, a Uruguayan team in New York and Wolves played in Los Angeles. We were there for six or seven weeks and won the Eastern League. It was wonderful, a big adventure. I'd studied art at school and used any free time to visit the Smithsonian Art Institute in Washington."

Football continued to give Buchan a chance to extend his cultural knowledge.

"For the next three or four seasons Aberdeen played pre-season in Holland or Germany. I went to art galleries and saw the Rembrandts. None of the other players came with me. After seeing how they worked for a few years I came to the conclusion that footballers only saw airports, stadia, hotels and discos. I wasn't a fan of discos where you couldn't hear what people were saying."

Buchan was established in the Aberdeen team and life was good, but near disaster struck in the summer of 1968.

"I drove to see a friend who had a testimonial game in Inverness at the end of the season. I'd been offered a place on a coach, but wanted to drive. I spent all season travelling on coaches and anyway, I'd bought a mini, which became my pride and joy. The milometer had been clocked back, but I didn't know that.

"I was with a mate who had had a few beers after the game. I was teetotal back then, but I offered a lift back to one of the referees who lived on the way to Aberdeen. I dropped him off and got lost. My mate was drunk and of no use. I'd left my maps in Aberdeen and of course there were no mobile phones in those days. Then there was a snow storm – in May! – and the sheep came to the side of the road to shelter. I fell asleep about 30 miles from Aberdeen and crashed."

Buchan's mini had spun off the road and into a stream. "I broke my ankle, and my mate was lying in the car in a ditch in a drunken stupor in some pain," he says. "I could see a farmhouse about a mile up the road. I tried to walk there, but then a car which had been coming in the other direction from Aberdeen stopped. They were two lads who were going out fishing at four in the morning."

The driver recognised Buchan.

"They took us both back into Aberdeen. I offered to report the accident from the first phone box we passed, but they said, 'No, if you've had a drink then report it in the morning.' I hadn't had a drop."

Buchan's injury meant he missed the first 11 weeks of the next season, and there was a postscript to the accident years later when he went for his Manchester United medical.

"Doctor McEwan, who still goes to games at Old Trafford, did the medical. I told him about my previous injuries like the ankle and how I'd also broken my collarbone at school.

"'I can see that,' he said, having studied the X-rays. 'Anything else?'

'No.'

'When did you break your ribs?'

'I didn't. I haven't.'

'You have.'"

Buchan must have broken them during the car crash and never realised.

"At this time Aberdeen were the second best team in Scotland after Celtic," states Buchan. "Eddie Turnbull was the coach. He'd played for Hibs when they had their 'Famous Five' forward line. Turnbull was the best coach that I ever worked with – he was a million miles ahead of the rest, the best that ever drew breath. He handed out 17 free transfers when he took over at Aberdeen. Pittodrie was transformed from a rest home for ageing pros from Southern Scotland."

Turnbull made Buchan captain in 1970.

"I'd broken my leg and was coming back. I passed the team sheet for the reserves one day and saw my name on it. I told Eddie that I wasn't ready.

'I know you're not,' he said, 'but I want you to get a shirt back over your head'."

During the game Buchan went in for a 50/50 in a challenge with "a man mountain". He came through it and went on from there.

In the Scottish Cup final Aberdeen beat a Celtic team who had been good enough to reach the European Cup final in 1970. The crowd at Hampden Park was a paltry 108,000.

"We played Juventus, who included Fabio Capello, in the Cup Winners' Cup in 1971. They had some team. We lost 2-0 away, then drew 1-1 at home."

Buchan was playing for Scotland's under-23 team "in six inches of mud" at Derby in 1972 when he found out that United were interested.

"Aberdeen's manager, Jimmy Bonthrone, [Turnbull had gone on to his first love Hibs] told me that three clubs had expressed an interest after that game, Leeds, Liverpool and Man United," says Buchan. "Man United wanted to talk to me, and Aberdeen needed the money after a fire had burned down half the stand."

Buchan packed his overnight bag and travelled south to meet the United delegation at a hotel in Belshill near Glasgow, where Sir Matt Busby's mother lived.

"Matt Busby came to see me, accompanied by manager Frank O'Farrell, secretary Les Olive and coach John Aston. O'Farrell explained that he was building a new United and that he wanted me to be part of it.

"It was explained to me that David Sadler was having problems with his knees and so I'd be replacing him. I could see a first-team place. I had looked at Leeds and there was Norman Hunter in my position. I looked at Liverpool and there were Emlyn Hughes and Tommy Smith. People later said to me, 'If you'd gone to Liverpool you could have won all those trophies'. That was true, but they could have been Central League [reserve league] medals because I might never have made it at Anfield."

United offered £110 a week for the player who was now a Scotland international and who had made 134 appearances for the Dons.

"Money wasn't my priority. I'd been on £40 at Aberdeen. I was also to get £1,000 in bonuses regardless of how I did at Old Trafford. Not to mention a £6,500 signing on fee, paid over three years. I told them that I would make a phone call and went to speak to Eddie Turnbull. He said, 'Go, it's a great opportunity for ye'. I wanted him to say that. I'd pretended to be Law – the city's most famous football son – Best and Charlton on a street in Aberdeen as a kid. Now I was to play alongside them. I agreed to sign."

Law wasn't the only Aberdeen-born footballer to end up at Old Trafford. Alex Dawson, John Fitzpatrick, Graeme Hogg, Ian Moir and Thirties star George Mutch all came from the Granite City.

United had offered £125,000 – a record fee surpassing those of Law and Willie Morgan.

"Aberdeen snapped their hands off," says Buchan. "I subsequently found out that United would have gone to £150,000."

He was United's record signing, but not for long.

"Much to my relief, Ian Storey-Moore topped that a few days later with a £180,000 transfer from Nottingham Forest."

Buchan would be a far bigger success at Old Trafford than Storey-Moore.

From the meeting in a Belshill hotel, Buchan travelled immediately to the North East.

"United had an FA Cup replay at Middlesbrough which had to

be played in the afternoon because there was a ban against using floodlights."

He made his debut the following Saturday at Spurs on 4th March 1972.

"I was up against Gilzean and Chivers – a man mountain but a gentle giant with it."

United lost 2-0 and would finish that season eighth in the league.

"When I joined United it was a curious mixture of legends and players who would not have got a game in Aberdeen's reserve team. It was that bad. I couldn't believe how bad the defence was."

United's new centre-half stood out in training.

"Paddy Crerand took me for my first session and timed me making 40 yards runs. He had to look twice at his watch because he couldn't believe the times I was doing. But what I was doing was normal in Aberdeen."

Buchan moved to a club-owned house in Davyhulme with his wife while he looked for a place to buy in Sale.

"We were gazumped on our first house before buying a place in Brooklands. Well, you'd call it Brooklands if you were posh, but it was actually Baguley, Manchester 23. My nearest neighbour was Stewart Houston, and we'd go for a pint in the Woodcourt."

He'd just turned 23.

"I met my first wife in a pub near Aberdeen airport. She was working behind the bar. I was the local hero, the captain of the team. I went to the pub to present a cheque for £3,000 to a Mrs Patterson who'd won a spot the ball competition in the *Green Un*, the Aberdeen equivalent of the *Pink* [Manchester's now-defunct Saturday football newspaper, printed, as its name suggests, on pink paper]. She owned the pub."

Buchan's eye was caught by the barmaid.

"I asked Mrs Patterson where the barmaid worked during the daytime. I'd never done anything like that before. She told me that she worked at the dentists in Crown Street. I looked in the

Yellow Pages and rang the dentist to ask her out for a drink. She agreed. I also found out that she lived in the pub!

"Mrs Patterson could have easily said, 'She lives upstairs because her dad owns the pub.'

The captain of Aberdeen would spend a lot of his free time in the living quarters of the pub with his future wife.

"A bell would ring during busy times and my girlfriend would go down and help serve. I would help out and take orders, do a bit of a work as a waiter. I was allowed to pull a pint one day too."

Buchan and his wife settled immediately in Manchester, where he steadily became one of United's most influential players, only missing one or two league games over the following five years, but he agrees the club he joined was a troubled one.

"Too much time was taken to break up the '68 European Cup winners," he opines. "There was too much loyalty shown to some of the older players – though some of them could still have played, like Bobby Charlton. He was a fit man and could have played longer, but I think Bobby was heartbroken by what was happening to his club."

United's slide began almost as soon as the club won the European Cup in 1968. In successive seasons the club finished 11th, eighth, eighth and, in '72/73, 18th. By that time, the team was an ageing and transitional one which failed to win until the tenth league game of the season. Frank O'Farrell had been in charge since 1971.

"I was very impressed with Frank when I saw him on TV, but I don't think he gave [coach] Malcolm Musgrove enough authority," says Buchan. "And while Sir Matt used to say 'go out and enjoy yourselves', he had had the luxury of having so many match-winning players in his team that he could give them free rein. The problem was that after 1966 – when England won the World Cup playing 4-3-3 with a system Alf Ramsey thought was best suited to his players – all of a sudden every team started playing 4-3-3 and tactics became more of an issue. A lot of the older players at United didn't want to be organised because they'd never been organised."

Personal issues also got in the way.

"We signed a goal machine called Ted McDougall, but he never got the service. Players wouldn't cross the ball to Ted – it was personal. Ted was a good player. He tore us apart in a pre-season game playing for Bournemouth."

United were destroyed 5-0 at Crystal Palace on 16th December 1972 and this humiliating defeat signalled the end for O'Farrell.

"Don Rogers ran riot," recalls Buchan. "But by that time Frank had lost the dressing room. Whatever ideas he had, most of the older players did not want to hear him. I had a sense of loyalty to him because he'd signed me. I trusted Frank, he was an honest man, but Frank O'Farrell lost his job on Davyhulme golf course."

Matt Busby used to play golf with several senior players, usually including Willie Morgan. Despite Buchan's beliefs, to what extent they influenced Busby is debateable.

Glorious as it was, Sir Matt Busby's 1968 European Cup victory cast a shadow over his successors for years to come. It is often said that when the newly knighted Busby retired in 1969, he left an ageing and declining team. But this is only true to a point. Foulkes, Charlton, Crerand, Brennan and Law were the wrong side of 30, but at 28, Stepney, Dunne and Stiles were in their prime; Aston, Kidd, record new buy Willie Morgan, and Best, the finest player Britain has ever seen, were good for years to come. The problem was that the drive, the ambition, the aim of the club, had been to conquer Europe for Busby and the boys who had perished at Munich. And once this had been achieved, the impetus diminished.

Whoever followed Sir Matt was going to have a difficult task. But (and this might be the lesson from history that those arguing about Sir Alex Ferguson's future replacement have failed to take into account) the men chosen for the job would in all probability have been unequal to such a massive task whether the old man had been on the other side of the world, never mind upstairs, willing to offer advice. The first nominee, Wilf McGuiness, lost his hair in the attempt. His successor was Frank O'Farrell, from Cork, the first Irishman and so far only Irish manager of Manchester United.

O'Farrell, a former West Ham player and member of the so-called West Ham Academy, whose members famously discussed tactics in Cassatari's cafe and included Dave Sexton, Malcolm Allison and others, had impressed in all his previous managerial jobs. When O'Farrell arrived at Leicester City in 1968 the club were on their way out of the First Division. He rebuilt them and took the Foxes to the 1969 FA Cup final where they lost to Manchester City. Leicester were then promoted back to the First Division, winning the Second Division title in 1971. O'Farrell was in negotiation with the East Midlands club for a new contract when Manchester United approached the 45-year-old in 1971.

With Jock Stein and Dave Sexton both turning down the United job, he hadn't been the United board's first choice, but he was considered bright, honourable, well behaved and tough.

"Matt [Busby] came to my house in Leicester one Saturday and offered me the job undercover," O'Farrell recalled when he spoke to the author in 2007. "United offered me £12,000 a year and I could probably have got that at Leicester – £15,000 was the going rate for a First Division manager. Matt told me that there was work to be done at Old Trafford and that it would take three to five years to sort it out. He offered me a five-year deal, plus bonuses. I was flattered and asked for a few days to talk it over with my wife.

"I rang Matt back and we agreed to meet at a hotel near Derby a few days later. Matt turned up in a Rolls Royce with [United's then chairman] Louis Edwards. Matt was nervous that there were people around and that we would be spotted together. So we went down a 'B' road and pulled up in a lay-by. It was all very surreal. I asked Matt to repeat the offer he had made to me on

Saturday. He did. Louis interrupted and said: 'No, Matt it's £15,000'. So, by not saying 'yes' on Saturday I was £3,000 better off.

"The question was why Matt had wanted me on the cheap and there was always a question mark in my mind about him. The Board had agreed £15,000 for a new man and he only offered me £12,000. That seemed strange but I accepted the job – for £15,000.

"Old Trafford was big. I was impressed by the size of the place. They were building a new stand with executive boxes."

On his first day O'Farrell decided to grasp his first nettle. "Matt was working from what had always been the manager's office," he explains. "He said that a new office was being built for the new manager. But I was uneasy with that and said to Matt. 'Before I came here the press were speculating that no-one would come here because you would still be here. It will be symbolic if I don't use what is regarded as the manager's office.' I said it in a polite way and I had to say it. I was impressed by him but I wasn't overawed and I was confident in myself. Matt relented and moved his stuff out.

"I'm quite a polite person but if I have to say something I'll say it. Jimmy Murphy, who had been treated very badly when he left the club, asked me how I had shifted Matt out of his office and I said that it was important that I was recognised as the manager. On that count you could say that we got off on a bad footing. I wasn't anybody's fool, but it was symbolic and important."

O'Farrell's Old Trafford tenure started well, in terms of results anyway. In his first season at Old Trafford, 1971/72, United won all but two of their first 20 league games and headed the First Division by five points at Christmas. This lead was achieved without a single signing, but by reorganising the existing players and giving a few young players, including Belfast-born Sammy McIlroy, their debuts.

"The results were an illusion though," insisted O'Farrell. "When

I looked at the team I thought that their reputations were better than their performances. George Best was a genius though, easily the team's best player."

O'Farrell increased Best's wages to give him the financial parity with Denis Law and Bobby Charlton. Best repaid O'Farrell by frequently absconding from club duty as his private life became ever more indulgent. "I dropped him on more than one occasion and he would invariably score two goals on his return," admits O'Farrell.

O'Farrell requested other changes which he viewed as progress. "The problem was that, whilst Louis Edwards was chairman, Matt was the real power behind the throne."

That wasn't a problem when United were winning. "Matt had a column in the *Express* and he wrote that I was probably the best signing he had ever made. That was after six months," says O'Farrell.

It was, however, a problem when United stopped winning, and they registered just two more league victories after 1st January. In February 1972 Leeds humiliated United 5-1 at Elland Road. Best later went AWOL from training, claiming to be in Belfast, terrified about the safety of his family during the Troubles.

"Unfortunately for George, I was actually in Belfast myself discussing a move to Manchester with George's parents," remarked O'Farrell wryly.

What was clear was that an ageing United side needed radical surgery, especially in front of goal. As Buchan pointed out, Ted MacDougall from Third Division Bournemouth wasn't given much help to make the step up to the higher level of First Division football. Wyn Davies from Manchester City did no better. Ian Storey-Moore's career was truncated by injury. But Frank O'Farrell did spot one gem, buying Buchan.

"Martin was intelligent and had the right attitude," said O'Farrell of his captain, "and he gave United 15 years service. Martin wasn't always popular with the other players, though, because he played his guitar and learned languages. I liked him because he was different. He was a good player and a family man and I enjoyed his company. After the trouble I had suffered with George Best, Buchan was a breath of fresh air."

O'Farrell preferred meeting supporters and promoting the club to the social drinking and playing golf with Matt and the lads. There was an inner clique at Manchester United and neither the manager nor the club captain were part of it. They were outsiders at their own club.

Results failed to improve and O'Farrell's relationship with Busby became more strained.

"At one club function, after a few drinks, Matt said to my wife, 'Your husband is an independent sod, why don't you get him to talk to me?' I invited Matt for a coffee in my office the following Monday, as I did most Mondays. I didn't sit at my desk and look down at him or anything like that, but I asked him about what he had said to my wife.

"Matt mumbled on before saying, 'I didn't think you should have dropped Bobby Charlton.' With that Matt was interfering with my team. He also said, 'I don't think Martin Buchan is playing so well.' He was picking on Martin Buchan who wasn't playing badly at all. From then on it was only a matter of time before the situation disintegrated. He shouldn't have gone to my wife."

The early form in the 1972/73 season was disappointing, and then came that 5-0 defeat to Crystal Palace.

"I got sacked in Christmas week, 19th December 1972," stated O'Farrell. Unaware that the board had already made up their mind about O'Farrell, David Meek wrote an article entitled 'Be Fair To Frank' in the *Manchester Evening News*. The club thought that Meek was being deliberately cunning and banned him indefinitely from travelling to matches on the team coach. No reporter has been on it since.

"I had to sue United for breach of contract as I had three and a half years left," remembers O'Farrell. "I had to sign on the dole at Salford Labour Exchange for the first time in my life too. That felt embarrassing, humiliating, as I'd never been on the dole in my life. The manager of the Labour Exchange could see my embarrassment and used to let me in the back door.

"United took nine months to pay up my contract. I had to get a solicitor and then a QC. I'd seen the judges' influence on the Manchester United board and I was worried that I might come up against one of them in court. I said to my QC, 'What chance have we got if I come up against one of them?' The QC said, 'I wouldn't worry as I'm a Manchester City supporter and if I get Busby in the witness box I'll be able to cross examine him.' Just as the case was coming to court, United settled. They didn't need to put me through that though.

"A lot of good came out of me getting sacked. A friend of Matt's came to me and offered me a £10,000 interest-free loan, a nice gesture as I had a mortgage to pay. Another person who I'd never met before said that I'd had a rough time. He invited us on his yacht around the Med. It was wonderful and all paid for. We went to Rome. Gestures like that balance what I thought of United. All this is over 30 years ago now, it's all in the past and I survived it."

O'Farrell's replacement was the ebullient, wise-cracking Docherty. The 1968 hangover was now at its most obvious. Best had become a liability, Law and Charlton were nearing the end of their careers – Charlton retired at the end of Docherty's first season, Law was sold on to Manchester City. But in truth the entire club was living on reputation. "We thought we were too good to go down and then we went down," says Buchan. "I was devastated."

Buchan received several offers to leave that summer. He declined them all because he wanted to get back in the First Division with United. He also welcomed a new signing to the club, his brother George who followed him down from Aberdeen.

"My brother could do everything that Keegan could do but better," says Buchan. "He was stronger and could run faster, but he just had that missing ingredient of self-belief."

George Buchan, a forward, made four appearances as sub for United before moving to Bury in 1974 after a season at Old Trafford. He left at the end of United's relegation season.

"George's wife was a schoolteacher and he joined Lancaster after Bury. He went to college to become a teacher himself and worked at a secondary school in Oldham for many years, teaching English and PE.

"Relegation gave the Doc time to clear all the dead wood out. He did. I also saw no reason why we couldn't come straight back up. Lou Macari maintains that the Second Division was a piece of piss. Well he can't have been playing in the same games as I was because it was tough. We were the big fish and opponents raised their game against us. That's what footballers do because they think, 'If I have a good game against this lot then they might fancy me.' It was their cup final, their only chance to play against Manchester United."

United's travelling support was enormous.

"There was trouble, but most of it would happen at train stations or away from the ground. There was a right battle on the terracing behind the goal at Notts County at the end of the season, though. I couldn't help but watch."

Buchan's partner at the start of the Second Division season was Jim Holton, a 13st 5lb Scot for whom the fans sang, "Six foot two, eyes of blue, big Jim Holton's after you." The song was factually incorrect for Holton was actually 6ft 1in. And while he may have been inclined to go after any player, he may have needed a motorbike to catch him. Most top English clubs had a fair complement of Scottish players in the Seventies and United had more than most after the Doc brought in no fewer than six Scots: George Graham, Alex Forsyth, Lou Macari, Holton, Stewart Houston and Jim McCalliog.

"Jim Holton was a big, aggressive centre-half. He was predictable in a good way. I could understand how he played and adjust according. I couldn't always do that with defensive partners. Jim was brought from Shrewsbury without the Doc ever

48

seeing him play," says Buchan. "The Doc still got the credit though."

Paddy Crerand had been responsible for Holton signing in 1972.

"I would go to a lot of games in a scouting role," recalls Crerand, "watching forthcoming opponents or checking out players United wanted to sign. I went to see one player at Shrewsbury, but it was another who caught my eye. Jim Holton was playing at centre-half and I loved centre-halves who were good in the air and frightened the life out of forwards. Harry Gregg, my former United team-mate, was manager at Shrewsbury. I went to see him in his office after the game and enquired about Holton. Harry said, 'You'll like him because he's Scottish and a Celtic supporter'. I went back to Tommy Docherty. Harry battered the Doc over the transfer fee, getting £80,000 out of United when he should have been paid £40,000, but that didn't matter because Jim turned out to be a great player. He was one reason why United stayed in the First Division and weren't relegated in '72/73."

Holton bought a pub in Coventry after he'd finished playing.

"He got Tommy Docherty to open it," says Buchan. "I got to hear about this and drove down to Coventry for the grand opening. Jim was delighted to see me. Tommy cut the tape and as he did it, he said, 'Nice to see Martin, one of Jim's old colleagues, come along. Trust an Aberdonian to drive 100 miles for a free half of lager.'"

Holton died aged 42 after suffering a heart attack while at the wheel of his car near his home in Coventry, where he'd stayed after four seasons with Coventry City.

"I was on holiday for ten days. I didn't buy any newspapers while I was away. Jim died and was buried while I was away. I knew nothing of his death until I returned. I was devastated. I later found out that he had a heart defect which had never shown up. He could have died at 21. I'm just thankful that I had all those good years with him."

Buchan pauses to recall the memory of Holton. Behind him in

his office there's a signed picture of Sir Matt Busby on the wall. His reverie is ended by the intrusion of happier memories.

"But I have to say that Jim was a bugger as well," laughs Buchan. "While he was playing he was also a partner in a heating and cavity wall insulation firm. He used to drive the other people mad. He'd go up to their office after training, have a cup of tea and answer the phone by saying, 'Hello, Crazy Foam'.

"The company was supposed to be selling sophisticated insulation filling to help heat your house. He didn't take things too seriously."

Injuries dogged Holton and he moved to Sunderland in 1976, where he played just 15 times.

Not even Holton, however, could displace Macari as King Prankster.

"Macari was the court jester and Ashley Grimes was his number two," he explains. "I stripped next to him in training for ten years. We both grew up in tough Scottish backgrounds and were of the same mindset – don't let the bastards ever see you hurt."

Buchan may use Macari's surname to refer to him sometimes, but the pair of opposites were close friends: "I liked a pint, Lou had never drunk in his life. He used to say, 'If you lot could see yourselves at two in the morning talking through bubbles then you'd never drink again.'"

Macari loved it when Gordon Hill joined the club.

"He was someone he could use all of his pranks on," says Buchan. "We stayed in one hotel near Middlesbrough and Lou called Gordon's room, but Gordon didn't know it was Lou. Lou pretended to be from Tyne-Tees TV and told Gordon that he wanted to do an interview with him."

Macari also told the story when interviewed.

"I offered him £500 – over a month's wages," recalled the perpetrator.

"He pretended to be calm, but as soon as the phone went down he was telling all of the other players. It was one of his first away trips and he wasn't used to our pranks. We organised for a cab to come and get him and told the cab company to take him to Tyne-Tees TV.

"Hilly got the cab to the studios, but nobody there knew anything about it. There was supposed to be a sports programme on at 10pm and that's what he thought he'd be on. We waited for him to come back to the hotel and, when he did, asked why he hadn't been on television. Quick as a flash, he explained that he'd made a mistake and that he'd actually been on the radio.

"Another Macari trick involved tickets. Each player would get two season tickets per season and a further two tickets per match if they were playing. As captain, I would be given these complimentary tickets and told to hand them out. I also had to distribute tickets for the players' lounge after the game. For me, the players' lounge was somewhere to have a relaxing beer after the match, yet there were so many people in there that I struggled to get a drink because all the glasses had gone."

Buchan tried to bring some order to the situation.

"I would strictly ration players' lounge tickets," he explains. "Unbeknown to me, Macari would go to Ken Merrett [later club secretary] and get extra tickets. Despite my best efforts, I could never understand why there were so many people in there. Macari was a rascal.

"Ron Atkinson once tried to hold a team talk. Macari and Grimes were giggling in the corner. Ron wasn't happy and said, 'That's the problem at this club, too much whispering in corners.' Macari stood up and faced up to Ron, all five foot six of him and announced, 'If I have anything to say about you . . . then I'll say it behind your back'.

"The two years back after promotion were the happiest in my career," Buchan claims. "That team would have given the '68 European Cup a good game, Ron Atkinson's best team a game and Fergie's best team as well.

"We used to train on one quarter of the Old Trafford pitch each Friday morning and you felt like you could touch the anticipation. After training we'd go up to the old wood-panelled directors' lounge and have a pot of tea. We'd go through the match the next day and what we were going to do. The Doc went to do his press briefing, but none of the players rushed off. We were so confident that we felt we could give any team a two-goal head start at Old Trafford and still beat them. A lot of the credit for that mood must go to Tommy Docherty and Tommy Cavanagh."

Cavanagh divided opinion among players, but Buchan, perhaps surprisingly, was one of his supporters.

"He was a good right-hand man for the Doc and later Dave Sexton," says Buchan. "He did a lot of the coaching and kept it simple. He didn't have anyone in the dressing room before a game. A director would come down and say, 'I just want to wish the lads all the best'. Tommy would cut them short and say, 'I'll pass on your best wishes'. Then he'd turn to us and say, 'See all those friends of yours in the Playboy club. When you are sucking air through your arse at twenty to five on a Saturday afternoon, they will not help you. Only the boys in here can help you. We're in this together.'

"We were the best team in the country when it came to winning possession back. We didn't have any crunchers in the middle – players like Gerry Daly, Lou Macari, Stevie Coppell and Sammy Mac couldn't tackle a fish supper, but they were quick and would poke the ball away. They wouldn't give the opposition a chance to settle.

"Jimmy Greenhoff was our Eric Cantona. His experience helped us a lot. Sometimes I felt that I could stand at the centre of defence and close my eyes before playing a ball up to Jimmy or Pancho. I was that sure that one of them would be on the end of it.

"I was lucky to play with the greats, Best, Law and Charlton, but they were not my era. If you had been a fly on the wall in the United dressing room, you would never have guessed that Best had been one of the best players in the world because he was so unassuming. No, [Willie] Morgan was the one who strutted, but he wasn't fit to lace George's boots," states Buchan in a tone of uncharacteristic harshness.

Buchan admired Best's talents and intelligence.

"I once saw George play Scotland on his own for Northern Ireland," he recalls. "He might not have been big, but he was a strong lad who could look after himself. I had immense respect for him.

"George had a very quick-witted sense of humour. One of the nicest things that ever happened to me was in a lounge at Old Trafford in the early 2000s. George was with Mick Hucknall and introduced me by nudging me in the ribs and saying, 'Mick, this is Martin Buchan. Now that lad could play.' I felt seven feet tall."

Of Buchan's "era" he singles out one player.

"Stevie Coppell was the best player in that side," he says. "He was intelligent as a person and a player. He worked hard for the team. And we could have won the league in 1976 if we hadn't been distracted by the cup run, especially with players like Coppell in the team, and I'll go to my grave thinking that. A lot of the lads got distracted by the magic of the cup. They were seduced by the glamour of the competition and thought they would be millionaires with the proceeds from the players' pool. We fell apart in the league when the lads had reached Wembley."

United reached the final after beating Derby in the semi on 3rd April. The preparations for the match had not gone smoothly.

"We booked into the Palace hotel in Buxton, but were ordered back onto the bus after Tommy Cavanagh saw the state of the rooms. He wasn't happy. So we stayed at Mottram Hall instead."

United beat Derby 2-0 with two goals from Gordon Hill.

"Hilly was a great player in his day, yet he was subbed in both the '76 and '77 FA Cup finals. He scored 18-20 goals per season, but with the chances he had he should have been looking at 30 goals a season. He really believed that he was Merlin, but he could never understand why the full-back used to cut out his 65-yard cross-field passes to Steve Coppell. It could happen three or four times a game and it infuriated everyone."

Buchan once clipped Hill on the back of his head during a game.

"It was to remind him of his defensive responsibilities," he recalls. "He just wouldn't track back with his man. I had just shepherded a player to the half-way line and then got back to win a header. The ball went for a corner and I was sucking air through my arse. Gordon said, 'You do that again and I'll kick you in the bollocks.' The incident was all over the papers."

Buchan was not one to cultivate his relationship with the press.

"I didn't talk to them," he says. "I didn't not get on with any of them, except for Meeky [David Meek of the *Manchester Evening News*], but I didn't give my number out like Macari did. It was to my detriment that I didn't. I think I might have got an award if I'd been more pally with some of the press."

Buchan's best season was widely considered to be 1976/77. Emlyn Hughes won the Football Writers' award for 1977 after Liverpool had won the European Cup. Buchan had a far better season than Hughes that year, but he wasn't a European Cup winner.

Following victory over Derby in the '76 semi-final, United lost three league games in April 1976. There was another defeat in the FA Cup final on 1st May 1976.

"We were overwhelming favourites, but Southampton were no mugs," says Buchan. "They were full of hard-bitten professionals with Lawrie McMenemy in charge. He was a good man manager rather than a master tactician. Every time I see a clip of their goal, Bobby Stokes gets further and further offside. Was he offside? I don't know. There was only one camera, you didn't have nine or ten angles like now."

There is one Buchan legacy of the 1976 cup campaign. United released a record, a seven inch single. The official title of the Decca release was Manchester United FC – *Manchester United*. The leaden singalong tune reached number 50 in the charts. The B side was *Old Trafford Blues,* penned and sung by Buchan, who took his music seriously, and included lines such as, 'Then there's Alex Stepney, the grandad of the team, He's been playing football since 1917'.

Leeds United were United's opponents in the '77 semi-final and could have proved a stumbling block.

"They were a good side, but we didn't have a problem against the good sides. United could match the best, our problem was that we couldn't go to Coventry on a wet Wednesday night and grind out a result. That's why we didn't win the league."

How good were Liverpool? Buchan hesitates.

"They were a very good side but I hesitate because I watched the game recently on ESPN and thought, 'Actually, I wasn't that good a player!' There were big differences between then and now. Every pitch is perfect now. We played on a mess of a pitch at Maine Road."

After lifting the FA Cup against Liverpool, Buchan celebrated for "a few days".

"I liked a pint, but I was sensible with it," he says. "There wasn't a drinking culture among players, but we'd had a great night drowning our sorrows after the Southampton game a year earlier. That was better than the night following the victory in '77."

Buchan very nearly wasn't there at all for the '77 final against Liverpool. United were hoping for a first major honour since the 1968 European Cup nine years previously and the first of Tommy Docherty's five-year reign at Old Trafford. Yet five days before there was a meaningless fixture at West Ham to complete United's league season.

Buchan was involved in an awkward challenge with Trevor Brooking.

"Trevor fell right on top of me and did my knee ligaments." The Doc had rested just one player, goalkeeper Alex Stepney, who made way for Paddy Roche. Other than that it was expected to be his cup final side. The nightmare scenario, an injury to a key player, had happened to the club captain and lynchpin of the defence.

The severity of the injury only became clear after the game.

"My knee started to stiffen and was really sore by the time we'd got back to our hotel," he says.

That didn't stop Buchan going out to Quaglinos nightclub to see Bill Fredricks, who sang with The Drifters, perform.

"I'd become good friends with Bill," says Buchan. "He would stay at our house when he performed in Manchester. My two kids, Lesley Ann and Jamie [who became a professional footballer for Aberdeen among other Scottish clubs], called him 'Singing Bill'. I went to see him with Tommy Jackson and he was great, but I couldn't walk when I got up in the morning."

It wasn't as if Buchan could relax at the hotel either.

"We were moving to the Selsdon Park Hotel south of London, while Wembley is North West London. It was a stupid place to stay but Southampton had stayed there the year before, as had a lot of Cup-winning teams."

But there were bigger problems for Buchan than the location of the hotel.

"I couldn't walk without crutches and told the Doc that he might as well give me a train ticket back to Manchester because I was fucked. He would have none of it. Laurie Brown, God bless him, worked tirelessly on my knee, but I can remember having a beer on the Wednesday night and saying that I wasn't going to make the game."

United needed Buchan. The Reds had already lost one defender, full-back Stewart Houston who would be replaced by Arthur Albiston. According to the experts, United's weakest link would be Albiston as Liverpool winger Steve Heighway would quickly shred the confidence of the callow 19-year-old and United would be exposed to the wily European champions elect. That was the script. Albiston didn't read it, besides, as he'd say to anyone who questioned his experience who would listen, "I had already played 30 or 40 times".

Miraculously, there was some improvement in Buchan's injury the following day.

"I was running by Thursday afternoon," he says. "I had my fitness test on Friday morning which consisted of me standing in some five-a-side nets wearing strapping and kicking the ball from a standing position. I survived. The Doc said, 'You'll be alright.' I played with a lot of strapping."

The fans didn't know that he'd been injured, but early in the final, Buchan went in for a 50/50 in the centre circle with Liverpool's hard man Tommy Smith.

"I got through it," recalls Buchan. "And I knew then that I'd be alright. The rest is history . . ."

Buchan became the first player to captain FA Cup winning sides in Scotland and England following a 1970 triumph with Aberdeen.

"Work your bollocks off for 20 years and you end up as a pub trivia question," he jokes.

United returned to Manchester the following day after beating Liverpool.

"We transferred from the team coach to an open-topped bus in Bowdon. We then started going through Altrincham towards Manchester. I was quite friendly with members of the licensed trade, including a pal who ran the Wheatsheaf, so I made sure that I had the cup as we passed the pub. They were all outside cheering and I shouted, "half seven". Sure enough, I went back to the Wheatsheaf at half seven that night. Just me and the FA Cup. The Doc had told me to look after it and bring it back in the morning."

Tommy Docherty, the man who had described Buchan in 1977 as being "better than Bobby Moore", was dismissed soon after.

"The moral climate of the time and the fact that United was a very Catholic club meant that I wasn't surprised when he was dismissed," says Buchan. "The irony was that of the team that won the club, the only Catholic player was Lou Macari. I was outraged during the talk of possible successors when Johnny Giles came into the frame. The papers listed his plus points, with one saying, 'Crucially, he's a Catholic.' That made me angry. Football is not a racist industry. If somebody came into a dressing room, all that should matter was whether he could play or not. Skin colour or religion should not be an issue and it isn't now."

Buchan stayed, Dave Sexton joined as manager and new sign-ings arrived like Gordon McQueen from Leeds in 1978.

"Gordon wasn't always the easiest to play with, just because he didn't do the expected," says Buchan. "The crowd would wind him up and he'd go on these charges up front, his giant legs taking him there quicker than any other player. There was no catching McQueen.

"We did a lot of set pieces with Dave Sexton. One day, Gordon piped up, 'Boss can we not just do that one where he puts the ball in and I head it into the back of the net and save all this messing about?'"

Buchan has his own views on why Sexton didn't prosper at Old Trafford.

"Dave's biggest problem was that he couldn't handle the press. The Doc would meet them after we'd had our players' briefing on a Friday and they would roll out of Old Trafford at 4pm having had a couple of glasses of wine and with so much material that they didn't know what to leave out the next day. Unfortunately with Dave, they didn't get anything. He was wary of the press because he didn't trust them. He lost his job after winning seven games on the row at the end of the season, including going to Anfield and beating Liverpool. The press had the knives out for him.

"Dave Sexton was the nicest man that I ever met in football," Buchan continues. "When we reached the 1979 FA Cup final he bought every player a lovely Seiko sports watch. I bumped into him eight or nine years later and told him that it needed a new battery!

"Dave was not a dour man like some claimed. He was studious and would love to read biographies, but he had a good sense of humour and would come back from helping coach England with some wonderful jokes. If Dave had a fault it was that he never switched off. He was always thinking about football. He was a keen student of European football and rather than take us on tour to play a team of Spanish waiters, he took us to play Hadjuk Split and they put six past us. They tore us apart."

Over a century had elapsed before United signed a player from outside the UK and Ireland. Jimmy Nicholl was born in Canada, whilst Forties winger Charlie Mitten entered the world in Rangoon, Burma. Both, however, grew up in Britain. United's first continental was Nicola Jovanovic in 1980. The Serb defender looked like the Incredible Hulk and boasted a model wife. She wasn't the only one who made an impression.

"We played on an icy training pitch for his first kickabout and Nicola was dancing on the ice. He was brilliant. I thought, 'I wonder if Dave Sexton is trying to put a bit of pressure on me?' because I was negotiating what would be my last United contract."

Buchan and Macari discussed the new £500,000 signing. Buchan was worried.

"'He's good isn't he?' I asked Macari.

'If he's worth £500,000,' said Lou, 'Then you must be worth at least £250,000'."

Alas, the 'sublime Serb' couldn't establish himself in United's first team and returned to Belgrade after just 25 games, along with a club-owned BMW. Martin Edwards later described him as the worst pound-for-pound signing in his time at the club.

The author tracked Jovanovic down to Slovenia in 1999 and went to interview him in the capital Ljubljana, where he found an amiable ex-player who had mixed feelings about his time in Manchester.

"The people were very friendly and Manchester was a big club like Red Star, but the technical level was much lower than at Red Star. The coaching methods were not advanced. I did not like Tommy Cavanagh and the players drank too much alcohol to be professional athletes."

"Nicola was a lovely lad," says Buchan. "He was six foot three, but shrunk to four foot nine when he went to head the ball. He was trying to learn English and would obviously make mistakes, like when he asked my Jewish friend if he was 'Jevvish.'"

Buchan signed a three-year contract in 1980 which would take him until the age of 34. His final contract was worth £850 a week in the first year, £1000 in his second, £1250 in his third. His United testimonial was against an Aberdeen side managed by Alex Ferguson at Old Trafford in August 1983.

"I asked adidas if they wanted to supply a kit and they said no. So I asked a friend who worked for Puma. United wore a Puma kit and the people from the club's sponsors, Sharp Electronics, were there and they were not happy that their logo was not on the shirt.

"I came out with £53,000 tax free after my testimonial which I put into a house in Aberdeen.

"Supporters come up to me and ask me if I remember certain games and scorelines. I don't. Some supporters can reel off every scoreline and what time the substitutes came on. I remember incidents from games and my goals, all four of them!"

One of these was a screamer against Everton at Old Trafford in September 1978.

"We were losing 1-0 and it was late on in the game. We got a throw-in and I looked to play the ball to Jimmy Greenhoff on the edge of the box. I was about 37, 38 yards out. The crowd were encouraging me so I had a go. The ball flew into George Woods' top right-hand corner."

Buchan was summoned to be interviewed by John Motson for *Match of the Day* after the match.

"Well, Martin," Motson said. "That's unusual for you to score. How do explain that?"

"Well, John," replied the United captain. "I've just come back from the World Cup where I was getting shooting lessons from Arie Haan [the Dutch midfielder who played in seven different European finals at club level]."

"Really?" asked Motson.

Afterwards Buchan drove north to Aberdeen. He stopped in Stirling to watch *Match of the Day*. Most of Buchan's family are still in Aberdeen.

"That wasn't the best goal I scored, however," he says. "The best was on my derby debut against City. They beat us 3-1, but I crashed an unsaveable past Rob Hayley into the Stretford End net. I also scored a swerver against Derby and a good header from a Steve Coppell cross against Bolton – the year when they beat us home and away with Frank Worthington."

Buchan also remembers the 5-3 defeat at home to a West Brom side led by a young midfielder, Bryan Robson.

"Ah, the so-called classic when Cyrille Regis was a handful," he smiles. "Gary Bailey, who wasn't the bravest goalkeeper, got Man of the Match. He'd conceded five. I had a go at him after the game because he'd been at fault for a couple of goals, but Dave Sexton stuck up for Gary. Gary was a manufactured goalkeeper, a shot stopper."

Buchan and Bailey had heated words after Arsenal's late winner in the dramatic 1979 Cup final, but as Martin says, "How could I say anything to him when I was out on the wing celebrating a goal? I should have been defending."

After 456 United appearances, including six years as captain, Buchan moved to Oldham Athletic in 1983.

"Joe Royle signed me on a two-year contract worth £300 a week," he explains. "It was a free transfer, which was good because Oldham were skint. They couldn't afford a signing on fee, so I agreed to a signing off fee of £15,000 when I'd played two years. I had a few muscle injuries and only played half the games for Oldham during that time. I'd struggled with a calf injury at United. When Bryan Robson got the same injury, he came to me for advice and I told him that he would have to take a week longer than he would think.

"I was a good pro at Oldham and Joe was happy at my influence in the dressing room. After the two years I could have taken the £15,000, but I didn't want Oldham to think I had gone up there for a holiday and ripped up the letter saying they owed me £15,000. I took £4,000 instead."

Buchan was financially comfortable when he finished playing. As well as the testimonial money, Frank O'Farrell had advised him to take out a pension.

"I thought pensions were for granddads," says Buchan, "but thanks to Frank I was receiving £100 a week from the age of 35. That was good because I wasn't earning anything else.

In June 1985, Buchan had made that ill-fated move into management with Burnley, who had just been relegated into the Fourth Division for the first time in their history – 25 years after being English champions. They were also £850,000 in debt.

He then moved back to Aberdeen, where he split with his wife.

"I went for one job in Scotland and the man interviewing me asked what I was on. I told him that I was on £100 a week pension. He explained that I was earning more than him and I didn't get the job."

Buchan did a bit of driving for his lifelong friend, Ian Taylor. He also bought a black labrador, Charlie.

"He kept me sane and we'd go running," he recalls, "me and the dog. I'd do four miles, the dog would do 14."

Buchan then moved back to the north of England.

"I'd spent most of my adult life in Manchester so I moved back south," he explains. "I got a job with Puma, where I stayed for 12 years. Gazza was with Puma, then he went and crocked himself."

Buchan signed up Ryan Giggs to Puma, Robbie Fowler and David James. Brian McClair also scored a lot of goals wearing Puma boots, but Buchan's relationship with the company turned acrimonious.

"They had unrealistic aims for what they should get for the money they were prepared to pay players," he explains. Buchan took them to an industrial tribunal and won.

He started at the PFA in 1999.

"The PFA is a voice of reason," he opines. "We have a phrase 'For the good of the game' and I think we are. We've got practically 100 per cent membership. Very few footballers don't join. We nearly had a strike after I'd been here for five years. The biggest volunteer was Paolo Di Canio.

"Not everyone is a millionaire in football. A lot of players do get a lot of money and a lot of them deserve it," he says. "Sometimes players come to us with a problem and we tell them to read their contract because their club will often be right. But if we think a player has a good case then we'll fight tooth and nail for them." Buchan does not mean literally; his boxing days are over.

3

LOU MACARI

SKIP TO MY LOU

LOU MACARI

Lou Macari remembers picking up the telephone one night in 1973. Jock Stein, his manager at Celtic, was brief, but to the point: "Be ready in the morning. A car will pick you up. You are going south."

"My wife, quite reasonably, asked me where I was going," says Macari. "I told her that I didn't know and she understandably looked surprised.

"I'd never considered life anywhere other than at Celtic. I didn't sit down and wonder whether I was good enough to play elsewhere because I was so happy there.

"I'd won the league and the Scottish Cup in 1972. We beat Hibernian 6-1 in the final, when I'd scored two. But during the summer when the time came to renew my contract I went to see Jock Stein. I had no agent. I was earning £50 a week and wanted a rise. I walked into his room and was quite excited when his first words were, 'You've done well for me'." Stein then offered Macari a new contract worth £55 a week.

"I was stunned and got the hump," he explains. "I had no idea what the other players were earning, but I felt that it wasn't a big enough rise. I plucked up the courage to say that it wasn't acceptable and that I wasn't happy. I went away to have a think about things. I was married and had more responsibility so I returned to Jock a few days later and told him that I wanted a transfer, secretly hoping that he would make me a better offer because I didn't want to leave Celtic. None of this was leaked to the press."

Stein didn't increase the offer.

And so Macari found himself in a car along with assistant manager Sean Fallon. At no point on the journey was he told where he was going. Macari tried to work it out.

"When we passed Carlisle I realised that I wasn't going to Carlisle United, but my geography of England wasn't too good. By late afternoon we arrived at the Prince of Wales hotel in Southport. I called my missus and told her where I was. She said, 'Who plays in Southport?'"

The travelling party had tea and sandwiches before setting off again.

"The first time I realised where we were going was when we arrived at Anfield," recalls Macari. "Liverpool were playing Burnley that night and I was delighted to be there, and even more so after I had been taken inside the ground to meet Bill Shankly. What I didn't know at the time was that he and Jock were best pals and that he had told Jock to give him a nod if I was ever going to leave Celtic."

Macari thought it a great honour to be considered by Liverpool and Shankly.

"Liverpool offered me £190 a week – almost four times what Celtic had offered," he says. "I tried not to show any reaction, but inside I was shocked. I was also entitled to 5 per cent of the transfer fee, and Liverpool had agreed £180,000 for me. I sat there thinking '£9,000 and £190 a week!' I really thought that I had cracked it, that I was the top dog. I told Shankly that I was happy. He told me, "Go and watch the game and we'll sort everything out after."'

But the story was to have another twist. Also at the game, by chance, was former Celtic player Paddy Crerand, Manchester United's newly appointed assistant manager to new boss Tommy Docherty.

"I sat next to Paddy and watched the Liverpool players who I thought I'd soon be playing with," says Macari. "Paddy naturally asked me what I was doing and I told him that I was signing for Liverpool. He said that he was surprised because he hadn't read anything about the move in the papers. I told him the story about how I had been smuggled down. Paddy looked me in the eye and announced, 'Don't do anything, we'll take you'.

"I couldn't believe what I was hearing and set about working through the biggest dilemma of my life. My biggest fear was upsetting Shankly, who I had assured everything was fine. Paddy came back to me before the end of the game and confirmed, 'We'll definitely sign you'. It turned out Tommy Docherty was also at the game watching his son, who played for Burnley."

Despite the obvious attractions of Anfield, Macari felt that United were the team for him.

"They'd been my club in England and Best, Law and Charlton were still playing. I also had a nagging doubt in the back of my mind that I wouldn't get into the Liverpool team because they were flying."

The young star told Shankly after the game that he needed a bit of time to think about things.

"He was great with me," recalls Macari. "I caught a train from Lime Street to Glasgow the following morning and decided to speak to United. I rang Shankly and told him. He wasn't happy, but he said, 'It's your decision.' He then joked to the Liverpool press that he had only wanted to sign me to play in Liverpool's reserves. I thought that was quite witty."

Again, coincidentally, United's Glaswegian manager, Tommy

Docherty, happened to be staying at the Excelsior hotel in Glasgow where Macari went to speak to him.

"He asked me what Liverpool had offered and offered me £200 a week, £10 a week more. United then rang Jock and Celtic upped the fee to £200,000 – which meant I would get an extra £1,000 signing-on fee. I signed for United in Glasgow that day."

"People think with a surname like 'Macari' that my parents must have been Italian, but they were both born in Scotland." Macari was born in Edinburgh in 1949 and spent his first year in Newton Grange, a mining village.

"A family rift meant we moved to Leytonstone in East London when I was one. Dad was in the British Army in the Second World War and represented them at football. Along with my mum, he encouraged me to play the game, and as a kid I used to watch him play on Hackney Marshes. I would retrieve the balls that flew wide of the goal – at that level of football I was kept quite busy. I was an only child and Dad had a motorbike with a sidecar which I loved travelling to football in. We'd often watch Leyton Orient play at Brisbane Road, but then we moved back to Largs on the Ayrshire coast."

There Macari became a Celtic fan.

"One of the most vivid memories from my youth is watching Celtic train at the Inverclyde training ground behind my house in Largs. My hero was Jimmy Johnstone, and I'd sneak in to watch him train, just me and my football. Some of the Celtic coaches would watch me juggle my ball and one day, when I was 13, they called me over and invited me to juggle a ball in front of them. That felt like a great honour."

Largs boasted a restaurant called Macari's.

"It was in the family, but my father was cut out of being involved in it because of the family rift," he says. "Instead, Dad travelled to Glasgow each morning where he worked in catering. It was hard graft, but he never complained."

Macari's father died when he was 18.

"He was only in his late 40s and had cancer. At least I think it was cancer, because nobody had ever told me. I'm thankful that he saw me make it as a footballer."

Largs was a good place to be a teenager.

"There was plenty of fresh air from the sea and the town was busy with tourists from Glasgow before they started getting cheap flights abroad. I'd play football most nights, either in the street or at the home ground of Largs Thistle, the local junior team. I also liked the amusement arcades and I would run there and back – about two miles. I loved the machine where you had to flick the ball into a hole using metal flippers. I'd also go fishing, sometimes twice a day. There was an abundance of fish like cod and mackerel. I would hire a little motorboat by myself, catch 30 or 40 mackerel and take them home. There is a famous story about the time Jimmy Johnstone took a boat at Largs after a night out when he was training with the Scotland team, but he ended up in distress and had to be rescued."

Macari would soon attract attention, but for his football rather than angling skills.

"St Michael's, my school team, was very good and some of the better players in it started to get noticed. I was a centre-forward who scored loads of goals, and at 15 I received an invitation to train at Celtic Park two nights a week. I was happy, but at no point did I ever think that I would become a professional footballer. I supported a team who would soon become European champions and didn't ever consider myself good enough to play for Celtic."

He used to catch a train after school to Glasgow every Tuesday and Thursday. Celtic paid his travel expenses and demanded punctuality in return. "I'd catch two buses from Glasgow Central to Parkhead. It would take me just over two hours in each direction to get to training which started at 7pm. I would be nervous all the journey in case I was late. Jock Stein used to stand at the front door and he would shout, 'Come on, Sir, what's this? Why are you late?'

"We'd train for two hours on the track around the pitch. We'd wear flat shoes and do a lot of running in front of those vast, empty terraces. If we trained well, our reward was 15-20 minutes playing football behind the goals. I was very committed, as were my parents. They would drive me everywhere, and I appreciated that.

I played for Scotland Schoolboys against England at Southampton. We got beaten, and I hardly got a kick. Physically, I was weak compared with English players like Brian Kidd, who was three or four inches bigger than me. I remember thinking that I didn't have a career as a footballer ahead of me. There were hundreds of talented Scottish players, and dozens moved south of the border every season, a flow that has all but dried up now."

Macari was 17 when he was summoned to meet Stein to find out whether he had a future at the club.

"I was very, very worried before I went to see Jock Stein to hear the news and had absolutely no idea whether I was going to be kept on or not," he says. "I went into Jock's office, a simple, sparse room, and he said, 'You've done well and we'd like to keep you on.' I was delighted, but tried not to show it."

Not that he had signed up to a life of riches.

"Oh no, we used to clean the boots of the first-team players and sweep the terracing after first-team home games," he says. "We'd start at the back and brush the rubbish down step by step towards the pitch: half-eaten pies, cans, chewing gum, Macaroon bars, everything. By the bottom there would be a huge pile, which a rubbish truck would pick up. It would take us a full day, and we did no training on a Monday because of the cleaning. It never bothered me and I never found it an ordeal. What I found harder to take in was that I had just left school, and suddenly I was seeing players everyday who I idolised.

"On my daily journey from Largs I sometimes met Gordon McQueen, who was in a very exciting St Mirren team, and we thought we were the bees' knees," he recalls, smiling. "One morning Gordon and I were at Paisley station and some young kid was hanging about. We gave him some money and told him to go and get us some fish and chips. He never came back. Aside from fish and chips, I avoided temptation and never touched alcohol. Jock left us in no doubt that alcohol and cigarettes were taboo, and I've still never touched either.

"I went to Celtic matches as a fan in the mid-1960s and travelled to games home and away with a supporters' club which ran coaches. My life was Celtic, and if Celtic didn't win life was a nightmare. I watched the Lisbon final on television. Live games were a rarity, and I was excited about the match for days before. I didn't think that Celtic would win; I just couldn't see how we could beat Internazionale. But we did. I went to see the victorious team return to Celtic Park a few nights later. They were paraded around the pitch in front of a packed stadium on the back of a truck, which travelled at five miles an hour.

"Celtic's 1967 European Cup win has never got the credit it deserves and I believe it remains one of the greatest achievements in the history of sport. Jock Stein brought young players through and signed more experienced players who hadn't blossomed else-where. It was management of the highest order."

Macari watched Manchester United play Benfica in the European Cup final a year later.

"A lot of Celtic fans had a connection with United because Paddy Crerand had played for both clubs, and because United had world-class players like Denis Law, George Best and Bobby Charlton."

Macari was desperate to go into the first team, but Celtic had their own way of making sure young prospects knew their place.

"When I signed professional forms with Celtic, it was listed that I had signed from a junior side called Ashfield. It was a way around the rules and would have allowed me to play for them if I didn't make it at Celtic. Celtic actually said to me, 'If you don't make it here you can play for Ashfield'. That kept my feet on the ground, my expectations in check. Fear of failure was a powerful motivation.

"The guidance and upbringing from Celtic was first class. There was no way I could get carried away or big headed. That was down to great management."

Outside football, Macari's private life was going well.

"I'd met my future wife, a New Yorker called Dale Marie, when I was at school. Her family had come over to work at IBM in Greenock. We got married in New York. When I look back at my life, it's hard to explain why I made certain decisions, but I just did. Marrying Dale was the best decision. You can be lucky in life and I was lucky with Dale. We bought a place together in Largs and I continued travelling to Parkhead each day, hoping that I would break into Celtic's first team."

Celtic reached the European Cup final in 1970 with many of the players who had won the European Cup three years earlier.

"I considered it a tremendous honour and privilege to be training with players of such high quality on a daily basis," recalls Macari. "The following season I made my first-team debut. You know what, I can't even remember who it was against, but I remember cleaning the terraces the day after. One reason I can't remember is because making your first-team debut was not a big deal. Jock didn't make a big deal out of anything, not even winning the European Cup, but a lot of people made a fuss about me and the players I came through the ranks with: David Hay, Kenny Dalglish, Danny McGrain and George Connelly. We were termed the 'Quality Street' gang by the press. All of us went on to have long careers and I believe that was because of the grounding we got at Celtic."

Macari's first big game was the 1971 Scottish Cup final.

"The only thing on my mind was collecting a cup-winners' medal," he says. "I was named sub, but that was fine by me and I still felt part of the team. That medal was snatched away from me minutes from the end when Rangers equalised. After the game, we boarded a bus straight to a training camp at Seamill Hydro hotel by the beach. Nobody phoned their wives for permission or anything, and nobody was allowed to touch alcohol. If players sneaked out for half a shandy and got away with it then they thought that they'd really pulled a fast one on the manager."

He didn't know if he would be playing in the replay.

"Jock only ever named his team an hour before the game. When he announced the team, I was down to start in the replay at Hampden, which surprised me because I thought the team had played well in the first game. I scored the first goal with a little flick at the near post. It's only recently that I've seen a replay of the game on television. After 15 or 20 minutes, I went on a run and the commentator said, 'Well, didn't I tell you that the little boy was nippy?'

"Before I knew it, it was ten o'clock and I was sitting at Hampden Park with a Scottish Cup-winners' medal after we'd beaten Rangers 2-1. It was the greatest moment of my life and all my family were there. They had gone to the game thinking that I would be substitute at best. I'm very happy that my dad saw me win the Scottish Cup before he passed away."

The celebrations didn't stop in Hampden.

"I went with my parents back to Largs after the game, and we stopped on the way for fish and chips. A Celtic supporters' bus turned up. I didn't give it too much thought because I considered myself a Celtic supporter. They viewed me slightly differently and the next thing I knew I was being carried around the chippy on someone's shoulders with everyone cheering and shouting my name. Mum and Dad watched on, a little worried for my safety but very proud. At that moment I think they realised that all the effort they had made with me had been worth it. For me, it set the seal on a great night."

Macari established himself in the Celtic side the following season, but there was still no superstar lifestyle.

"Each day we would put on our training shoes at Celtic Park and then run to Barrowfield, carrying our boots with us. We ran through the streets, trained and then ran back. I was on £35 a week when the man in the street was on around £10 a week. There was no feeling that I'd hit the big time . . . that didn't come until I got my first car."

Macari enjoyed his first European campaign with Celtic.

"We played in the European Cup and beat BK 1903 Copenhagen, Sliema Wanderers and Hungarian side Ujpest Dosza in the quarter-finals. I got the winner five minutes from time in a 2-1 win in Budapest, and I remember Jock saying that it was Celtic's best-ever display in Europe. I scored against Ujpest in the return leg at Parkhead in a 1-1 draw. We were then paired with Inter Milan in the semi-finals – the team Celtic had beaten in Lisbon."

Five of the Lisbon Lions – Jim Craig, Bobby Murdoch, Billy McNeill, Jimmy Johnstone and Bobby Lennox – remained in the side. Inter still had three players from the final.

"We drew 0-0 in Milan, and I felt we were unlucky not to nick a win. Neither team could score in Glasgow, and it went to penalties after extra-time. Dixie Deans missed his and we were out, but Europe was a great experience for me."

Macari was surrounded by top players.

"Kenny Dalglish became a great, but goalscoring was a problem to Kenny as a youngster, and he missed more than he scored. The remedy was simple. Jock would say, 'There's a bag of balls, there's the net. Spend time every afternoon putting the balls in the net.' Kenny wasn't born to be a world-class footballer, but he worked so hard that he became one."

Veterans like Jimmy Johnstone and Billy McNeill still continued in the side.

"Billy's 'Caesar' nickname was appropriate – he was our leader and captain. I really looked up to Billy because, despite him having led Celtic to European glory, he still used to put extra training in each afternoon. All the youngsters respected him for this and followed his example. A lot of us became Celtic and Scotland regulars, partly because of Jock and partly because of players like Billy. We used to ask Billy to go and see Jock for various perks, and he always came back with the same result: nothing. Jock set our win bonuses and didn't tell us what they would be until after the match.

"Jock was tough, but aside from a few little remarks I can't recall a bad word said about him. The respect for Jock was immense, and I was in awe of him, frightened of him even. He would check on everything. When we were away he would send somebody up to your room if he thought you were even having a Coca Cola. It would be poured down the sink because you were not allowed fizzy drinks. Jock controlled what we ate – there were no chips and evening meal times were set rigidly."

Jock did allow his players to go to the Vesuvio restaurant after games in Glasgow on a Saturday.

"The bill was paid by Celtic, but we were not allowed to have a drink. There was uproar one Monday morning when Jock called a team meeting because he'd seen a cigar on the bill at the Vesuvio.

'Which smart arse had a cigar?' Jock demanded. It had been Tommy Gemmill and he got a ferocious dressing down. And all because he smoked one cigar."

Whereas Glasgow Rangers had the better team in the early Sixties, Jock Stein had got the better of them by the late Sixties and early Seventies when Celtic won nine league titles in a row.

"Despite us being the dominant team, there was a real hatred when we played Rangers," explains Macari. "When you are brought up in an environment like I was, you loathed Rangers. I can remember being on supporters' coaches returning from Celtic matches and being stoned by Rangers fans on the way back to Largs. Even if I had been good enough, they would never have signed me because I am a Catholic. That caused resentment, but I respected Rangers' players and the referees, who probably had the toughest job – officiating an Old Firm game."

When Macari came to United in 1973, he was struck by the contrast with the orderly regime at Celtic. "Everything was different at Old Trafford, and not always in a good way. The discipline was far more lax than it was at Celtic, the quality of training much poorer, although there wasn't much to separate the two clubs in terms of the standard of football."

However, Macari had joined a club in a state of flux.

"One year all these great players like Law, Best and Charlton were there, the next they had gone. They were replaced by players who were not fit to lace their boots. With the benefit of hindsight, I should have looked at what Tommy Docherty had done at previous clubs where he had quickly made lots of changes. Yet, in spite of the changes, there wasn't a day when I didn't enjoy myself at Old Trafford.

"I couldn't wait to get down to Manchester to start training ahead of the first game against West Ham. I was excited because I was set to play against Bobby Moore, the England captain who had lifted the World Cup."

Macari made an immediate impact, scoring a point-saving goal in a 2-2 draw on 20 January 1973.

"There's a great photo of Bobby Moore lying on the floor watching the ball go in the net, which I'm sure every Scot would appreciate."

Macari's team-mates included several other Scots like George Graham. Tartan scarves and the odd kilt began to appear on the Old Trafford terraces.

"United was probably the wrong club for 'Stroller'," says Macari. "He was cool on the ball and did things in his own time. Inevitably he was also compared to the legends who had played before him. I liked George, he was good company and a good player. He was up for a joke, and I was sad when he left."

If Macari found it hard to settle in such a disrupted team in his first few months, the next season, 1973-74, would be worse. "You could tell how lacking in confidence we were because it took us an hour to find a way past Plymouth Argyle in the FA Cup at Old Trafford at the start of the year. There were only 31,000 watching us, but I got the goal which took us through. We didn't get another win until I got a goal at Sheffield United, and that was in March."

In March 1974, Macari was sent off in a fiery derby at Maine Road, a decision which he still believes to be unjust.

"Mike Doyle chopped me down. I fell on the ball and threw it in his direction. Clive Thomas, the referee, sent both of us off. We refused to go. I don't think Mike deserved to go, and I certainly didn't. Clive ordered both teams into the dressing rooms. He then came into our dressing room with the chief of police, who ordered me not to go back out. The pair then went into the City dressing room and said the same to Mike. We stayed put. Imagine that happening now?"

United were heading for relegation, but it's a myth that they had Manchester City to thank for the drop, courtesy of a Denis Law back heel.

"There were two league games remaining, and we had to beat City to have a chance of catching Birmingham. Norwich and Southampton were in the same position. Three of the four would go down."

Macari was on the pitch for what he describes as "one of the most iconic moments of the Seventies".

"There were eight minutes to go when Denis scored his goal. Pandemonium broke out and fans stormed onto the pitch. Police horses soon followed. We were taken into the dressing room and told to wait as police restored order. It never happened. We were told that the match had been abandoned and that the score stood. We were down, but Denis wasn't responsible. Birmingham got the win they needed to stay up. We could have won and we would still have gone down."

A lack of goals had been a major problem for United, they had scored just 35 in 42 league games. Macari had managed a paltry five, with opinion divided over whether he was best utilised as an attacker or midfielder. Perhaps through lack of striking options, Docherty played much of that winter with a defensive, unexpansive 4-5-1 formation, the diminutive Macari obliged to spend his time haring after the hopeful, yet largely pointless long balls that were the team's one attacking tactic.

"My decision to choose United over Liverpool wasn't looking good," he admits.

Macari scored more in the Second Division the following season, his 18-goal tally the best return of any of his 12 seasons at Old Trafford.

"Over a million fans watched us that season and we averaged more than 48,000 at home, a remarkable figure for a Second Division team. We had bigger crowds than all the First Division clubs, and any doubts I may have had about not going to Liverpool ended as I scored in the final game of the season against Blackpool."

Lou was loving life at United.

"Just staying away in hotels the night before a game was brilliant, though I always got my own room. Other players roomed together, but I wanted a good night's sleep with no interruptions.

"Just getting on the bus at Old Trafford to go on an away trip was magical. We went by bus to every away game apart from those in London, which we travelled to by train like they do now."

The team coach was split into two sections.

"I would be in the card school at the back," he explains. "Me, Alex Stepney, Gerry Daly and Paddy Roche would be the hardcore members. While the educated ones would sit at the front with their books. Martin Buchan would be at the front. A lot of the other players didn't understand him. He was immaculate in everything he did. If there was a meeting at 4 o'clock then he'd turn up five seconds before four. It was as if was hiding around the corner looking at his watch so that he couldn't possibly be late."

Buchan later had competition in the sartorial stakes.

"When Ray Wilkins arrived he outdressed us all," says Macari. "He had a handkerchief in his jacket pocket and shoes from Carnaby Street. The Chelsea players always thought that they were the best-dressed boys."

Macari didn't seek to emulate Wilkins' dress sense, but was determined to take him down a peg or two.

"I nailed his expensive shoes to the dressing room floor," he smiles. "Someone had suggested that Ray was a bit over the top and I decided, 'Let's have him'. I got the nails and the hammer from the groundsman a few minutes before the end of training. Ray came back in and had a shower. All the other players knew what was going on and none of them wanted to miss it. I wanted him to stand in his shoes and then be stuck to the floor, but he went to get a shoe and it didn't move. He had to take it in good humour and he did."

Macari is another of those players who is critical of Docherty's style of management.

"At the start of the '75/76 season the Doc told Steptoe [Alex Stepney] that he would be second-choice 'keeper to Paddy Roche. Alex was a senior figure at the club and had kept United in the 1968 European Cup final, but he didn't kick up a fuss, even though you could tell he wasn't happy. On the Friday before the first game of the season, Alex was sent to train with the reserves, as was the norm if you weren't in the first team. It all seemed so wrong to me, a real slap in the face to a European Cup winner."

Stepney, however, would be required after all.

"Paddy Roche's dad had passed away and he needed to go back to Dublin. Alex came back into the first team dressing room, but there was no kit for him. Tommy Cavanagh was taking training and was very fussy about appearances. Alex cobbled together some kit and joined the session, to be met by Cavanagh having a go. It took a lot to rattle Alex's cage, but the next thing you know Tommy was picking himself off the floor. Alex had punched him square on the chin."

Macari was not immune from Docherty's quixotic behaviour.

"Soon after arriving at Old Trafford, I was told to play a game with the kids at Mossley in the hills near Manchester. Not the reserves, the kids. I couldn't understand it, and when I asked the Doc he offered no explanation. I decided that I wasn't going and told the Doc. He told me that I would be in trouble if I didn't go. The PFA advised me that I should go, so I went. The Doc tipped the press lads off that there would be a story. He wasn't expecting me and was shocked to see me in Mossley. He then sent me home."

Macari was baffled.

"He just turned on me, and I've no idea why. Maybe it was because I'd not scored enough goals for him since arriving, but it was all very confusing."

For all that, Macari claims to have liked the Doc personally.

"He was a witty man, one of the boys," he attests. "He could be a hard man if you crossed him. The chairman, Louis Edwards, who wanted to be one of the boys, loved the Doc and his company. Louis would always throw a party in his room at the end of the close-season tours. The players liked Louis. His son Martin was misunderstood too. He was a good chairman and popular with the players. He was never a big egotist like a lot of chairmen – and I can tell you that from experience."

United finished third in the league in 1976 and reached the FA Cup final.

"Maybe we started to believe our own hype a bit towards the end of the season," explains Macari. "It was an exhilarating season, but we limped across the line at the end. The FA Cup final against Southampton summed up our weaknesses. The bookies had made us the shortest-priced favourites for years and Southampton were not given a prayer. With the game 0-0 at half-time, doubts started to enter our minds. We couldn't see ourselves scoring, though I flicked a corner on for Sammy McIlroy, who hit the woodwork with a header. With seven minutes to play Jim McCalliog, a former United player, slipped Bobby Stokes through. We couldn't respond. Tommy Doc said we would be back next year to win the cup. Everyone agreed, without really believing it."

Macari invested some of his money into a chip shop on Chester Road close to Old Trafford.

"There was a shop run by an old lady which sold jumpers and knitting needles," he explains. "I went in one day and asked her if she wanted to sell it and she said yes. My intention was for my mother to come down to Manchester and run the shop, but she died not long after I'd bought it."

The fans who sang "Lou, Lou, Skip to my Lou, Skip to my Lou Macari", a song which had been started by Celtic fans, now had somewhere tangible to skip to. Macari's wife worked there along-side other relations.

"I went in a few times and saw how much hard work it was," he explains. "I never did serve behind the counter, but my wife did. And I still own it."

The 1976/77 season saw Macari play 53 games for United – the most of his career in one season. United were in Europe for first time since 1968/69, in the UEFA Cup where opponents of the highest quality awaited.

"We played Ajax, who had won three European Cups on the spin in the Seventies. They beat us 1-0 away, setting us up for the game at home. The atmosphere was as good as I had known and I felt ten feet tall when I opened the scoring. Sammy McIlroy got the winner. We were through."

Juventus were next, the Italians having overcome Manchester City in the first round. They were cynical and crude with their deliberate fouls. The Italians were constantly booed and called animals by an incensed Old Trafford crowd. They didn't care.

"Gordon Hill – our main threat – was kicked pillar to post by Marco Tardelli and the brutal Claudio Gentile, but he got the only goal of the game."

Hill's goal was seen as too slender a lead to protect and United's performance was roundly criticised in the press, with one paper noting, "United totally failed to produce sufficient variety of ideas, banging long shots at a goalkeeper as classy as Dino Zoff is a pointless exercise."

"My greatest prank was before that game," explains Macari, recalling a happier memory of the tie.

"I managed to cut the end off the socks of every Italian journalist who came to Manchester. The press had arranged a game against the English press lads the day before the match at the Cliff. As they played, I put all the sock ends in the teapot and took great delight when I watched them drink their tea through the keyhole. They were making noises as if they were enjoying the traditional English tea. Then they started putting their socks on and pulling them right up over their feet. They didn't have a clue what was going on."

Macari was a compulsive prankster, as the accounts of Gerry Daly, Martin Buchan and Paddy Roche confirm in this book.

"I once put a dozen dead bluebottles under physio Jimmy McGregor's lamb at The Cliff," he smiles. "He started eating it and was really enjoying the food. He was whistling while he ate, and I watched him, hidden away in the kitchen. Then the bluebottles started to appear. He looked disgusted then he shouted, 'Macari!'"

Macari considers his greatest achievements at Old Trafford to be his performances in the 1977 FA Cup.

"I scored in the fourth, fifth and sixth rounds. Then we met Leeds in the semi-final. As we lined up, Gordon McQueen, then of Leeds, shouted 'Come on, lads, we've only got to beat a bunch of fucking midgets!' It was intimidating but funny at the same time. We just thought, 'Right, we'll see about midgets.' I'm only five foot five inches tall, but I take great pride in not being bullied or intimidated by anybody. We won 2-1."

Liverpool were next in the final.

"All the goals came in five mad minutes at the start of the second half. First Pancho for us and then Jimmy Case for them. Then the ball was played up to the halfway line. I outjumped one of the Liverpool lads, flicked it on, turned and headed for the box. The ball broke to me again. Jimmy Greenhoff was almost in my way. He was trying to get out of it because he knew he was in my line of vision. His movement distracted me a bit. I mishit the shot slightly and later learned that it deflected off him into the net. I knew it wasn't a brilliant shot, but I also knew it would end up in the back of the net. I wasn't bothered how it got there − all that mattered was that we were going to win the FA Cup."

The first Macari knew of the scorer of the goal being in dispute was when Greenhoff walked into the dressing room holding the golden boot − the prize for the winning goal in the FA Cup final.

"I had been waiting for someone to give it to me, but wasn't that bothered that Jimmy kept it. The main thing was that we beat Liverpool."

Macari didn't join in the drinking at the post-match party at the team hotel.

"I'd sit and watch the lads drink and laugh to myself as they did things they wouldn't dream of doing sober," he says. "Sensible people like Ray Wilkins and Steve Coppell would come alive. Gordon McQueen was a funny lad sober. When he was drunk he was funny enough to have made a living on the stage."

Like so many of United's players in the Seventies, the 1977 FA Cup was to be Macari's only major trophy at United.

"I didn't win the league with United, but the competition was far tougher then. Nottingham Forest and Derby County both won the league in the Seventies. Forest had Trevor Francis, Larry Lloyd, John Robertson, Martin O'Neill and Peter Shilton. They won the European Cup twice. We played them when they were European champions in 1979 and beat them 3-0. I don't know how because they absolutely battered us.

"Leeds and Liverpool had very strong sides with great players. Ipswich were a fine side. There were eight or nine teams genuinely in contention to win the league because the money was more even. Derby were better payers than United for example. Players would leave United, join clubs like West Ham and see their wages increase."

With the best players spread around more teams, the chances of one team dominating the league were lower. Six different teams were crowned champions of England in the Seventies, more than in any other decade. Nine different teams finished in the top two, although United were not one of them.

"United never had the consistency," explains Macari. "We destroyed Everton 6-2 at Goodison on Boxing Day 1977. It was best performance I was involved in at United – and I'm not just saying that because I got a couple of goals. Yet we'd lost the two games before that, 2-1 at West Ham and then we were taken apart by Forest and lost 4-0 at Old Trafford."

United finished 10th in 1977/78.

"If we won a game, then we'd would go to the Crossford pub

in Sale afterwards. The players would be joined by the press lads once they had finished their match reports. We'd mix, and there would be fans in there too.

"The players understood that the journalists had a job to do and we largely got on well. If they did something underhand – and I don't mean give us 5/10 when we felt we deserved 7/10 – then you would just ignore them. Some of the married lads would drift home at nine, others would stay out later. We'd go to Soames Casino in town – the owner is one of Fergie's closest friends and now runs Les Ambassadeurs in London – and they would give us a free meal because we played for United. You could even have prawns!"

Macari would usually go home to Sale after the casino.

"Others would get home at nine the next day," he says. "I honestly don't think it had a great effect on the players when they came into training on a Monday."

The United players earned good money compared to the man in the street.

"I was on £200 a week, and the average wage then was about £30," explains Macari. "So we had money, but not enough to push the boat out, to go to the South of France for a few days after a game or to retire once we'd finished playing. We really valued our win bonuses, which you only got when you played. So everyone was desperate to play – that was a good thing."

Macari was almost ever present for United between 1973 and 1981, never playing fewer than 38 matches per season.

"We got to the FA Cup final again in 1979 after knocking Liverpool out in the semi-final replay," he says. "We drew 2-2 at Maine Road after Alan Hansen had equalised for them eight minutes from time. There was a lot of needle in the match, and Emlyn Hughes tried to take the piss out of Gordon McQueen in the tunnel afterwards by saying how Liverpool were going to win the replay. Big Gordon just banged him one. And we won the replay.

"Our new manager, Dave Sexton, came into the dressing room

at Wembley before the final against Arsenal and sat a magnum of whisky on the floor in front of everybody. 'This is what we all need today,' he said, 'bottle.' He got what he wanted, to a degree, when we fought back from 2-0 down in he last five minutes. He must have thought that we'd drunk it because the equaliser went to our heads and Arsenal got a winner."

Macari thinks that Sexton was misunderstood.

"He was football through and through and had no other interests," he explains. "At the end of one end-of-season tour we ended up in Hawaii for a week. It was brilliant. Waikiki Beach, Honolulu, Pearl Harbour, we did them all. Five days in we started to get concerned as we hadn't seen Dave. He'd been in his room watching nothing but American sport, absorbing everything. When he did join us he wanted to organise a football quiz. When you are in Waikiki Beach there are a lot of things competing for your attention. A quiz is not one of them."

New faces had arrived at Old Trafford by the end of the Seventies, including Mickey Thomas.

"He admits that he was overwhelmed by playing for United," states Macari. "We'd turn up for training and Mickey would be nowhere to be seen, despite his car always being one of the first there. He lived in Rhyl and would drive over every day. When training started, he'd suddenly appear. He'd usually been with the reserve players, where he felt more comfortable. Yet he was fine on the pitch."

Sexton was replaced by Ron Atkinson in June 1981. From playing 44 games the season before Atkinson arrived, Macari, 32, played 12 in Big Ron's first season.

"I was sub a lot, and that was okay with me. Of course I wanted to start, but I had to be more realistic. I did come on for Kevin Moran in the 1983 League Cup final, but I didn't make the team for the FA Cup final a few months later. There were no offers to renew my contract.

"I spent 11 years at United and had a testimonial game against Celtic in 1984. Over 44,000 turned up for arguably the best night

of my whole career. Over 20,000 Celtic fans came – which I found
a great honour because I'd left the club many years earlier."

Macari moved to the West Country after Old Trafford to
manage Swindon Town.

"I'd not given management much thought and didn't know
what was in store, but I set about trying to do things in the way
Jock Stein would have done. We had a discipline and routine. I
stressed the importance of fitness and got a good response. We
were promoted from the Fourth Division to the Third and then
to the Second."

Macari was attracting admirers. Ken Bates approached him and
offered him the Chelsea job.

"I agreed to that, but then he tried to install an assistant who
I didn't know and I said no. West Ham offered me their job in
1989, replacing John Lyall who had been there since 1974. That
was going back to my roots in East London. I had a bit of trouble
with players in the first two weeks, when Paul Ince was pictured
wearing a Manchester United shirt. I was threatened by his agent
Ambrose Mendy, who was a bit of a lad and didn't want me to
stand in Paul Ince's way, while I wanted to keep one of our best
young players."

Matters reached a head as West Ham were about to leave for
a pre-season game.

"Paul was pictured wearing the Manchester United shirt in a
paper. Now I had a problem. United had not spoken to us. I was
determined not to let Ince leave, no matter what Mendy said. But
that picture changed everything. United got in touch and offered
£2 million. The fee was agreed, and Ince went to Manchester
before failing a medical. West Ham settled for £1 million up front
with the rest payable over a certain term. Ince was gone."

Macari went soon afterwards.

"I was involved in an Inland Revenue investigation about players
receiving undeclared payments. Everyone was at it in the lower
divisions, receiving extra money for winning games. The Inland
Revenue wanted to shake up football and sort out the problem

of undeclared payments. They had a tip-off about Swindon and investigated from there. I was soon embroiled. It was very distracting and eventually I went to the secretary and suggested that I stand down. West Ham wanted to stick by me and the fans did. I should have stayed, but I stepped down to concentrate on the trial. I went to court and got found not guilty. The chairman was found guilty and jailed."

Macari's next job was at Birmingham City.

"I went without a contract on the understanding that if I won anything I would be looked after. I took Birmingham to Wembley where we won the Leyland DAF Cup. Over 40,000 Birmingham fans went to Wembley and we had a great day out. The chairman gave me a cheque for my work and I thanked him, went outside and had a look at the amount. My bonus? £1,800. I expected about £20,000. I went back in and told him that it was an insult. He told me to write out my own cheque. I didn't, but cashed the one for £1,800 instead. Stoke City called a couple of years later and we had a great time. We won promotion and went to Wembley, winning the Football League Trophy. I was happy at Stoke and had a five-year contract on the table, but then Celtic offered me the manager's job in 1993."

Celtic were a club in turmoil.

"Attendances had plummeted and fans were boycotting games. Some were even standing outside the turnstiles trying to stop other fans going into the ground. There was trouble in the board-room and takeover bids talked about too. The club was facing bankruptcy. The advice given to me by people in football was not to go near the place.

"But I had been a lad who followed Celtic and then played for them. To manage them was an opportunity that I could not turn down, even though there was the possibility that I could find even more problems at Celtic. The temptation was too big and I took the job.

Celtic was that big a mess I didn't really know where to start. The biggest problem was in the dressing room where there were two camps of players – and they both disliked each other. I started to get to the bottom of why they disliked each other and there were lots of reasons, many of which didn't involve me. There was no money to bring players in; that had been spelt out to me before I arrived. It was a case of making do."

Fergus McCann became chairman six months after Macari arrived at Celtic Park.

"Results had been up and down. I was at Celtic Park on the night that the takeover was completed. I was alarmed that Celtic were now controlled by people from overseas, but my main concern was for my job. The following day, I received a phone call from a journalist. He said, 'You are not the chosen one. Just be ready to lose your job.'"

"We played at St Johnstone that day. McCann walked into the dressing room and barely acknowledged me. He shook hands with a few players, who he was on first-name terms with. I started putting the plot together."

For the next month McCann didn't speak to Macari once.

"His office was 25 yards from mine. The first time I spoke to McCann was at the first board meeting, but even then football matters were over in a flash. There was no great desire to get the football team up and running, but there was no way that they wanted to keep me. I just had to bide my time, knowing that I didn't have much of a future.

"Still, I tried to do my job. I would try and get improved contracts for promising young players who were on £200 a week – players who went on to play for Scotland. I would take them to McCann and he would rip the contracts up and ask what right I had to negotiate contracts.

"I quickly felt that the club were looking to get rid of me without me paying up my contract. I would travel to matches to look at players. McCann told me that it wasn't my job to look at players. The relationship was awful, the communication always negative. He said that I couldn't go on holiday in the summer. I told him that I was going to the World Cup in America to try and find players who were good enough to play for Celtic. He told me that I wasn't. He offered a compromise – that I could go to games on the condition that I returned to Glasgow after every game with a report on the match. It was quite ridiculous. I felt that he was trying to build up a portfolio to get rid of me. We only communicated through solicitors. I went to the World Cup and was told that I was being sacked because I didn't have permission. I sat next to the Rangers manager, Walter Smith, at the first game.

"'I've just been sacked,' I said.

'What do you mean, you've just been sacked? What for?'

'Coming to the World Cup.'

He couldn't believe the situation.

"I took Celtic to court citing unfair dismissal. The trial lasted a month at the Crown Court in Edinburgh. At the end of it, the judge, Lady Cosgrove, was very critical of Mr McCann's conduct towards me, but had to stick by the rule of employment law. I lost the case. It cost me a lot of money. What started out as a dream job for me turned into a nightmare.

"My feelings for Celtic have not changed. I still feel like I did when I was a fan. The McCann episode was unfortunate. I was realistic – new boards bring their own people in. That wasn't a problem for me, but I felt I could have been treated better. I could have gone there three or four years later and it might not have been as bad. Celtic got their reward with McCann in the shape of a vastly improved stadium. McCann got his reward when he sold his shares on."

Macari went back to Stoke, then to Sheffield United with Steve Bruce and to Huddersfield, but football would seem inconsequential in 1999.

"I lost my lad, my youngest son Jonathan, who took his own life," explains Macari. Jonathan, 19, had been a young forward at Nottingham Forest. His body was found hanging from a tree in Stoke.

"It was easily the worst thing that has happened in my life, and my outlook changed dramatically. What did results matter when

I'd lost my son? The bereavement meant that my life changed. I found it difficult to think about management, to give it the energy and attention I should have done. There were times when I wanted to get on with things, and other times when I felt guilty because I somehow felt at fault. People told me not to feel guilty, but I did.

"People say that time heals. It doesn't. That's a load of crap. You can't forget. If you are in a family in which death is pushed aside then I suppose you can, but my wife has pictures of Jonathan all around the around the house. I'm not saying that I agree with that – maybe I would have preferred no pictures – but everyone does their own thing.

"Your life ends that day to what it was previously. There is nothing that can compensate for it."

Macari had to carry on.

"You have to," he says. "Bad things happen in life to everyone, it doesn't matter who they are. I have a family to look after, but I just wish that I had one more to look after."

The death made Macari question his faith.

"I was brought up a Catholic and used to go to church, but as time has gone on I have looked at religion differently. Some people who are very religious would say that my son took his life for a reason, but I'm sorry, I don't agree with that. Some people have suggested grief counselling too, but that would not be worth my while because I cannot accept that what happened was unavoidable."

Macari had known players take their own lives before.

"Alan Davies, my old team-mate at Manchester United, did exactly the same in 1992. Alan was a quiet lad and a tidy footballer. You would never think that he was capable of taking his own life, but then you don't think that of people do you?"

Davies was found dead in his car at the age of 30.

"I saw him play for Swansea at Stoke a few days earlier and he seemed his normal self, the happy fella I knew at United."

The Macaris had little privacy in bereavement.

"Reporters surrounded our house, and for the first time in my life I refused an interview," says Macari. "I just didn't have any answers to their questions and I still don't. I've spent hours wondering about what I could have done differently with Jon. It's too painful for me to go to his grave often, but when I do I see the headstones next to his. One was 86 when he died, another in his 70s. Jon was 19. Who knows what he might have gone on to achieve?"

Macari decided not to return to management afterwards.

"You have to be patient as a manager, you have put your arms around players or listen to their demands. I knew I couldn't do that any more. I couldn't listen to a player tell me that he felt hard done to when we'd lost our son. It all seemed so trivial, people worrying about getting into play-offs.

"Jon's death has become the defining event of my life," Macari explains. "You like to remember the great things that you've done – isn't that what life's about? But none of my achievements in football mean as much to me now. My judgement and decisions were usually right in my career. In the one area that really mattered, looking after my son, I did not make the right calls. I didn't get it right when it mattered, and that's a hell of a thing to have on your conscience.

"I started getting back on track by doing some television, and I scouted for the Republic of Ireland too. I enjoyed that, even if I missed the day-to-day involvement in football. I'm enjoying my life again and doing work for MUTV and other commentary, but I'd like to get back into management. If I don't, well, I've had a great career in football and I've been lucky enough to play for Manchester United and play and manage the team I supported as a boy."

The interview in the bar at Manchester's Malmaison hotel is drawing to a close.

"The game has completely changed from when I played," he concludes. "Everything about football has changed, and I'm not just on about the stadiums, the pitches, the media and the money.

People have come into the game and convinced everybody that if you sit down and eat a bowl of pasta then you'll play better than if you eat a plate of steak and chips like we used to.

"The most I ever earned from football was £420 a week at United. A few years ago, a friend was selling an apartment in a posh part of Altrincham. He knew that a fringe United player was looking for a place, and I called the player. The apartment was £900,000. The price was no problem to him — and this for a player not even established. That made me think that something had gone badly wrong with football."

4

GORDON HILL

MERLIN

The English accent with the tinge of cockney stands out a mile on the lush playing fields north of Dallas.

"Good lad," shouts Gordon Hill, "Well done, yes Johnny, yes!"

The former Manchester United and England winger is clad in a full red kit and boots as he bellows instructions to 14 young players who form part of United FC − a club of several youth teams and around 80 players near Hill's home which has been going on since 2004 in the Texan city.

Hill first played on loan in America while a 20-year-old with Millwall. Later in his career − after spells under Tommy Docherty at United, Derby County and Queens Park Rangers − he played for several American clubs, before moving full-time to Texas with wife Claire and their son Sammy.

Back in the Seventies, Reds idolised the chirpy cockney and the Scouser Steve Coppell on the opposite wing.

"We played great football under Tommy Docherty," recalls Hill. "He bought attacking players like myself and Steve Coppell, wingers who played the United way. Stevie was the worker, I was the entertainer. We thrilled the crowds and terrorised defenders. We were a young team who beat Ajax and Juventus in Europe."

United fans labelled Hill 'Merlin', as in the magician, and 'King of all Cockneys.' Doc's Red Army also sang a song to the tune of *Save Your Kisses For Me.*

Training finished, Hill drives back to his house in McKinney, where he agrees to recite the words to the song in his back garden as he tends to his flowers.

"Bye bye, Derby, bye bye . . . because we beat you 2-0, with two goals from Gordon Hillllllll," he sings with a smile as he recalls his greatest moment, scoring both goals in the 1976 FA Cup semi-final which took United to Wembley.

From the Thames to Texas, Hill has led an eventful life.

"I was born in Sunbury-on-Thames in 1954, a small and beautiful riverside town," he says, from the comfort of his sofa. "My father was a gardener at Hampton Court. He never drove, but cycled to work with a spade across his handlebars. He worked at the Water Board too, but had to retire when he put a drill through his foot. He had a lot of responsibility, what with nine kids. Dad liked a drink down the local pub and I'd often find him there, but I spent most of my time playing football."

Six of the nine children were boys.

"My big brother, Sid, was on Brentford's books and Graham was on Chelsea's," explains Hill. "I was on QPR's books. Tottenham and West Ham wanted me to sign for them when I was 11, but my parents didn't want me travelling across London on the Tube."

Tottenham's seduction efforts amounted to sending a young Hill six match-day programmes and a signed autograph sheet accompanied by a letter saying that they had been watching him and wanted him to sign.

"Tottenham played in North London," he says. "I was way out west of London. And still at school."

Hill stayed with QPR, though he wasn't a supporter of any of the London clubs.

"I watched Chelsea because my tennis coach could get tickets, but only when I wasn't playing."

A tennis coach and a village by the Thames are not typical footballer backgrounds.

"We lived in a council house!" laughs Hill. "The area was affluent, but we weren't. And the tennis coach was at the local youth club. We came from a very humble background. We wore hand-me-downs, but we were happy. We had to put money in the television for it to work, and we only got a phone when all the children chipped in after they had moved out. We all agreed to buy one so that we could call the house, which was the hub of the family. Apart from me, the family never moved far away, and mum was the head of the family. When we started earning we'd give her money. She never asked for it, but we gave her enough to go to the bingo – which she loved.

"Years later, when my mum came to watch me in the 1977 Cup final, word got out in the stand that she was my mum. United fans were bowing to her, and she was very embarrassed by it. She didn't enjoy that attention at all. She would give attention to other people and was a great giver. She'd give you the cardigan off her back, but she didn't like attention from others."

Hill played for Sunbury Celtic and wore number 10. At 14, he was playing an open-aged league for his brothers' Sunday team, Sunbury Casuals, where the other players paid his subs. School came a distant second place to football

"I wasn't a scholar," he states. Many who know him would agree. "Though I loved wood and woodwork. Wood smells nice. I hated metal and metalwork. Metal makes me cringe, but I found working with wood like a release and I started an apprenticeship in wordwork. I would have been a pattern maker – an elite carpenter, and I mean elite. I would have made precise patterns for foundries, but football took over."

His brother Sid was training pre-season with Southall, a semi-pro team, when he invited young Gordon along.

"Sometimes I was allowed to take part," he explains. "My problem was that I wasn't very big. But I could handle myself."

Even though he was only 17, Hill was without a club, but it was his own doing.

"I had walked out on QPR. I didn't like the system and one of the coaches told me to get my hair cut. I told him that I didn't play with my hair, and that was that. My hair wasn't even that long. So Southall asked me if I'd like to sign for them, and I said yes."

Hill played for six months in front of crowds of anything up to 700.

"I scored 22 goals in no time before Millwall came in with an offer of a trial," he recalls. "I had two trial games and did well. That was it. Millwall offered me a professional contract when most lads my age at clubs were on apprenticeships."

He didn't take long to think about it.

"Signing as a professional, even at Millwall, was a highlight of my career. That's when I knew the road was open. When somebody tells you they want to sign you as a pro it's a wonderful moment. I was bouncing off the walls. I was on 25 quid a week and thought I'd won the lottery. I was training with Millwall legends, and my priority was to establish myself in the first team."

That didn't take long.

"We had an away game at Carlisle," he says. "I was going along for the ride and never expected to play. Normally we would have travelled there by train, but a strike meant we took a bus which took forever. We had an hour to rest at the hotel and then went to play the game. I came on as sub and ripped my marker to pieces, setting up the equaliser. The eight-hour journey home didn't seem so long. Benny Fenton, the boss, was the man who gave me the early confidence to succeed."

With a defence containing indomitable left-back Harry Cripps (the substantially built Millwall cult figure) and an expansive midfield which featured Eamon Dunphy and Keith Weller, the Lions came within a point of promotion to the First Division in 1972, a year before Hill joined. Those older pros could be merciless in their mickey taking.

"You had to be so sharp, and I was young and naïve," says Hill. "They knew that I liked tennis and got one of their mates to ring me in the hotel before an away game at Bournemouth. They pretended to be from local television and said that they wanted to interview me about tennis. I agreed to it and went down to reception where the rest of the players were laughing at me. I ended up having an imaginary game of tennis with Harry Cripps, with the sofa as a net and all the players watching."

Hill's style was open to interpretation, and Dunphy later wrote, "You never knew what he was going to do. Which makes him impossible to play with. And he gives the ball away too much. He has learnt a little, but I doubt his capacity to learn much. And he's not very good at picking people up. When you say to him: 'watch the full-back,' he just watches him race away. He literally just watches him." Dunphy, who hadn't made the grade at Old Trafford, poked fun at Hill at length in his 1976 autobiographical diary, *Only A Game?* now considered a classic of football literature. The mockery in print is a huge, if back-handed, compliment, because also what comes through loud and clear is the envy of Hill's abundant, natural talent and that Millwall fans loved him.

Hill returned the compliment, feeling relaxed even at the notorious Den.

"It could be a cold place to come for people who came to cause trouble, but it was the warmest place to play, especially as a youngster," he says. "The crowd could be harsh and the fans were quick to react if I did something wrong. It was love and hate, but the hatred would be followed by more support."

Millwall's following was notorious.

"A lot of villains were in the stands and the players' bar after," recalls Hill. "I knew a lot of the younger guys who went on to be villains. I was on the same wavelength as most of them because

I was a working-class boy. They loved football and I loved playing football for their team. I'd go down the pie and eel shops on the Old Kent Road with them."

Hill doesn't deny that the reputation of Millwall fans being hooligans was sometimes deserved.

"There was one game against Luton when Don Shanks [Stan Bowles's gambling partner and later boyfriend of Mary Stavin, the 1977 Miss World who, clad in a diaphanous baby doll nightie, was the blonde Swedish stunner in George Best's 'Where did it all go wrong, George?' anecdote] whacked me near the touchline. A Millwall fan jumped out of the crowd and chased him. Don legged it. The fan was carted off and Don said to me at half-time, 'These fans are mad.' He still clattered me in the second half . . . again a fan jumped out from the crowd – the posh side with seats this time – and chased him. I could hear him saying, 'Leave Merlin alone or I'll fucking kill you'. Most of the Millwall fans were dockers, and the real hardcore stood in the Cold Blow Lane end."

Until the early 1960s, Millwall were the only club allowed to start home games at 3.15pm, specifically to allow nearby dockers to finish their morning shift.

"A lot of the trouble at matches stemmed from fans trying to take each others' end," explains Hill. "I never saw any fans take the Cold Blow Lane End. A hundred Millwall fans would fight a thousand if it meant protecting their end."

Playing on the wing meant that he was closer to fans than most.

"I saw a lot of incidents where fans came on to the pitch. I must have looked worried, and one fan told me, 'Don't you worry son. You'll be protected, but we're gonna sort this lot out good and proper.' I think you had to be a Millwall person to understand how the club worked."

It wasn't only the fans who were characters.

"We trained on a cinder pitch in Deptford. We'd walk from the Den under the railways and train. Then we'd walk back to the ground. Harry Cripps would get his little silver Jaguar washed by the apprentices. We had another player whose brother ran a fruit and veg stall, so we never went short of fresh veg. There was another who used to sell clobber from the boot of his car. A lot of goods came in off the docks, from sugar to petrol. You could get anything."

Hill was making the left wing his own.

"I stood out and got a lot of praise," he says. "I knew that bigger clubs were watching me, but I was happy at Millwall and not looking for a move. Happy playing in front of 13,000 people who loved me every week."

Millwall knew that they would be selling their prize asset. When Hill was offered a three-month contract playing in Chicago in the summer of 1975 it only served to increase his profile.

"I felt like I was going to the land of Al Capone," he says. "The former United defender Bill Foulkes was the manager. I knew that United had been watching me, but I think Bill pushed the point because I was ripping defenders to shreds in America. I was getting MVP [Most Valuable Player] every week [for Chicago Sting] in front of 3-4,000 people and played in the All-Star team with Pele. He told me that I was "an English Brazilian" and said that he loved watching me play because of the way I danced with a ball. Imagine hearing that as a kid, from Pele?"

It would begin a lifelong affinity with the United States, and self-confidence was seldom an issue for the winger.

"I was classed as the best volleyer in the world," says Hill. "I wouldn't let the ball hit the floor, I'd strike it as it came out of the air. At England get-togethers, Ray Wilkins would say, 'I've never seen anyone strike the ball like that'. I had pace and a low centre of gravity, and I would try anything."

Bill Foulkes described him as the most exciting player in the American league – and included Pele in that assessment.

Hill returned to England after scoring 16 goals in 22 games in his three months in Illinois, a superb strike-rate for a winger that would become the hallmark of his career.

"Arsenal and Tottenham were watching me, but I went back to Millwall," he says. "Tommy Docherty was putting the final pieces to his Manchester United plan. United had been promoted back to the First Division, and Docherty was looking for someone to replace George Best."

United made their move in November 1975.

"At half-time during a League Cup game, the Millwall manager told me that I was not going back on. I asked him why and if it was to save me for Saturday. He told me that I wouldn't be playing for the club again because the bank had told Millwall they had to sell me. News of a bid from United had only just arrived. I was disappointed to go off, but excited about United."

Hill had to meet the Millwall manager the next morning at Euston station to get his ticket to Manchester.

"I took my boots and travelled north. Apart from the Chicago trip, I'd never travelled out of London by myself before."

Gordon Clayton was waiting for Hill at Piccadilly. Hailing from the West Midlands, Clayton had been a goalkeeper at United and a close friend of Duncan Edwards. Mainly a reserve 'keeper, he played only twice for the first team in his six years at Old Trafford but worked at the club in the Seventies. He died in September 1991 aged just 54. He is referred to in the introduction to this book.

The two Gordons hit it off immediately after Clayton said, "You are United. Your style is United."

Hill was taken straight to Old Trafford.

"I was overawed by the place," he says. "One of my brothers had a poster of Best, Law and Charlton on his bedroom wall, and now I was being asked to join the club they'd played at. I was taken to a room where Louis Edwards, TD and Sir Matt Busby were sat down."

Edwards began with an insult, saying, "You're a flash London bastard, but we'll cut you down to size."

"It didn't put me off, and United didn't need selling," recalls Hill. "I would have played for United for nothing. I signed a contract without actually realising how much I would get paid a week. I had to ask later and was told that it would be £125 –

double what I'd been on at Millwall. I had a signing on fee of £3,500 too. United would also pay for my lodgings. They told me that they were putting me up in the Piccadilly Hotel, but I was to watch United play that night."

The match was a League Cup derby where the score ended up Manchester City 4 Manchester United 0.

"I thought it couldn't be true, United losing 4-0," he says. "Colin Bell got carried off the pitch, and the injury was so bad that he would never be the same again." City would go on to win the League Cup, which would be their last trophy for 35 years.

Hill returned to the Piccadilly and stayed there until renting a place in Buxworth in the Peak District, 18 miles south east of Manchester.

"All the other players lived around Sale, but I wanted to be in the countryside," he explains. "I'd never lived in the country and wanted to live near the hills. There was fresh air and a good local pub owned by Pat Phoenix, Elsie Tanner from Coronation Street."

Hill lived there with his first wife Jackie. "I married when I was very young," he explains.

Hill's transfer fee was £70,000.

"Even at the time it was a fairly modest fee," commented Tommy Docherty later. "Gordon was a fast, direct winger who was not only a maker but a taker of goals. He had tremendous ability, and his attitude and character were first class." Over time, Docherty would sign Hill on three occasions.

"Ken Ramsden, one of the United secretaries, pointed me to a financial adviser," he explains. "He told me not to take my signing on fee but to start a pension. I could never thank them enough for that advice. It wasn't a huge pension – it's £400 a month now – but I have been drawing it since I was 35."

Hill didn't have an agent, but there were other offers of money.

"*Shoot!* magazine offered me some money to do a column each week which was ghosted by a journalist."

Hill made his United debut v Aston Villa on 15 November 1975.

"It was hard," he recalls. "The standard was much higher than Milwall, and I got cramps after the game." The United line-up was: Stepney, Nicholl, Houston, Daly, B. Greenhoff, Buchan, Coppell, McIlroy, Pearson, Macari and Hill. Docherty's team was complete. United won 2-0.

He travelled back to London after the game.

"I'd travel by train, first class," he says. "I'd never travelled first class, but United paid for my ticket. I bumped into my old Millwall team-mates. They spotted me. They were not in first class and had played at Bury, and I was soon in normal class having a few beers. I wasn't one for heavy drinking and never found pubs fun, but I'd left a mark at Millwall and it was time to say goodbye properly."

He was an immediate success at United, with fans praising Docherty for the signing. And he would go on being a success in each of his three years at the club. His goalscoring record of 51 goals in 132 appearances is one of the best ever achieved by a United winger.

Hill liked living in the hills, though after a year in Buxworth he moved to Bollington so that he could be nearer Macclesfield train station and the connection to London.

"I stayed there for a long time," he says. "Joe Corrigan and Rodney Marsh lived nearby, but Marsh was never my cup of tea, even though he was a Londoner. I remember him from being a kid at QPR. He was arrogant then and he hadn't changed."

Hill was an ever present after his debut and played 33 games through to the end of 1975/76, scoring 10 goals including both of those against Derby in the FA Cup semi-final at Hillsborough.

He'd also shown his volleying talents earlier in the competition when United knocked out Peterborough at Old Trafford.

"That tie was settled by a wonderful piece of skill by Gordon Hill," recalled Docherty later. "He was 25 yards from goal when the ball was played to him wide on the right. I expected him to control the ball and lay it off. Instead he conducted a half-turn of his body, got his head over the ball and volleyed it with his left foot. Eric Steele [the current goalkeeping coach at Old Trafford] stood frozen to the spot. A matter of a second after leaving Hill's boot the ball jerked the centre of the net into he shape of an elbow. It was a tremendous goal."

Hill was always determined to do better.

"I used to watch *Match of the Day* each week and see their Goal of the Month. Then I'd say to myself, 'You can do better than that.'"

Those semi-final goals are undoubtedly his most famous United moments and his personal favourite.

"That brace was the highlight of my whole career," he says. "The first one stands out. I was in the middle and played a one-two with Gerry Daly, who was at the left edge of the penalty area. I took one touch, and as Roy McFarland ran to close me down I bent a left-footer into the top corner. We were going to Wembley.

"United fans took over Hillsborough and everyone was singing. We stopped at Mottram Hall to celebrate after the game and there was a wedding reception on. They invited us in, and *Save Your Kisses for Me* was playing. Tommy Docherty began singing away – but with the words to the United version. We were so happy to be going to Wembley for the first time since 1963 in the greatest cup competition in the world."

Hill's greatest match was followed by arguably his worst in the final, but he wasn't alone.

"The 1976 FA Cup final was a nightmare," he says. "Everybody expected us to beat Second Division Southampton, but the day got to us. That season they'd brought out the card system, where they held up your number for substitutions. It was towards the end of the game, and we were losing 1-0 when I saw number 11 go up. As I walked to the bench I turned to Tommy Docherty and said, 'What? Fucking me?' and he said, 'No, the whole fucking team'. Even though I was so disappointed I had to chuckle."

Docherty was later more pointed in his criticism.

"Semi-final hero Hill found no headway against Southampton's experienced skipper Peter Rodrigues," he said. "As he wilted away, I moved to substitute him."

Unfortunately, that cup final was the only game in Hill's entire career which his dad attended.

"He never came again because he thought he'd bring me bad luck."

Hill had settled in and loved life at United.

"Teams hated coming to Old Trafford — they could smell us too. Our kit smelt of Five Oils, a preparation used in massages which no other team seemed to use. Teams would smell us and say, 'That's Man United.' All we had to do was open the skip."

While he was hugely popular with fans, his personality wasn't to everyone's taste. His birthday is April Fool's Day, and some considered it to be very apt.

"I was a quick-witted and funny Londoner," he says. "It wasn't arrogance, but I've always felt that smiling is the best way to make people feel at ease. I did impressions of everyone off the television. If I got just one word right then people would laugh. Norman Wisdom was my favourite and I wore a cap to carry it off. I did John Wayne, Max Bygraves . . ."

At one stage, Hill was photographed as frequently by the tabloids in a Wisdom-trademark peaked cap and ill-fitting buttoned-up shirt as he was in a red shirt.

"I was a bit of a joker and didn't see eye to eye with everyone," Hill continues. "Martin Buchan once clipped me round the head during a game for not picking up a player. I saw red and went after him. I told him that if he did again I would kill him. The ref pulled us to one side saying, 'I've never sent two players off from the same team for fighting, so calm down.' Martin was a good lad, but you don't have to be best friends with people you work with. There were 12-15 personalities in that dressing room. We may not all have got on well off the pitch, but when we went out on to the field the respect for our team-mates kicked in and we were the best young team in the country."

Buchan gave a hint of his opinion of Hill in the lyrics to his

Old Trafford Blues song, which became the B side of the 1976 Cup Final single, *Manchester United*:

> *Then there's Brian Greenhoff, he's got lots of skill*
> *And he really needs it to play with Gordon Hill*

The 'different personalities' in the team manifested themselves in unusual ways.

"Gerry Daly took his driving test," recalls Hill. "He was picked up from The Cliff in an old Ford Cortina and a few of us watched out the window. Gerry made himself at home by opening the window and having a cigarette. Then we saw him drive away along a path. He later told us that the driving instructor had said, 'Mr Daly, you can come off the path.'

Daly did pass his test.

"His car used to have bumps all over it. I pointed this out to him by showing him the marks and dents on the bumper. He replied, in all seriousness, that it was made like that.

"Gerry bought a powerful car off Jim Holton and crashed it early one morning. The police came and told him to clear off. Gerry came in to training the next day and had a go at Jim because he hadn't told him that the car had power steering.

"We locked the Doc in the toilet on the team coach on the way back from one game. After a while he just kicked the door open and steamed out looking to see who was responsible.

"The Doc barged out and grabbed David McCreery – the player sat closest to the toilet. The Doc banged David's head against the coach window and then went back to his seat. McCreery wasn't the one who had locked his manager in the toilet, but still no one owned up.

"We'd put Mentholatum – wintergreen – or Five Oils on the toilet seat. Players would go in and sit there reading the programme and come out in pain."

Not everyone appreciated Hill's brand of humour.

"Hill might be termed an enigma; or to put it another way, he was scatterbrained. But my, how he could play," said the former Busby Babe John Doherty, who remained close to the club. "He had a left peg to die for and, for a winger, his scoring record was nothing short of sensational."

Hill scored 22 goals in 55 games in 1976/77, his best season for United. He also won the first of his six England caps.

"I played for the under-21s at Old Trafford against Hungary. England manager Don Revie told me that I was travelling with the first team. That's when I thought that I'd really made it as a player."

His England debut was against Italy in May 1976 and he played European football for the first time that year.

"We knocked Ajax out of the UEFA Cup," he says. "We had a great young team and met Juventus in the next round."

United struggled to break the Italians down.

"Gordon Hill, with an explosive volley, was the player who could breach what was an experienced and superbly organised Juventus defence," purred Docherty. "Victory over Juventus showed me how far this young team had come."

United were defeated 3-0 in Turin, but the point had been made. One reason Hill played 55 games that season was because United excelled in cup competitions. It took two replays to separate United and Southampton in the FA Cup and two replays against Sunderland in the League Cup. Still in the FA Cup, United entered April facing a schedule of 13 games in six weeks. A tough league match against an Everton side who had knocked United out of the League Cup with an emphatic three-goal victory at Old Trafford was decided by two Hill goals, one scored with typical aplomb.

"Hill had the ball 35 yards from goal," recalls his manager. "And he decided to chip the goalkeeper. It was delightful."

A Hill shot in the FA Cup semi-final against Leeds later that month cannoned off Paul Madeley and was picked up by Steve Coppell. United won 2-1 and were back at Wembley against Liverpool.

"We were the underdogs but won 2-1," says Hill. "I had a better game than a year earlier and, though I felt very tired, I was substituted for tactical reasons. We were winning and the gaffer put David McCreery on to hold things a little tighter."

"After the game the press wanted us all to pose for pictures with the cup in the bath. Wembley's old bath was about six feet deep and they put about four feet of water in it. So we threw in the lid and then the cup itself, but the guy who'd filled the bath had forgotten to put cold water in. Stuart Pearson was aching so much he'd put Fiery Jack on his legs. He jumped in and nearly got third-degree burns. He jumped out without touching the sides. He looked like a lobster. We all stood looking at the cup at the bottom of the bath. It had taken us a year to win it, but it was still out of reach."

Hill rises to the defence of the FA Cup as a competition.

"It's the most important domestic cup in world football," he says. "Every player wants to pick up the FA Cup. Playing for your country is the icing on the cake, playing in a World Cup is icing too. But lifting the FA Cup is best of all. Every team in the country has a crack at it. It runs almost all year round from August until May. You could go to little grounds, real David v Goliath matches every year. There's always upsets, and isn't that what football is about?"

On holiday in Ibiza in the summer of '77, Hill's relaxing off-season break was soured by a chance meeting with Sammy McIlroy.

"Heard about the Doc?" asked McIlroy. "He's been having an affair with Mary Brown. United will cane his arse for that. There's a lot of religious people at the club."

Hill was very concerned.

"The Doc was a player's man, a hard man but a likeable rogue. If he was going to stab you in the back then he'd tell you a week before he did it."

The Doc had so many facets to him. "On one hand he was the best coach I played under because he was a great one for inspiring you to perform to your best. I coach kids now and I'm careful not to over coach a youngster. I try to see what he's already good at and help him do it even better."

"On the other hand none of us trusted him. Martin Buchan got £1,500 for the players for winning the FA Cup. It was in a suitcase and he told the Doc to keep it until after the summer as the players had gone away. We never saw that money again."

Hill still sticks up for the man he usually calls TD.

"He had a self-destruct button which he'd press every three years," he says. "He did so much good at United but took a lot of stick because he got rid of Crerand, Willie Morgan, Bobby and Denis Law. He had to let some of the older players go even though that didn't make him popular. The Sixties had been fabulous for them, but United weren't winning when the Doc arrived. He built a new United. We'd play at 100 miles per hour, but it was all controlled. We played great football under him. We knew what we were doing. We thrilled the crowds and terrorised defenders. They would hate playing against me and Stevie Coppell. We were totally different as players and people, him a Scouser who was at university and me a cheeky Londoner. Far more teams were in contention for the title than now, but we were going to win the league, I'm sure of it, then the Doc got sacked."

Dave Sexton took charge in time for the 1977/78 season and Hill feared that his style would not be to Sexton's liking.

"He didn't take to me," says Hill. "I found him a difficult guy. We couldn't come off the training field until we'd done something perfectly . . . even if that was at walking pace. He was the wrong person for the job at that time."

Despite his anxieties, Hill started every week.

"We played St Etienne in the UEFA Cup and then Porto in the next round. They beat us 4-0 away and left us with too much to do at home in the second leg."

Hill blames Iran for the defeat in Portugal.

"We played a friendly game to promote good relations with Iran," he says, recalling the now largely forgotten match on 24th

October 1977 against Iran B in Tehran. United won 2-0 in a game that had been requested by the British government to promote exports to the Middle East.

"We had to have vaccinations for smallpox and cholera. It wiped us out. We lost 4-0 at West Brom away a few days after the Porto game too."

Sexton's first season was not a success. Out of the League Cup in August, the FA Cup in the fourth-round stage and Europe before Christmas, United finished a disappointing tenth position in the league.

"I still think that Dave wanted to stamp his own authority on the team because what he managed that first season was the Doc's team. He started to sell players off who were key to the Doc's team and replaced them with Leeds players like Joe Jordan and Gordon McQueen. He should have built on the team, not replaced it."

Hill had started every league game, scoring 19 goals in 45 appearances, when Sexton called him into his office one Friday afternoon in April 1978.

"He told me that I would be playing in the reserves," he says. "He was trying to unsettle me, and it worked. I'd felt that for a while, felt that there was a vendetta against me. Those suspicions were confirmed. I was told after the game that United had accepted a bid for me."

Hill's suitor was none other than Tommy Docherty, manager of Derby with a bid for £250,000.

"I had been looking to sign a direct flying winger and Gordon fitted the bill perfectly," wrote Docherty later. "Word reached me that he was unhappy at Old Trafford. Gordon had caused me no problems at United. He put everything into his game, was a model professional and had been happy. I couldn't understand what had happened to make him feel so unhappy in such a short space of time. It was insinuated that some of the United players had singled Gordon out for mickey-taking, but he was big enough to take all that in good heart.

"During my time at United, Gordon picked up a head injury

when challenging in the air for the ball. As a precautionary measure we had him sent for a scan. When a reported asked if he was going to be fit for the following match he replied, 'I think so. I've seen a doctor who took a scan of my brain, but he found nothing.' It was a verbal gaffe and the players ribbed him about it for days, but he just laughed it off."

"I was off to Derby," sighs Hill. "It all happened too quickly. I returned to Old Trafford two days later to pick up my stuff and saw 'Sexton Out, Hill In' graffiti on the wall. The fans were worried that he was breaking the team up, which he was."

The Londoner had played for United for three seasons. He'd just turned 24.

Hill went public with his feelings, which drew an uncharacteristic response from Sexton, who said:

"The fact is that Gordon is a very selfish player. The other lads have had to do a lot of work to accommodate him." If Hill had been so problematic, why had Sexton started him almost every week?

"Derby were a prestigious club and my wages were far higher," says Hill of the move, "but they weren't Man United."

Derby didn't work out for Hill. He'd been virtually injury free at Old Trafford, but that luck would run out on 30 August 1978 – just four months after leaving the Reds.

"I'd scored the winning goal in a League Cup tie against Leicester when I attempted a slide tackle on George Armstrong. I didn't need to make that at the end of the game. I went in and my knee split. It scared the crap out of me because I couldn't move my leg. My left leg bent sideways instead of forward and back and I knew immediately it was a bad one. It's haunted me ever since. Why did I have to make that tackle? I was supposed to be in *Superstars* [a popular TV programme where sports personalities did a number of physical challenges] the next day too."

Hill had shattered his knee ligaments.

"It was career threatening," he says, wincing as he strokes his dog. "They put my leg in plaster for three or four weeks, but the surgeon warned that I might never play again. I stood up with tears in my eyes."

The plaster came off a few weeks later.

"When my leg came out of plaster it was like a chicken's leg."

Hill wouldn't play again for 18 months.

"I came back at the start of the next season and did a pre-season running up and down the stands at Derby. My knee felt heavy because my cartilage was being crushed and was deteriorating."

The stricken winger's life went into a spin.

"My marriage had fallen apart, I'd lost my England place and my knee was knackered," he says. "Mentally, I was gone. My wife had gone back to London and left me with nothing. She emptied my bank account. She took my daughter too. I was going to buy a house from Charlie George but suddenly didn't have any money and had to live in a hotel. I would go and sit in a wine bar each night in Derby and have a bottle of wine to get rid of the pain."

Hill was still not much of a drinker.

"I did it to feel happier," he says. "I was still training each day, but it was a long, hard, road. I could have packed it in quite easily.

"I really resented women because of what had happened to me and I sat in the bar cursing with anger one night. I felt horrible. I went back to the hotel and there was a reporter there. My ex-wife had written a piece in a paper slaughtering me. It said that I didn't like Manchester, and it accused me of being unfaithful when that wasn't true.

"I used to get up to 400 fan letters a week, and one was from a mad fan claiming that she had slept with me. My ex-wife took it as gospel and I was guilty until proven innocent."

Hill felt that he was being kicked while he was down.

"I was so, so low."

One night it came to a head.

"I went to the wine bar and a thought just came to me. It was very clear. I knew that drinking every night wasn't me. I got up, put the cork in the wine and said, 'Goodnight, you won't see me again.' I doubt that anyone there believed me, but I never went back. I didn't want to end up like so many other footballers, sat at the end of the bar talking about the past."

But Hill's luck was about to turn.

"A friend offered me a house in Ashbourne, and the bank offered me some money to buy it. I had help from friends kitting it out."

The physio also began to go well.

"I worked really, really hard. I was with other patients and they would wince if they had any pain. I would put myself through far more. I didn't want to be there. I wanted to be playing football."

Eighteen months after the tackle, he played again.

He also met a new partner, Claire, an air stewardess, who he's with to this day. She recalls meeting Hill.

"He was down when I met him and tried to get me involved in his problems, but I wanted to stay clear. If his ex-wife walked down the street I would not know what she looks like. I felt like she wanted to destroy Gordon, for him to go like George Best."

The divorce was not amicable.

"I haven't seen my FA Cup winner's medal since the day I received it," he says. "She won't give it back."

Tommy Docherty had been dismissed at Derby while Hill had been injured. He would have doubtless fared better if a fit Hill was in the team and scoring.

"Colin Addison was the manager and he told me that he wanted me to stay . . . but that there had been an offer from QPR, where I'd played as a kid. They were managed by TD . . ."

After just 24 games in two seasons, Hill left Derby in 1979 for a transfer fee of £175,000.

"Being in London was better because I had to go through the divorce," he says. "I started well at QPR but I hadn't got over my knee psychologically. I was always worried that it would go again. I did get back playing but was never the same. I'd lost a yard of pace, so I never played for England again. I had to rebuild my game, dropping a bit deeper and becoming a left-sided midfielder."

Hill was to play just 14 times for QPR in two seasons.

"Terry Venables replaced TD and told me that he was bringing new, younger players in. He told me that I was welcome to go if another club came in for me. I was only 28."

Canadian Club Montreal Manic, who played in the NASL, made an offer for Hill.

"I just thought, 'Fuck it, I'm going'," he says. "I'd gone through the divorce, though my ex-wife tried to play silly games when I wanted to get a visa for Canada. And my attitude about my knee changed from being scared of a repeat injury to being 'if it goes it goes.' Maybe I should have had that attitude at QPR."

Hill got what he craved in Montreal, first-team football every week.

"I did a pre-season and felt good. We played in South America pre-season in Uruguay, Peru and Paraguay. We played a game against Marseille and I scored two goals. They put an offer in for me, but Montreal didn't want to sell me. I had a great first season [he scored 18 goals in 36 matches]."

"Montreal was a lovely city," adds Claire, who made the move too with their son Sam, born in 1980. "But the politics made it difficult for us. There was a movement who wanted independence and some strong anti-English sentiments."

As his career wound down, Hill then started a tour of the USA. From Montreal he moved back to his old club, Chicago Sting.

"Then I played for San Jose Earthquakes, New York Arrows, Kansas Comets, Tacoma Stars, Twente in Holland and HJK Helsinki in Finland. Some of those American clubs were in the indoor league which ran then. I loved the American way of life, and that's one reason why we are here now."

The Hills moved back to England after the spells in Finland and Holland.

"Twente wanted me to stay another season and I did enjoy playing against teams like Ajax, but we wanted to move back home."

Hill signed part-time for Northwich Victoria, who were managed by his former team-mate Stuart Pearson. The Vics were his last club.

"I had a sports shop in Macclesfield too," he says. "That was a nightmare and we sold it. Broke even."

Hill then did his coaching badges and briefly managed Nova Scotia Clippers, Chester City and Hyde United.

"I was doing bits for MUTV and other media when I got a call from America. They said that they were looking for top-class coaches to coach in youth football. As I had my green card, we decided to go for it and have lived in the US since 2004. We love the lifestyle here and I have my own little club, United FC. It's not linked to United, but we wear red and white and I'll steer any diamonds towards Old Trafford if I spot them."

He watches United games from home, but has mixed views about modern football.

"The pitches are a dream for skilled players. I would have thrived, but the diving drives me crazy. If you dived in my day you were called a coward. These days they take a dive and then look at the referee and hold up their hand, pretending to wave a card, trying to get a guy booked. It's cheating."

And, of course, there aren't enough wingers.

"A good winger who can cross the ball is worth his weight in goals. Wingers should be nurtured because flair has been lost from the game."

The remnants of Doc's Red army will doubtless agree.

"I miss the good old days at Man United," he concludes. "It's that everyday camaraderie that you miss. I had a great career, but that injury came at the wrong time for me. I would have had 50 England caps if my knee hadn't gone. But I'm proud that I was United, proud that, despite being there for just three years, I am part of the history of that great club."

5

STUART PEARSON

PANCHO

STUART PEARSON

"I got a call from the secretary of Hull City who told me there was a club interested in me. He wouldn't tell me which one, which I found ridiculous. I told him I wasn't going to London without knowing who it was. He told me I wouldn't be disappointed." Stuart Pearson is sitting on the terrace at his home of six years overlooking the luxurious La Manga golf complex in Murcia, on Spain's eastern coast, recounting his less-than-happy memories of how he came to sign for Manchester United.

Without agents or chief executives getting involved in transfers in the 1970s, managers were free to wheel and deal, which suited Tommy Docherty down to the ground. Second Division or not, in the summer of 1974, United's need for a goalscorer was acute. Top scorer in 1972/73 had been Bobby Charlton, who managed six goals. In the following relegation season, Sammy McIlroy had matched his paltry total. Docherty's answer was to turn to his old club, Hull, where Stuart Pearson had been top goalscorer for the previous three seasons.

Pearson had prepared carefully for the encounter with what he assumed would be representatives from one of the London clubs when he was handed the train tickets. "Only George Best had an agent, so I asked Tony Kaye, the ex-West Brom player, who knew football inside out, for advice. He told me to ask for £150 a week and a signing on fee. 'If they ask you what you want,' Kaye instructed, 'ask them to make you an offer'.

He found out from Terry Neill, Hull's manager, whom he'd been told to meet at the Russell Hotel, that he was wanted by 'the biggest club in the world'.

Pearson went to the hotel room of Tommy Docherty, who was down in London for the 1974 cup final. "Paddy Crerand was in there too. The Doc said, 'Come on, Stuart, let's have a chat. What are you looking for?'

"'Make me an offer,' I replied, following the script.
'£80 a week.'
'TD, I'm on £85 at Hull. I want at least £100.'
'Done.' Docherty immediately put out his hand to shake on it.

"Like a pleb, I shook it." Pearson's voice betrays his frustration at what he sees as gullibility, even after all these years. He phoned his wife, Sue, back in Hull and then his parents.

"I should have been happy. But I was just deflated."

His well-warranted belief that he had been sold short rankled with him throughout his years at Old Trafford.

Not long after, assistant manager Paddy Crerand took the new signing for a night out in London.

"He was with a mate who paid for champagne. I saw him pull a wad of notes from his pocket and nearly fainted. I'd never seen money like it."

Pearson found out afterwards that United's top earners were on £160 a week and that he was at the lower end of the pay scale.

"I love the Doc to bits, but my only gripe with him is that he didn't offer more. It wasn't his money and he could have upped his offer."

To add insult to injury, the punitive tax system of the mid-1970s meant Pearson saw little of his signing-on bonus.

"Tax was around 85p in the pound. I got a five grand signing on fee, spread over the course of my two-year contract. I got one wages payment of £3,000. You know how much of that I actually received? £420.

"I'd promised my mum a fridge freezer. They were £350 at the time and they're still that price nearly 40 years later." So his signing on fee effectively paid for a fridge freezer for his Mum's council house in Hull.

Pearson was born in Hull and grew up on a council estate in Cottingham just outside the city.

"You don't think it's rough at the time, but when you see the good things in life which football brought us, I realise that it was rough," he explains. "The people were all sound though, working-class people like my dad who was a painter and decorator or my mum who did a bit of cleaning. Others were trawlermen who earned what seemed like huge amounts of money. They were tough fellows. The people looked after each other. I had a happy childhood – except school."

Given that Pearson disliked "learning" and "being told what to do", school was unlikely to be a happy experience and passing the 11-plus exam always an unrealistic prospect for someone who describes himself as a "useless" student. The eldest of four children, he did like gymnastics, football and he was the cricket captain. He was also a good boxer.

"I could have gone into boxing or football," he muses. "I used to go to Hull Boys club and had a few fights, but I was more into football."

Pearson used to watch second tier Hull City on a Saturday and stand on the Bunkers Hill terrace with mates.

"Rugby League was as big as football in Hull, but I was always a football man and used to love watching Hull City. I also liked

Leeds United and Manchester United because of players such as
Best, Law and Charlton, but Hull were the team I watched live.
Standing on the terrace there with my mates was fantastic – like
a mini Stretford End. I watched a lot of super players, who, for
one reason or another, weren't playing in the First Division."

Hull were promoted to the Second Division in 1966. Their
Boothferry Park home held 42,000 and was one of the best outside
the First Division. Crowds rose to 20,000. It was a good time to
be a Hull City fan and Pearson would end up playing with many
of his former heroes, but the journey from fan to terrace favourite
would not be straightforward.

Pearson got his chance at Hull aged 15 because of a gallon of
paint.

"My dad worked for a company who got the job to paint
Boothferry Park," he explains. "Dad loved playing football and he
saw one of the coaches and offered him a free gallon of paint if
he'd give me a trial."

Pearson impressed sufficiently in the trial games to keep training
at Hull, although he wasn't offered professional terms until he
was 19.

"I left school and there were no jobs around for a dummy like
me," he says. "I went for a few interviews before joining a government scheme to learn to be an electrician, a joiner and a linesman.
I decided to be a linesman – a physically hard job which entails
putting huge telegraph poles into the ground from which wires
could be hung. It was hard and the lads I worked with were rough
diamonds, rugby league players, big lads."

After a long day's work, Pearson would go for three or four
pints each night to wind down.

"I was still training twice a week for Hull and playing with their
juniors or reserves. I wasn't offered a contract because I wasn't
good enough. And I wasn't good enough because my fitness levels
were nowhere near high enough."

A full English breakfast most mornings didn't help either.

"I was in bad shape when I signed professional at 19 and it

took me a full season to get properly match fit," he explains. "In my first session with the first team I felt I'd done okay but I was feeling a bit tired. When a team-mate pointed out that that was just the warm up before training, I realised how far I had to go."

Still, Pearson was highly regarded.

"One of the coaches, Andy Davidson, used to give me extra training sessions in the afternoons. They helped."

Pearson made his first-team debut at the end of his first professional season.

"I didn't play particularly brilliantly, but the players were fantastic with me. They really encouraged me and I felt part of it. At the start of the season I'd felt that a few of the players didn't rate me and maybe that's why they didn't encourage me as much as they might have done."

Hull were a selling club and let their star striker, Chris Chilton, move to Coventry in 1971 for £200,000. Hull's assistant manager, that man Tommy Docherty, said publicly that he wasn't concerned about the loss because he expected Pearson to be better.

"He goes out and runs and never wants to stop," said Docherty. "He will be the answer to our goalscoring worries."

Pearson would be starting the following season as first-choice striker alongside Wagstaff, and the Doc's words rang true: Pearson scored 31 goals in 67 matches for the Tigers. Already happy at the "family club" which was Hull, the striker was happier still after meeting wife-to-be Sue in Bailey's, one of Hull's top nightclubs.

"I fancied her and asked her for a dance, even though I didn't like dancing," he recalls. "Then somebody said to Sue, 'Do you know who that is you are dancing with?' She didn't have a clue that I was a footballer, which afforded certain advantages in Hull when it came to girls. We started dating."

Sue wasn't attracted to him because of money.

"I was on £9 a week," says her husband of nearly four decades. "I'd been on up to £20 a week as a linesman at the electricity board."

Pearson's wages rose as the young striker became Hull's most valuable asset.

"I would give my mum a third of my wages as keep," he says. "I was soon earning £30 and giving her £10 a week – a huge amount."

Mrs Pearson spent the money well.

"She would buy steaks just for me, which left my brothers wondering why I was getting special treatment."

The diet may have been relatively luxurious, but it still wasn't suitable for a professional athlete. "I was still eating a lot of fry-ups, and all these years later I still do," he says. "My favourite meal is still a fry-up or meat pie, chips and beans. I had gastric problems at Hull and had different types of tests. My diet was contributing to the problem. They also told me that I was colour blind, which I never realised. If I'm playing snooker then I can't tell the difference between red and brown. That never affected my game, though."

Food wasn't far from Pearson's agenda on the pitch either. After one game at Sheffield Wednesday, he was sent off for calling the linesman "a bloody onion." A newspaper headline the following day read, 'Onion Stu Lands City In A Pickle'.

"I hadn't called him an onion," he says all these years later. "I'd called him a fucking idiot. When I spoke to the press after the game, I was embarrassed at what I'd actually said and fabricated a story that I'd called him an onion."

Pearson's goals started to attract attention from other clubs. Previous manager Cliff Britton had known how to bring him down to earth if needed.

"He'd look at me, shuffling with my hands in my pockets, and say, 'And what bloody good have you done Pearson? You might as well get back up a pole.' He was dead honest and said it like it was. I respected him and there was no back chat."

Cliff Britton was replaced by Terry Neill who "created a wonderful team spirit."

Neill brought in Tommy Docherty as his assistant. Docherty, in turn, brought in Tommy Cavanagh as a coach. The pair would go on to work at Manchester United, with Cavanagh having a reputation as a tough disciplinarian.

It was Docherty who gave Pearson the 'Pancho' nickname – after United's 1950s striker Mark Pearson.

"Docherty had been manager at Chelsea and Porto so becoming assistant manager at Hull was a big step down," says Pearson.

Nevertheless, Docherty took the job seriously.

"The Doc was a stickler for discipline. If you weren't on time for the coach then it would leave without you. We all had a laugh one day when the Doc was late. One of the players told the bus to leave and we set off. That was not appreciated at all by the Doc."

The two Tommys could see clear potential in Pearson.

"I was coming back from injury and they gave me a fitness test before one reserve game. It was a kind of bleep test and I broke all records at the club. I then scored a hat-trick in the reserve game. Tommy Cav said to me after, 'You keep going son and you'll play for England.' That was a strange thing to say about someone who was not even a regular in the first team. He saw something."

What?

"In those days I was so aggressive," explains Pearson. "I would smash into people, even in training. I wasn't that big, but nobody could knock me down. If they did, I would dust myself down, laugh at them and do it again. I probably got sent off too many times early in my career."

Pearson could play a bit too.

"As I became more experienced I showed that and cut back on the aggression a touch."

In December 1973, Pearson heard that Manchester City were interested.

"I was told that the bid was dependent on whether Mike Summerbee went to Leeds or not. He didn't leave so nor did I."

Six months later, he joined United instead. Pearson had watched his new club struggle the previous season.

"United was a huge name but they'd just been relegated – even with all these big-name players. From the outside I thought they needed three or four new players including myself. I wanted to join United."

The total fee was £222,000 and included a player – Peter Fletcher – who went in the opposite direction.

Fellow striker Fletcher had played twice and been sub five times for United since joining in 1969. He later played for Stockport County and Huddersfield Town.

Pearson remembers, "Tony Kaye also told me to ask for an ex gratia payment from Hull as I'd not cost them a penny and they were about to earn a great deal from selling me." He raised the point with Neill, who told him that he'd had a word with the chairman and there would be no payment.

"Even to this day I'm disappointed by that," says Pearson. "It was obviously a lie. I'd done everything for the club and for him. I was on £85 a week and due a new contract."

"My one regret is that I couldn't buy my mum and dad a house. Football has been good to a lot of people, including me, but these players today should be so grateful for the money they earn."

United's new signing could afford to buy himself and his wife a house in Manchester. Just.

"We looked in Sale and found a house. Nobody from the club helped us like they do now. We found a house for £12,000 but I couldn't get a mortgage as I only earned £100 a week. United couldn't help me so I ended up going to a City fan who sorted us a mortgage out. We later became good friends."

The Pearsons had other commitments having planned their wedding in Cottingham for Christmas '74.

There was also the small issue of Stuart's tonsils.

"I had them taken out just after signing for United. I kept getting a sore throat and used to get ill all the time. I saw a specialist and he told me that I needed my tonsils out. What a horrible operation that was. The doctors told me not to drive for a week. I drove straight back to Hull that day, which took four hours in those days before the M62 was built."

Finally, Stuart Pearson started training as a Manchester United player – albeit nine pounds lighter than before his operation.

"I couldn't believe how good the atmosphere was at a club

which had just been relegated the year before. I was surprised that they'd been relegated too because there were great players there like Martin Buchan, Alex Stepney, Sammy McIlroy and Lou Macari – though I soon realised that the Doc hadn't worked out whether Lou should be a midfielder or a striker. I was more concerned that Lou used to put Fiery Jack (a fiery muscle pain relief ointment similar to Deep Heat) in my underpants. At first I considered battering him, but he would do tricks on everyone, even players who were twice his size like Big Jim Holton."

Revenge was not a simple matter against the dressing room menace from Largs.

"Sometimes Lou would do it if a player was getting a bit too big for his boots. He'd come back from training and find the ends of his shoes cut off. Or he'd set up non-existent meetings with the press for players. Players would shower and then go to meet a journalist in reception of The Cliff or a hotel. There would be nobody there.

"Lou didn't drink so you couldn't slip something into his coke because he could smell it. He had a sharp mind and was aware that he was a target for pranks. Yet he'd stay out all night with us, and when everyone got a bit inebriated he'd take advantage."

Pearson scored on his home debut, a 4-0 victory over Millwall, the first United game outside the top flight since the 1930s and, in football parlance, he never looked back.

"I just thought, 'We're away here,' as I ran away to celebrate," he says. It was the first that fans saw of his celebration, pumping his arm like an uppercut, fist clenched. "Maybe it was because I was a boxing fan who loved Ali, Frazier and Sugar Ray.

"If I had to use one word to describe the celebration then it would be 'violent'," he says, "the adrenalin was pumping and that's how I always celebrated, as if I was knocking somebody out. I was probably inspired by Denis Law's celebration, though mine was far more aggressive."

The fans, who were also not shy of showing their aggressive

side, loved it as much as Pearson enjoyed life in the Second Division.

"It was amazing," recalls Pearson. "There was a bit of trouble with fans, but we were taking so many to matches that the small grounds couldn't cope. We played great attacking football and we thought we could go all season undefeated."

United were no Invincibles – they lost against Hull for one – yet they led the table throughout, winning 26 of their 42 league games, drawing nine and losing seven. "We thought that if the opposition scored two then we'd get three," adds Pearson. "We only knew how to attack."

After seven wins and two draws from the first nine games, United were the only unbeaten team in all four divisions. The first defeat came at third-placed Norwich City on 28 September, with Ted McDougall, the striker discarded by Docherty, scoring both goals.

Norwich were United's opponents in the League Cup semi-final in January 1975. Pearson was injured for both legs as United drew 2-2 at Old Trafford before losing 1-0 away – a game preceded by a sabotage attempt as the wheels to the United coach were tampered with.

"The fans were not a problem for me," says Pearson. "They took to me straightaway and sang 'I'd walk a million miles for one of your goals.' That was Denis Law's song and he was the original King. He could still get in any all-time greatest United side and I was a similar type of player. I had quick feet and was always around for any rebounds. I was a penalty box player, but I was never going to be as prolific as Denis. I liked to play well and that meant more to me than not scoring. Great goalscorers are not like that. Ruud Van Nistelrooy didn't care how he played as long as he scored, whereas I used to love beating players and setting team-mates up. If I scored then great, but it wasn't all that mattered."

Pearson finished United's top scorer with 17 from 36 games.

"I had a few injuries which caused me to miss a dozen games so it could have been more, but the fans were happy and I felt really proud that they gave that song to me too." Really proud.

"My chest would be out, my blood pumping and I'd think, 'This is fucking brilliant'. I was in awe of the Stretford End. You had 15,000 people caged behind a fence singing at you. Wow."

Pearson smiles as he recalls his relationship with United fans.

"I felt very close to them, maybe because I'd stood on a terrace myself for years and idolised footballers. Sometimes I would walk to the touchline and tell the fans to calm down a bit. They could look like an angry mob, but they loved me to bits. The only danger was of them kissing me to death. I could sometimes see over-crowding on the terracing and wanted to protect United fans. They were getting squashed and sometimes they had to climb over the fence and jump onto the pitch – but they were not invading the pitch like the police thought. Often, problems arose because there were so many fans packed into a confined area that the terrace would break its bank like a swollen river."

United fans were not always the aggressors either.

"Rival fans would wind the United lot up and provoke them by spitting or throwing things at that. We had some rough lads who used to defend their corner and win most of the time. I could understand why they acted like they did."

Clubs didn't know how to deal with the Red hordes. Oxford United tried a "let's be friends approach" and hung a banner across the goal saying, "Welcome the Reds". Sir Matt Busby also opened a new section of the ground the day before the match and subsidised buses were laid on to transport fans from the train station to the ground. Not that all the fans travelled by train. United had 32 supporters' clubs across Britain and most would send a full coach to every home and away game.

It didn't work as United lost the game 1-0 in front of Oxford's biggest crowd of the season. An Oxford director was assaulted outside the ground by a group of 200 Reds who were locked out.

United recorded the highest away crowd of the season at all but two venues, and demand for players' tickets was always high.

"We'd get a couple for each match and Lou or Martin Buchan would ask me if I had any spare tickets. They had probably promised them to fans."

Pearson was one the main beneficiaries of another one of Docherty's signings – Stevie Coppell, whom he found a more conducive partner than Coppell's wing mate, Gordon Hill.

"Stevie – or Popper as we called him – was a team player with a great engine. He was the opposite of Gordon Hill. His first priority was to help the team. He would try and get at the full-back and cross the ball to me first time. As a striker, if you know what your wingers are going to do then that gives you a great advantage. Hilly was the opposite. He'd beat his player and then I'd make my run thinking that he was going to cross it. I'd make my run, but he'd come back again onto his right foot and then cross it. It was too late, I was out of the game. Hilly was actually a better crosser, and when he did it right he was fantastic. He had the best left peg at the club too and got lots of goals. Hilly was hugely talented, but he could be frustrating to play with too."

Coppell was signed in February 1975 from Tranmere Rovers for just £40,000. His impact was immediate and United were unbeaten for the remaining 11 games of that season. Coppell wasn't your archetypal footballer, even though he entered the world in the football factory, and later Wayne Rooney's home, that is Croxteth.

"I was a full-time economics student at Liverpool University who played part-time for Tranmere," recalled Coppell later. "Football was a bonus as I'd resigned myself to not making it.

"Apparently a couple of Liverpool directors had been watching me, then halfway through my second year at university I got a call telling me Manchester United wanted to buy me and that Tranmere had agreed a fee. It was like a dream." Even then the fee was tiny, although United would have to pay another £20,000 if Coppell made 20 appearances. He would make 395 – not bad for a player who trained on his own in Liverpool after signing.

"I told Tommy Docherty that I had an option to delay my studies, but he said, 'Absolutely no chance, football can be finished at the click of your finger, academic qualifications are with you for life.' I'm eternally thankful for him saying that."

Coppell, the student United professional, studied in Liverpool, training alone, except for a weekly Tuesday night session at The Cliff.

"It would never happen now, and it would only be with a character like Doc that that happened then. Docherty was a major influence on my life and I still love him to bits."

Coppell has every reason to, for despite not having seen him play, Docherty introduced him to first-team action immediately.

"I came on as a sub for Willie Morgan against Cardiff in the old Second Division four days after signing. It was 0-0 and I was so frightened the first time I got the ball that I just crossed it. Stuart Pearson – who had lent me some boots – scored. I had a hand in another goal and we won 4-0.

"It was beyond a fairytale," he reminisced of his debut. "And despite winning trophies, that day was my highlight as a United player. My heart was jumping out of my chest, and I've never had another experience like it. I wasn't running; I was floating across the grass. Words do not do the experience justice; it was a drug-like euphoric trance. I've had a few operations, and it was like that little pleasant stage when you've just been given the anaesthetic. Only multiplied by a hundred."

Coppell's thrilling runs and slick skills ensured he became a regular, and at one point in his eight-year Old Trafford career he played 206 consecutive league games – a club record unlikely to be broken.

"There were no problems with me studying in Liverpool and playing for United either. I had good friends, and if United didn't have a midweek game I'd play in goal in the university inter-departmental league. We got to the cup final, losing 6-1 to Geography, not one of my better games!"

The bizarre concept of playing for United at Anfield at the

weekend, and in Anfield for economics midweek became the norm. And being a Liverpudlian didn't cause problems either.

"United fans appreciated it if you had a go. They don't like prima donnas, regardless of skill, they want to see commitment and effort. I'd have a bad game, but as long as I tried the crowd were alright. Whereas if you appeared big time then they would dig you out. Old Trafford could be a harsh and demanding environment."

Coppell, Hill and Pearson both finished the season as first-choice starters in the team which were crowned Second Division champions. Pearson decided now was the time to do something about his pay.

"I went to see the Doc and asked him for a rise. He told me that he'd go and have a chat with Sir Matt, before coming back to me to say that Matt said that I was halfway through a two-year contract and that was that.

"I pleaded and said that I was the top scorer and yet one of the lowest-paid players in the team. He wouldn't budge."

Despite being the best-supported team, United's relative parsimony was nothing new.

"The Doc tried to get Peter Shilton but United wouldn't sanction his wages," says Pearson. Other players were identified – Duncan McKenzie of Nottingham Forest and Mick Channon of Southampton were targets in the summer that Pearson had joined, but neither were tempted by the low salaries United offered.

"It wasn't until Bryan Robson was signed for £1.5 million in 1981 that United started to pay top level again."

Unlike his salary, Pearson's status was increasing. United's joint top league scorer in both 1975/76 and 1976/77 was more than just a target man. "I was probably too unselfish," he opines. "If somebody was in a better position to me I'd pass it to them. I didn't come as deep as Wayne Rooney would, though." He also received the first of his 15 England caps in 1976.

"I was in Australia on tour with United when I got the call to go back early and join Don Revie's first get together as England manager. I took 24 hours to fly back to Heathrow and we landed three minutes early. Then I had a three-hour delay for the flight to Manchester. I decided to get the train. I arrived in Manchester late at night and got up the first thing the next morning to go back to London for the meet up. There were about 70 players, and I enjoyed it. I loved Don Revie and enjoyed playing for my country, but nothing like as much as I enjoyed playing for United.

"At United they knew my strengths. I received the ball to my feet and I would make runs knowing where it would go. Playing for England was more direct. The full-backs would hump the ball forward in the air and if I had a big defender like McQueen marking me for Scotland he was going to win the ball every time."

Pearson played in the First Division for the first time in August 1975.

"Stepping up wasn't a problem for any of us. We didn't compromise the way we trained or played one bit. Stepney would still throw the ball to a full-back and one of the two forwards would make a run short to receive the ball, while the other looked for a longer pass. The Doc would shout, 'Change the play,' and the ball would then come through midfield. As a striker I always had to make myself available for anyone with a red shirt with the ball. I always tried to show and get an angle."

United's team spirit was a strength, though major fault lines began to appear on the return to the top flight. Willie Morgan, whom Docherty had appointed captain, describing him as the best winger in the world, became a peripheral figure. An intelligent Scot, Morgan had predicted United's relegation on television in January '74. Unfortunately, an eye injury and the arrival of Steve Coppell limited his appearances that season. The Docherty bonhomie stopped and the bitterness which eventually led to court proceedings started. One minute Morgan was offered a six-year contract with a testimonial, the next he was sold to Burnley for £30,000 in 1975, nothing like his true worth.

"I should never have left United," Morgan rues, ". . . should have waited until the Doc had got the sack, but I didn't have much choice."

Pearson saw less than a season of Morgan.

"It's not fair on me really to comment on Willie Morgan because by the time I arrived he had a major injury with his eye and was no longer the great player he'd been," he explains. "He had a major issue with the Doc too so that didn't help him."

Morgan wasn't the only person the Doc had "major issues" with. His relationship with assistant manager Paddy Crerand had become almost non-existent.

"The Doc would moan about Paddy – just stupid things. He'd moan that Paddy had been using the phone is his office and scribbling all over his paperwork. Paddy wouldn't have meant to do that! And Paddy would have the odd moan about the Doc, but it didn't affect the team spirit.

"Everyone got on with Paddy. He didn't do a lot of coaching but he was always there – he was assistant manager. If we were ever in a nightclub then Paddy would be sent in to have a scout around and clear us out. There were many occasions when we'd be in Slacks [George Best's club Slack Alice] on a Wednesday night and Paddy would come in and tell us to clear off."

Socialising in the daytime wasn't outlawed, and the United players had a number of haunts they'd frequent after training.

"United hadn't started serving food at Old Trafford after training at The Cliff so we'd go to Oscars, Bestie's place in town. We'd not drink alcohol, though; we just had a laugh together like the good mates that we were. We played golf twice a week too," recalls Pearson.

Not that these get-togethers were always teetotal.

"We'd drink in the Little B pub in Sale, where most of the players lived. We went out two evenings a week and had some great times. Maybe if I had my career again I wouldn't drink quite so much. I would have like to have played nowadays because while we were super fit, we could have been fitter. Roy Keane had 4 per cent body fat – none of us could have come close to that."

United did well in their first season back and headed the First Division table by the end of January 1976.

"We were a couple of players shy of being able to win the league that year," recalls Pearson. "Our squad wasn't big enough and we only had David McCreery as sub."

McCreery, another Belfast boy in the team, made 57 starts and 52 substitute appearances for United.

"David was one of the quickest players at the club. He'd been a striker and we called him Road Runner because he'd run and run. He scored some important goals, but maybe he didn't have the class of someone like Jimmy Greenhoff, who arrived later."

United's deficiencies were exposed in the league. Three draws – including a 0-0 home tie with eventual champions Liverpool – and defeat in four games saw the team slip to third, a position United would finish in their first season back.

"We started to suffer as we had the FA Cup on the go too," explains Pearson. "Maybe that was our priority. We had tough games like against Derby in the semi-final when I played against McFarland and Todd. They were as good as any defensive partnership."

Pearson and Rioch, two men who weren't shy of confrontation, would come to blows.

"He was having an argument with Sammy Mac and they were about to throw punches. I got in the middle of them and parted them. Bruce spun round and caught me one on the chin. He should have been sent off and he knows that, but it was no big deal to me. He should have apologised and admitted that he lost his head."

He didn't.

"So I tried to cut him in half during the game and failed. He made it look as if I did and I got booked. Bruce Rioch 2 Stuart Pearson 0. But we beat them to get to the final.

"Alan Hardaker from the Football Association came into the dressing room before the game. He stood in front of us like we were schoolchildren and said, 'Under no circumstances do I want any of you lot going to your fans after the game. It is not allowed'.

"It was a hot day and a poor game, with neither team playing well. Bobby Stokes' goal was offside but we would never have scored anyway. I was pleased for Jim McCalliog. He'd been at United before falling out with the Doc and joining Southampton. Now he had a cup medal.

"I wanted to thank our fans, even though we had been told not to. I thought 'sod this' and started walking to the United fans. The Doc came up and stopped me. I told him that it wasn't right that we couldn't applaud our fans. I wanted to say thank you, so did the other players, many of whom were in tears. We couldn't. It looked really bad."

The United players had to wait until the following day, when Manchester's Albert Square was filled with Reds.

"It was quite upsetting to come back to all those cheering supporters with nothing to show for it. The Doc promised them that he'd win the cup for them the following season. It was a risky thing to say, but it didn't seem it to me. I fully believed that we'd win the FA Cup to avenge how we felt and reward those fans."

The cloud had a silver lining as Pearson finally got the pay rise he was after that summer. "My contract was increased to £250 a week and Jimmy Greenhoff arrived later in the year. With my first England cap, 1976 was a good year with only the cup final defeat to spoil it."

Jimmy Greenhoff joined in November when the team were in the middle of a run of six defeats and two draws. Among those defeats was a 3-0 loss to Juventus in Turin which saw the team exit the UEFA Cup at the second-round stage. And another 3-0 defeat at Everton which meant the end of the League Cup campaign. Having been first in the table at the start of October, United slipped to 17th by Christmas 1976. The New Year saw an upturn in results, in part thanks to the signing of Greenhoff. Pearson and his former strike partner are close mates to this day, though they weren't at the start.

"Jimmy lived in Alsager and wasn't around much socially so he wasn't my best buddy. He was a great player, though, and made such a difference to the team. He could hold the ball and pass it well. He was a great volleyer, worked hard and scored important goals. Keegan and Toshack claimed that they had a telepathic relationship. The same was true of Jimmy and I. If I went short then I knew where he'd be."

Greenhoff was the catalyst for United's return to form. By the end of February 1977 they had climbed to 4th. In the same month they met FA Cup holders Southampton in an FA Cup fifth-round tie. Almost 30,000 crammed into the Dell – and given the severe limitations of the Saints' old ground which would only hold 15,000 as an all-seater stadium, the term 'cram' cannot be under-stated – to see a 2-2 draw. United won the replay 2-1 at Old Trafford in front of a near full-house crowd of 58,103. Greenhoff got both goals. The visit of Leeds in the league a week later attracted the season's biggest crowd of 60,612. United were on a roll.

United were true to Doc's promise and reached the cup final.

"The good thing about the Doc is that we never trained overly hard," he says. "We were like prize fighters who saved their energy for the ring. We'd tick over. He had us just right for the cup final. We were ready to play, ready to go to war against Liverpool, the best team in the world."

A vengeful Pearson was up for the game.

"I walked out onto the Wembley pitch and I was looking around the stands when I saw a banner which read: 'Jesus Saves – Pancho Scores the Rebound.' I was so happy when I saw that. It's the best banner that I've ever seen. I felt inspired. I was playing to a high standard and I genuinely thought I was the best player. I wasn't being arrogant, I just felt invincible. I felt that if someone kicked me then I would just get up and seek retribution so that they didn't do it again."

Pearson put United in front in the second half.

"Jimmy knocked the ball to me and I headed it on. I knew that nobody would catch me, but I had time to think. You'd think that you wouldn't, but it all happened in slow motion for me. I saw the ball bouncing on the edge of the box and thought, 'Clem's coming out, he'll think that I'm going to take a touch. Don't take a touch and hit it low. Don't hit it too early because the ball is bobbling about. Keep the ball down. You're at Wembley and you are clear through against Liverpool in the FA Cup final."

Pearson struck the ball low.

"Perfectly," he says with a winning smile. "Bottom left. Clem couldn't get it. Goal!"

The strike was in front of the United end.

"That was a bonus too," he says. "It was the highlight of my career, better even than scoring for England away in Argentina. To help stop Liverpool winning the treble. I knew what that would mean to our supporters, whose rivalry with Liverpool was far stronger than the rivalry between the two sets of players. I wasn't born in Manchester, I couldn't pretend to hate Liverpool, but I felt for the people who were keeping the club going, the fans. The fans who to this day should be looked after better. I hope I made a few of them smile that day in 1977."

The game was far from one sided.

"I thought it was one of the best cup finals ever, it could have gone either way," says Pearson. "My goal gave us the advantage, but Jimmy Case equalised almost straightaway, then my mate Jimmy got the second. Three goals in five minutes."

That's how it would stay, and both teams applauded each other at the end. Liverpool were good losers and several of their players sought out Stewart Houston, the full-back who had damaged his ankle two weeks before the final to shake his hand. His replacement, 19-year-old Arthur Albiston, offered him his winners' medal, an offer Houston turned down.

"I celebrated that night with my wife and parents," recalls Pearson. "They loved the big games, the trip down to London from Hull. They were so proud to see me play and to touch the FA Cup. That was the nice bit about an FA Cup final. The worst bit was getting phone calls off uncles that you'd never heard of asking for tickets. After a while I changed my number and gave it out to hardly anyone, so my parents would get calls or my brothers Keith and Neil. They'd pass a message to me saying that so and so had been on asking for tickets. I had to say no."

The massive high of the cup final success was followed by the low of Docherty's dismissal.

"I went to Old Trafford on the Tuesday after the game. I had hoped to see the Doc to get a new three-year contract which would give me parity with the other senior players who still earned far more than me. I was playing for England and they were on double my wages. The Doc told me that he'd seen the chairman about my contract and there was not a problem. The news of his relationship with Mary Brown had come out, and at first it didn't appear to be a problem. Then he got the sack. We were told that Sir Matt had put his foot down and insisted that the Doc's behaviour was not appropriate for the manager of Manchester United.

"I was shocked, but not as shocked as when Dave Sexton was appointed," says Pearson, who duly went to see his new manager to enquire about the new three-year contract. He told me that he'd have a word and came back to say that the club were not willing to sanction it. That was me and Man United just about finished there and then. I was also disappointed because we were so close to winning the league. Buying Peter Shilton would have won us the league in '77/78."

The Doc's departure left a personal void for Pearson.

"It was never the same for me at Old Trafford after that," says Pearson. "Dave and Tommy were chalk and cheese. Dave was lovely – everyone says that – but he couldn't handle the media or cope with the pressure. The media was easy for the Doc, he'd make a story up if he needed to.

"Dave was supposed to have a great reputation as a coach too, but I just didn't see it. He had us training twice a day but it didn't work. We'd gone from being spoiled with the Doc and given days off to play golf to being told that we had double sessions with Dave. We didn't need it. We were all playing regularly, there was no squad rotation as there was only one sub. We over-trained, we got tired. The mood changed with it. It was a shame because you don't like to see people struggle in life, but Dave struggled alright."

Pearson actually did fine under Sexton, scoring 15 goals in 39 appearances in 1977/78, but the following season was a disaster.

"I didn't play, I had three operations on my knee. I started playing squash in the summer of 1978 to keep fit. My knee seized up one day – cartilage problems. Dave thought I was sulking a bit. My knee blew up, it was all different colours and I was in agony. I was rushed into North Manchester General with a blood clot and was operated on immediately. I came round to see people staring at me. The man in the next bed had called his mates and told them that I was in the ward with him. They wanted autographs. I went mad at the fella, properly kicked off at him while still under the influence of anaesthetic.

"Three months later I needed another operation. I fell out with Dave because I wasn't happy with the United surgeon. I went with City's surgeon then and didn't regret that."

United couldn't wait for Pearson to recover. And Joe Jordan was signed as a forward.

"I'd had a few run-ins with Joe at Leeds," admits Pearson. "He was very competitive and so was I. That wasn't a problem to me. He turned out to be a great pal."

Jordan became first choice.

"Dave had paid £500,000 for him and was obviously going to play him before me or Jimmy. The first time Dave left me out, he called me into his office on the Friday and explained that he had to make a change. I knew he meant Joe, but kidded, 'You're bringing Jimmy back to play with me?'

'No, no,' he said in all seriousness. 'I'm going to leave you out and play Joe.'

'But I've scored seven in the last nine games, boss,' I said. 'Do you not think that I should be keeping my place?' I wasn't happy. If you're happy being left out then there's something wrong with you, but I could not blame Joe and I also understood that Dave needed to do something as we were not getting the results we needed. Sometimes as a manager you have to change things."

Pearson played just twice in 1978/79.

"Come the Arsenal cup final I was doing pre-season training," he says. "Harry Gregg was fantastic with me, but Dave told me in the summer of '79 that West Ham had come in for me, adding that he didn't want me to go. I said, 'Well, give me what I want and I won't go'.

'What do you want?' he asked.

'£500 per week like I've always said.'"

United offered half that.

After scoring 66 goals in 179 United appearances, Pearson left for Second Division West Ham in September 1979. The Hammers paid United £220,000 and Pearson got a three-year contract. Sexton also sold two other Docherty stalwarts, Brian Greenhoff to Leeds for £350,000 and David McCreery to QPR for £200,000. The money was used to pay a club record £825,000 for Ray Wilkins, who had been Chelsea captain at 18.

Pearson, meanwhile, would finally be suitably remunerated.

"West Ham paid me £500 a week," he explains. "I wanted to prove people who said that moving from Man United was a step down wrong. Financially it was a big step up and my time at the Boleyn was a success. I won three trophies – more than I'd won at Old Trafford and we had a great side with Alan Devonshire, Trevor Brooking, Alvin Martin, Billy Bonds and Phil Parkes."

West Ham beat Arsenal in the 1980 FA Cup final and reached the League Cup final against Liverpool in 1981.

"We drew 1-1 and Kenny Dalglish got the winner in the replay. He was a different class as a player – the best in English football. If I had to choose two strikers from all time then it would be Dalglish and Alan Shearer.

"I know Kenny well as he has a place near me at La Manga – we were out the other night. I hope he does well at Liverpool because he is such a genuine man – a witty, sarcastic fella who is great company."

West Ham were also promoted back to Division One, but Pearson still struggled with injury.

"My only disappointment there was that I didn't play enough games. I played in the big games, but my knee was never the same as it had been. It's arthritic and I just try and get by with it."

Pearson's young family had moved to London for the first two years of his three-year contract. Daughter Sarah had been born in '75, son Wayne in '79.

"They moved back to Manchester after two years and I moved into digs for a year."

Pearson also went on Jimmy Hill's lucrative "rebel tour" to South Africa. With sanctions imposed against the country under apartheid, British sporting teams were not allowed to travel.

"Hill wanted to promote football in South Africa. We also received a grand a match for six games which was great money. People said that we shouldn't have gone, but they didn't see the joy that we brought when we played in Soweto. The poverty was frightening. A young lad caught my eye on the team coach after the game. I opened the window and threw him my tracksuit top. Maybe I was out of order because I then saw him getting chased by 50 other kids.

"The tour was so controversial it came under enormous pressure. It only lasted three games, and then we went to Sun City for a few days and few rounds of golf."

Pearson's playing career was over and he moved back to Sale.

"The little bit of money I had went on a tiling business which didn't work. We undercut the main competitor by nearly half and it still didn't do any good. Maybe people thought we were selling seconds because they were that cheap. I'm still good pals with the two lads that I was in business with – which doesn't always happen. You hear many stories about players getting screwed."

In 1984, Pearson was offered the assistant manager's job at Fourth Division Stockport County alongside Les Chapman.

"Despite having very few resources, we were near the top of

Bobby Charlton talks with new United manager Frank O'Farrell at Old Trafford in 1971. O'Farrell was an intelligent man and a good manager, but felt undermined by Matt Busby and the senior players.

George Best and Tommy Docherty. The United manager recognised Best's talents and liked him personally, but had little patience for his off-the-field indiscretions. He also thought the Irishman had lost his explosive pace by the time he took charge.

A copper with a stick ponders what to do next after United fans have invaded the Old Trafford pitch and surrounded City's Denis Law in April 1974. The King of the Stretford End had just scored an unfortunate backheel which he refused to celebrate. That goal alone didn't relegate United for the first time since the War, but it was another nail in the Red coffin and United went down.

Young guns: United players in cowboy gear for a Christmas party in 1974. They are (from left to right) Sammy McIlroy, Willie Morgan, Stuart Pearson, Gerry Daly and Lou Macari.

Champions, of sorts. It's 26th April 1975 and United players celebrate their Division 2 Championship success after beating Blackpool 4-0 at Old Trafford. From left to right: Alex Forsyth, Stewart Houston, Brian Greenhoff, Stuart Pearson, Steve Coppell, Lou Macari and Steve James.

United's proud captain, Martin Buchan, lifts the Division 2 Championship trophy.

Stuart Pearson poses for a picture at Old Trafford in June 1975 as (from left to right) Brian Greenhoff, Stewart Houston, Jim Holton, Gerry Daly and Lou Macari wait their turn. Striker Pearson was an instant hit at United having arrived from Hull City the previous year.

As contrived Seventies photoshoots go, this one takes some beating. Tommy Docherty stands in between his 'shooting stars', Steve Coppell (left) and Gordon Hill in 1976. United's speedy wingers, who were as different on the pitch as off it, delighted fans with their swashbuckling style.

The calm after the storm. Dubliner Paddy Roche poses for his portrait photo in 1976.

Lou Macari in front of the Stretford End in 1976.

Another laid-back Dubliner, Gerry Daly, poses for his pre-season picture in 1975.

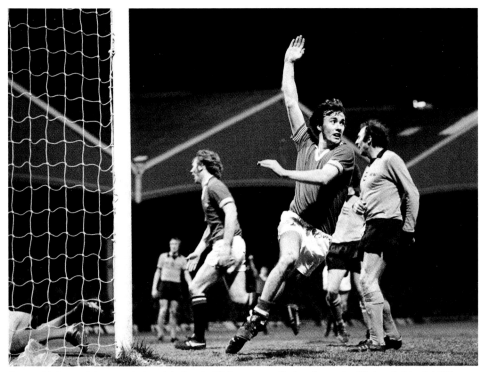

Sammy McIlroy celebrates a vital goal during the FA Cup quarter-final replay against Wolves in March 1976. United won 3-2 in a game which many players remember as one of the finest of the Seventies.

1st May 1976. Alex Stepney dives but fails to keep out Bobby Stokes' shot in the FA Cup final against Southampton. The only goal of the game, it gave Southampton the cup. Debate endures to this day about whether Stokes was offside.

Flag and banner-waving Reds at Wembley for the FA Cup final against Liverpool on 21st May 1977.
The Seventies were a high point for terrace culture.

'I'd walk a million miles, for one of your goals'… Stuart Pearson shoots to score United's first in the '77 FA Cup final.

The ball is on the way into the Liverpool goal as Lou Macari celebrates after his shot has struck Jimmy Greenhoff, arms raised, far right, for the winning goal in the '77 final. Liverpool goalkeeper Ray Clemence and full-back Phil Neal are helpless to prevent the goal that crushed Liverpool's dream of becoming the first English team to win the treble.

It's all smiles as Tommy Docherty celebrates with goalscorers Stuart Pearson and Lou Macari (or was he?) after United had beaten Liverpool. In what would become an increasingly rare display of Manc-Scouse bonhomie, both sets of fans applauded each other's teams after the match, United fans wishing Liverpool well in their forthcoming European Cup final.

Jimmy Nicholl, Jimmy Greenhoff and Alex Stepney celebrate with the FA Cup.

Groovy sew-on patches adorned the jean jackets of many young Reds in the Seventies, usually accompanied by scarves tied round the wrists.

Manchester United's only major honour of the Seventies, the 1977 FA Cup. Pearson, left, and Lou Macari hoist the trophy on the lap of honour.

The happiest fan in the world. A Red celebrates atop the Wembley crossbar in '77.

BOB THOMAS/GETTY IMAGES

Spot the missing man. Manchester United 1977/78 – the FA Cup winners line up for the team photo.
Back row (left to right): Tommy Cavanagh (Coach), Jimmy Greenhoff, Sammy McIlroy, Brian Greenhoff,
Alex Stepney, Jimmy Nicholl, David McCreery, Laurie Brown (Physio), Frank Blunstone (Assistant Manager),
Front row (left to right): Lou Macari, Stuart Pearson, Martin Buchan, Gordon Hill, Arthur Albiston, Steve Coppell.
Tommy Docherty had already departed.

Gordon Hill celebrates after scoring for United against Arsenal in November 1977. Arsenal won 2-1 and Hill's fortunes at United would subsequently slide under new boss Dave Sexton. Check out the no-man's land separating the home and away fans in the Scoreboard Paddock below K Stand.

Another win against Liverpool in '77 as United triumph 2-0 at Old Trafford in October. Sammy McIlroy celebrates scoring the second, joined by Jimmy Nicholl and Brian Greenhoff.

New signing Joe Jordan celebrates a goal against City at Old Trafford in March 1978. Close mate and compatriot Gordon McQueen checks Big Joe's armpits are fresh.

Oh no. Arsenal's Alan Sunderland scores a last-minute winner in the 1979 FA Cup final after United had come back from 2-0 down to level at 2-2 in the 88th minute. Several players still cite this as their lowest moment in football.

Where are they now? Opposite page, top row (from left to right): Sammy McIlroy, Martin Buchan. Middle row: Lou Macari, Gordon Hill. Bottom row: Stuart Pearson, Paddy Roche. Above, (top row): Jimmy Greenhoff, Gerry Daly. Middle row: Joe Jordan, Jimmy Nicholl. Left: Tommy Docherty.

Overleaf: One of the Red moments of the Seventies. Pearson, 2nd left, has scored the first goal in the '77 Cup final, as Lou Macari (10), Steve Coppell (7) and Jimmy Nicholl (2) join in the celebrations with the delirious United fans at Wembley.

the league at Christmas. We fell away in the second half of the season and were sacked."

Pearson then dropped a division to Northwich Victoria.

"The chairman was a balloon. We had no money but I had Gordon Hill helping me out and we scouted the best players from the league below. We were playing great football, but we were in the lower half of the table. I fell out with the chairman, resigned after an argument in which I told him to stick his club up his arse and was then persuaded to go back. Another fall out, a request to resign and a sacking followed."

Despite his knee problems, Pearson was still playing one type of football. In 1985 he played rugby for Sale. "The rugby lads and football lads mixed," he explains. "We'd wound each other up, but we became friendly and I used to go training with them. They showed me the ropes and I played a few games on the wing!"

Pearson later went to West Bromwich Albion, where Ron Atkinson was manager. "I knew Ron from when he lived in Manchester as United manager.

"I was bubbly, fit and he liked me about the place and joining in training. I used to drive there most days from Manchester. In the end I was invited to join the coaching staff. Ron eventually took the Atletico Madrid job and recommended Brian Talbot to be West Brom manager. I was a bit put out because I'd hoped that he'd recommend me, but maybe Brian was the better option because I was more of a player's man. Talbot wanted to keep me as his assistant and I got on fine with him for a while."

Sam Allardyce joined West Brom as a coach and Brian Talbot changed the team's tactics without consulting his assistant. Allardyce was promoted to assistant manager and Pearson was demoted to look after the reserves.

"The first team were humping it, while I had the reserves playing good football. We won the league, but Brian and Sam were sacked. I felt for Sam because you could see that he was a talented coach who would think deeply about football."

Pearson took over as caretaker manager at West Brom before

Bobby Gould got the job full time. His next job was at second-tier Bradford City as assistant to Frank Stapleton.

"It was great at first," he recalls. "We had a good chairman and achieved decent results on very little. We were two or three players short of a side that was good enough to get promoted to the Premier League. The chairman sold out to Geoffrey Richmond who I didn't have any respect for. It seemed that his ambition was to outdo Leeds because he married into the Cousins family who had been in charge of Leeds. He helped get Bradford into the Premier League, but they lived well beyond their means to get there and paid the price."

That was Pearson's last job in football.

"I didn't make enough money from the game to have a decent pension," he says. "The tax man took most of my Seventies' United money and Sue has had to work most of her life. People think that I'm rich, but none of us made much from playing. I bet Best, Law and Charlton didn't have £10,000 in the bank when they retired from football. The only thing I got from football was a nice house in Sale. We sold that and bought a place in Warrington, sold that and moved to La Manga in 2003. We've had a great time in Spain and met a lot of nice people. I'm a keen golfer [Pearson plays off four and has played off scratch in the past] and there are three fantastic courses. For a long time I flew back to Manchester for United home games to do the corporate lounges before matches. United were great with me.

"A diminishing pound and irregular flights put paid to that, but we're moving back to England because my mother-in-law isn't in the best of health.

"I feel honoured to have played for United," concludes Pearson. "People remind me of the bigger names all the time, but I was just as close to guys who would have been considered fringe players.

"Jim Holton was a bit of a townie who showed me Manchester at night. He got me in trouble with the boss and I regret not keeping in touch with him when he left. I'm not the best man for picking up the phone and Jimmy wasn't either. I think it's a footballers' trait, we're terrible at keeping in touch. I do think about the former team-mates a lot, though, even though I haven't kept in touch with a lot of them.

"George Graham – or Stroller as we called him – gave me advice about money. He read a piece I'd done at the start of my time at United where I said that I was one of the lowest-paid players and he gave me some advice. He was on twice as much as me and couldn't get in the team. He fell out with the Doc, but that didn't detract from the fact that he was a good, experienced player.

"I used to be paired up with Tony Young in training. He was a lovely lad, a full-back who didn't quite make it at Old Trafford.

"Mick Martin was the most underrated player at the club. He was a handful when I played against him for Eire."

Martin played 43 times for United, but won 52 caps for the Republic of Ireland and played almost 500 games in a career which also took in West Brom, Newcastle United and Vancouver Whitecaps, among others.

"Arnold Sidebottom was another who never quite made it at Old Trafford. He's another that I wish I'd kept in touch with.

"Tommy Jackson – or Keg as we called him as he was a bit heavy – was a great lad. Not seen him for years but I guarantee if I saw him tomorrow we'd have a great laugh.

"Chris McGrath was a very quiet, pleasant lad. Dave Sexton wanted him to come out of his shell so much that he concocted one of the most bizarre training sessions ever. He made Chris stand a full football pitch away from where we were training and then shout out all the players' names. I'd hear 'Panchooo' and I'd look around and see poor Chris. That wasn't good coaching, it just highlighted how shy the lad was. And that was the difference between the Doc and Dave."

6

PADDY ROCHE

BETWEEN THE STICKS

PADDY ROCHE

"I couldn't escape." Paddy Roche, United's second-string goalkeeper for much of the 1970s, is sitting on the sofa at his home, a three-bed semi-detached in Sale, Manchester. "I'd walk down the street to buy a newspaper and kids would come up and ask me my favourite colour. Before I had chance to reply, they'd shout, 'Indigo!'

"My mate was a teacher, and I used to help him coach the kids at his school but the boys would come up to me and say, 'My dad says that you are rubbish.' It was horrible because I'd never experienced it before. It took me a good while to get over it, if I ever did get over it. I'd never had nerves before that time. I've had them ever since."

When Paddy Crerand came to Dublin to speak to Roche about signing for United, he had explained that the second 'keeper, Jimmy Rimmer, didn't get on with Tommy Docherty. "Like a lot of people didn't and like Paddy soon wouldn't," Roche observes.

The club's first-choice goalie was veteran Alex Stepney, whom Docherty had sold to United in 1966 when he was Chelsea boss, for a then world record fee for a 'keeper. Stepney, as some of the interviewees in this book attest, was a safe pair of hands, a commanding figure who marshalled the defence from his box.

Both Roche and he were also talented outfield players, always first pick in five-a-sides during training at The Cliff. But eventually Docherty decided it was time for a change, partly persuaded by the excellent form that Roche was showing in the reserves.

"We won 1-0 against Norwich at home. I had been doing well and Alex hadn't been doing so well, so I was selected ahead of him. Then we went to Liverpool the next week."

Roche vividly remembers what happened at Anfield on the 8th November 1975. "It was an easy cross and I shouted clearly for it and then jumped high to collect it, so high that my foot collided with Brian Greenhoff's shoulder. Unfortunately, that knocked me off balance and the ball spilled from my grasp. Steve Heighway scored. A soft goal."

He winces as he recounts the incident that people still continue to remind him of today.

"The papers crucified me," sighs the Dubliner. "They slaughtered me. There was photo after photo. I'd actually played well aside from that mistake, but everyone highlighted that one.

"I found the criticism very difficult because I'd never experienced a downer as a player before. People were slagging me off and doubting my ability, which knocked my confidence. It was hard. I retreated into my shell and stopped answering the phone. Tommy Docherty kept me in the team, but he could have provided a lot more support."

The mishap at Highbury was to have a disastrous effect on Roche's future career and reputation, from which it never really recovered.

Paddy Roche had been spotted playing for Shelbourne, the team he had grown up supporting.

"I was born in Dublin in 1951," he says, "a place called Irishtown near Sandymount. It's a very working class area on the south side. I'm proud to be a Southsider. Northsiders are . . . different. We're more refined."

He is one of seven children, four of them boys.

"Two of my brothers played football. My elder brother was a centre-half for Shamrock Rovers who thought he was going to United at one point, but he kept getting bad headaches. My younger brother, Brendan, was a great player with Shelbourne until he broke his leg. Football was in the family."

Roche's dad was a handyman, his mother a housewife, hands full with seven to take care of.

"I played football night and day as a kid," he says. "We played Gaelic football and hurling too. I'd often play all three sports in the same day. On Sunday I'd play soccer and then go and watch Shelbourne in the afternoon. I was a Shelbourne fan and they had a lot of success in the Sixties. Tony Dunne, who played so many games for United, started out at Shelbourne and they played European games against Barcelona, Sporting Lisbon and Atletico Madrid. Their training ground was just behind our house. If it was foggy, I would wait by the bus stop and guide players to the training ground because they would always get lost."

Roche wasn't academic.

"I wasn't the worst," he smiles, "but I hardly had time to think about school work with football on my mind all the time. In fact I would commentate on imaginary games between Irish clubs during class. There would be classic games between Shamrock Rovers, who my mate supported, and Shelbourne, my team. English football wasn't as popular in Ireland as it is now. There was no television at home until I was 15 and the only English football news came in the Sunday newspapers which would arrive on the boat from Holyhead. They would often only contain half a report from the matches played on the Saturday. Irish football really suffered when English games started to be shown on television."

A local chip shop had a television with a huge aerial so that they could tune into BBC programmes.

"I would go there on a Saturday night to try and watch *Match of the Day*," remembers Roche. "The poor reception meant a really snowy picture, but we'd pray for a big long queue so that we could stand and watch. You could just about make the teams out, but if there was no queue we'd stand outside the window. It's the opposite of how it is now, with everyone spoiled with television access to the best of everything."

Shelbourne were one of the biggest clubs in the league.

"They would get average crowds of 4,000, and I loved going to Tolka Park," he says. "It was my dream to play for them."

Roche had joined a local junior team called Bolton Athletic.

"I was a centre-forward and we had a fine team and would win everything." Later, Roche's team-mates at United would rave about his ability as an outfield player in training, but he made his living as a goalkeeper, not a striker.

"In 1966 I was asked to play in goal in the finals of the Evans Cup, an Irish national cup competition. Our team had previously been beaten 5-0 by our big rivals, a team called Rangers, in a game at Shamrock Rovers' ground and our goalkeeper had a nightmare."

The team had their semi-final in the Evans cup against Home Farm the following week.

"Our manager told me that he wanted me to play in goal for the semi-final, simple as that. I had played in goal in training from time to time, so obviously he saw something. I don't think the other 'keeper was best pleased, but I saved a penalty and we won the game," smiles Roche. The manager then told him that he wanted him to play in goal all the time.

"I explained that I didn't want to be a goalkeeper. We did a deal whereby I played in goal until we were three or four up – which we were most games – and then I could come outfield. We won the final 4-0 and I played the second half outfield. At the end of the season my manager told me that he felt that I wasn't as good outfield as I was between the sticks and that he wanted me to play in goal permanently."

Meanwhile, Roche had attracted some attention over the sea in England.

"Frank O'Farrell, the manager of Torquay United, invited me to play with them for a year," he recalls. "I got the cattle boat from Dublin to Birkenhead. Then I took a train to Torquay. The journey took about 18 hours."

The lanky custodian enjoyed his time by the sea in Devon.

"I was an apprentice motor mechanic and worked during the day, training two mornings a week with Torquay," he says. "During my time there, Frank got the Leicester City job. Within a few years he would be manager of Manchester United."

Homesick, Roche decided to go back to Ireland.

"I returned to Dublin in 1969 but I didn't have to wait long to find out what I would do next. Shelbourne told me that I would be playing for them. No money or terms were discussed. I just agreed to play for them."

Roche went straight into the first team. He was paid £10 a week and earned £2 extra if the Shels won.

"I also continued to work as an apprentice at a place in Bray," he says. "I drove around delivering parts for garages. I liked driving and still do – it's been my job for years."

Roche had three seasons in the first team at Shelbourne.

"I made over 100 appearances and played UEFA Cup football against Vasas in Budapest. We lost 1-0, but I probably had the best game of my life."

The Vasas manager made it known through a translator that Roche was a 'miracle man'. Roche was also capped by Ireland in a European Championship qualifier while still a Shels player.

Not every game was so rewarding.

"We played Derry City, and a lot of their fans came down from Derry," he says. "I was having words with them behind the goal, nothing out of the ordinary. Then one of them shouted at me and held up some rubber bullets. I'd never seen them before and spent the whole game worrying about getting shot."

Roche returned to the garage one day in November 1973 where his boss told him that the Shelbourne manager had been on the phone.

"He said that I was going to sign for Manchester United. I told him to piss off, but he insisted that it was true. I realised that he wasn't joking. I was told to get back into my van and drive back into Dublin to the Gresham Hotel where Paddy Crerand was waiting to see me. Was I excited? Just a bit."

Tommy Docherty had spotted Roche on a scouting mission to watch Gerry Daly and Mick Martin in Dublin. And the 'keeper was so surprised at United's approach, he barely considered that the £65 full-time wage being offered at Old Trafford was actually less than what he was already earning.

"I just thought 'show me the way!' Money wasn't the issue.

"I didn't discuss any terms, just nodded. United and Shelbourne agreed a fee of £25,000 – a record for a goalkeeper in Ireland. I was hopeless with money but asked Shelbourne if I was due any because I'd not cost them a penny. They asked me how much I wanted. I didn't have a clue. I got £3,500. I would have taken a fiver if they had offered that."

Gerry Daly and Ray O'Brien were two Dubliners who had been signed by Tommy Docherty for United just prior to the arrival of his new 'keeper. O'Brien wouldn't get a game at Old Trafford and was transferred to Notts County for £40,000 in December 1973, subsequently enjoying ten years at Meadow Lane.

"I remember the two of them coming to see us play at Tolka Park. I thought Gerry was a prat when I met him for the first time," laughs Roche. "They both had long leather coats on, the type that you never saw in Dublin. Gerry had an English accent too – he'd only been there for a few weeks! I grew to like Gerry a lot, but my first impression was not positive."

Roche was married in June 1973 to Harriet, a Shels supporter who he had met on the team bus on the way back from a match. The couple had just bought a house in Dublin.

"We never lived in it. That's football. We moved to Manchester and rented a flat on Stockport Road in Levenshulme."

Full-back Alex Forsyth was one of the first to strike up a friendship with Roche when he arrived at United, and it's one which endures to this day. "Alex gave me directions to come over to the Pelican pub in Timperley for a beer. People would drink and drive then. I couldn't find the pub and got lost, but Alex and I became good friends."

Armed with a contract, wages of £65 a week, a pay-off from Shelbourne and signing-on fee, Roche had enough money to put down on a house.

"Ray O'Brien was selling his place in Timperley because of his move to Notts County. We bought that from him and we've been in the area ever since."

Roche and Forsyth would share the driving to training every day.

"Some players had cars, others didn't. I didn't. Most lived around Sale. We would pick up Lou Macari on the way to training."

Roche settled in and impressed. He was doing so well in United's reserves that Docherty publicly stated that he would be his number one in the 1974/75 season. But Docherty's announcement was premature.

"I was brought into the first team at the start of the pre-season," he says. "I was going to play, I was told that, but my dad died just before the season started and I went back to Dublin. Alex Stepney was given his place back. He played really well. I wasn't too concerned."

The two United goalkeepers got on.

"He was completely different to me," explains Roche. "He was far more worldly than me and knew the politics of football. He wouldn't help me a lot, but it wasn't his job to help me because I was trying to take his place. When I look back I think he was a good person."

Roche arrived at a club where Willie Morgan was the main man.

"Or he was until he fell out with the Doc," recalls Roche. "And if you fell out with Tommy Docherty that was it. Ask George Graham."

Roche finally made his debut in a Second Division game against Oxford away in February 1975.

"We lost 1-0 and the pitch was terrible. I was brought in because Alex was injured. I played the following week and we beat Hull 2-0 at home.

"We won the league and there was a great atmosphere among the players. I only played two games so I didn't feel fully part of the celebrations."

Roche admits that he was naïve.

"I believed everything that Lou Macari told me," he smiles. "I had no reason to think he was lying. He was always scheming, but I wasn't usually the butt of his jokes."

Although he was when Macari discovered his "peculiar" eating habits.

"It sounds stupid because I'm a good eater now, but I wasn't then. We'd go to places like Italy and I would turn my nose up at all this really good quality food in favour of sandwiches which my wife had made me for the trip. She made me sandwiches for all my trips abroad with United. I would eat these sandwiches every day until we got home."

This was a situation tailor-made for Lou Macari.

"After a while, Lou found out about my sandwiches," explains Roche. "He would try and nick them. I would be minding my own business and he'd walk past and drop one of my sandwiches on the floor. I'd see this and shout, 'That looks like my sandwich!' Of course he wanted to see my reaction."

Preventative measures were required.

"I would usually room with Gerry Daly or Alex Forsyth," explains Roche. "One of us would always keep the key so that Lou couldn't pretend to be us at reception, go into our room and steal my sandwiches. I used to imagine him creeping along the corridor on the lookout for my sandwiches. I used to have to hide them everywhere."

The nadir of Macari's pranks came when Roche and Daly were locked in their hotel room in Belgrade, a story which is told at the beginning of the Daly chapter. Roche laughs out loud at the memory of Daly screaming to him in a Dublin accent: "You fucking eejit, how could you let him take the phone?"

"Macari was childish," laughs Roche. "He was always up to something, even if it was just hiding your shoes. He was a good lad and a nice fella, but it got to the stage when I'd just watch him to see what he was up to. He was always alert. He never drank or smoked and would always stay up later than anyone else."

Then, finally, Roche's chance to replace Stepney in the first team arrived. After the Liverpool debacle, no relatively easy games awaited the shaken, new first-team goalkeeper,

Manchester City were United's next opponents.

"We lost 4-0. City played well, we didn't," he says matter of factly. "I didn't have a bad game. We played Villa in the next match and won 2-0. I did well, but got a bad knock on my shoulder."

Despite his injury, Roche was selected for the next game against Arsenal away.

"I was playing well until they had a corner. Most grounds had floodlights on pylons. Highbury's were mounted on the top of the stands. As the ball came in all I could see was the floodlights. There was nobody near me and I went to punch it. I missed the ball . . . which went straight in from the corner. I froze after that and the pressure really got to me."

It became every goalkeeper's nightmare.

"My bottle went. My confidence and concentration had gone," rues Roche. "I had gone for a cross, with nobody near me, but missed the ball completely. Confidence is everything, especially to a goalkeeper."

There was plenty of pressure off the pitch.

"People were ringing my house night and day, journalists mainly. I tried to be helpful at first, but then I'd see what they were writing about me, calling me butter fingers. I told my wife to tell them that I wasn't at home.

"The United crowd turned against me," he sighs. "That's a horrible feeling when you take to the pitch and you know that your own supporters are against you.

"I played later for Halifax and we were at Torquay once. I went into the bar after the game and a fella came up to me. He told me that he was a United fan and that he used to boo me when I came out. I told him to fuck off."

Roche had little support from his team-mates.

"Nobody really said anything to me and that didn't help my confidence either. Then I heard that Tommy Cavanagh had said something in the dressing room after the Arsenal game while I was in the bar. He said that I had cost the team three points. I'm told that Sammy McIlroy stuck up for me and told him that he shouldn't be speaking about me like that behind my back."

Sammy Mac continued to stick up for Roche. Although he later wrote that he believed this patchy spell cost United the title in 1976, he also commented, "A goalkeeper is supposed to have a defence in front of him".

Docherty called Roche into his office at The Cliff on the Monday morning after the game.

"He told me that he was going to leave me out for the next game. Stupidly, I told him that was fine because I was going to ask him to leave me out. That was the wrong thing to say, the wrong message to send out, but that's how bad I was feeling at the time. I wasn't sleeping, I was in shock."

Docherty told *The Times*: "I am leaving Paddy Roche out for his own sake. I have never seen a footballer criticised so constantly." Other pundits suggested that racism played a part in the barracking of Roche, with anti-Irish sentiment strong in some quarters because of the Troubles.

United beat Newcastle United 1-0 in the next match and then drew 0-0 with Middlesbrough. Stepney was back, and it took the under-fire Roche considerable time to recover his composure, if he ever did.

The 'keeper would be a target throughout his career.

"I played at Brentford and the home fans were great with me, they knew I was a decent goalkeeper. But away fans would taunt me wherever I went for years. I played until I was 38 and got abuse for 15 years, people calling me 'United reject'."

Roche wasn't finished at United, far from it. He made 53 appearances in what would be a nine-year spell at the club. To dwell on two inopportune moments isn't fair to a man who, it is not often remembered, made 53 appearances.

"I was United's reserve 'keeper for most of the time. There was no such thing as a substitute goalkeeper so I'd be with the reserves, Manchester United's number two goalkeeper, first behind Alex Stepney and then Gary Bailey. I played two different half seasons when they were injured. Twice, I got in [the side] for six months . . . and twice I got injured."

Roche played 23 of his United games in 1977/78.

"I got a Player of the Year award from a supporters' group in the Midlands that year," he says proudly. "My confidence had slowly returned and it helped when people like Steve Coppell said to me, 'You're a different goalkeeper, you can see that your confidence is back.'

The reason I lost my place was a hamstring injury. Sammy McIlroy told me to play through it so that I didn't lose my place, but it wasn't possible. I was out of the team again as Alex came back in. And that's how it was for a good while . . ."

He has happy memories from that time.

"We beat Everton 6-2 at Goodison one Boxing Day [1977] and played absolutely brilliant. That was my most enjoyable match at United."

And for the first time he could enjoy the wholehearted support of the crowd.

"The Stretford End was so loud," he says. "We played West Brom in an FA Cup fourth-round replay. Gordon Hill got us a late winner and we won 3-2, but the crowd were responsible for that goal. It was an inspiration to play in games like that.

"I played a game or two with Bryan Robson and he stood out

a mile, but Martin Buchan was probably the best player that I ever played with. He read the game well and had pace. He wasn't the best passer of the ball, but I used to give it to him easy. And he was very much a defender. If he went over the halfway line the crowd would start cheering.

"Martin was great to play with because you knew what he was going to do, whereas Gordon McQueen was unpredictable. You'd shout for a cross and he'd still go up for it before ducking at the last second. I'd not see the ball until the very last second.

"We used to get discounted meat off the chairman Louis Edwards. He was a big affable man with a huge place just outside Palma in Mallorca which we'd be invited to when we played pre- or post-season games there. He'd go to games with directors like Denzil Haroun and Mr Gibson. They were like something out of *Last of the Summer Wine*. We drew 1-1 at Stoke and Mr Gibson, who wore thick round glasses like bottle tops, thought that we'd won 2-0!

"Martin Edwards was one of the lads in the very early days. He'd play tennis with us on tours in the Seventies and was very normal.

"Tommy Docherty was larger than life, yet he'd get all the players to go to Mass on a Sunday, even when we were on tour. All the Irish lads would go."

Roche has happy memories of the majority of his time at Old Trafford.

"There were some good people and we had a great fun. We travelled the world – and that was just in one tour in 1975."

The attire for goalkeepers was very different in those days.

"Tommy Cavanagh wouldn't let us wear caps or long pants," Roche explains. "They wouldn't let you wear long pants even when the ground was rock hard. My legs used to get cut to pieces. It wasn't seen as a manly thing. The only time I was allowed to wear long pants at United was when the ground was frozen. And I wore normal woollen gloves for most of my career, either them or Peter Bonetti gloves – green cloth gloves with bits of rubber from a table tennis bat stuck to them. They were hopeless. The modern type of gloves started coming in towards the later Seventies. They were fine if they were very wet or very dry, but slippy and useless anywhere in between. I can remember Alex Stepney trying them for the first time and the ball went straight through his hands from a cross."

Footballs were also very different.

"There was a huge difference in gloves and balls between the start of my career and the end. The balls became more plasticky and lighter. It travels much further now. I used to really have to whack a ball to get it over the halfway line. Goalkeepers now just chip it.

"Pitches are perfect now, too, and like bowling greens. In the Seventies I played on some horrible sand and mud pits. They put so much sand on pitches in the winter that it was like playing on a frozen beach. That was dangerous for goalkeepers because the sand would affect your grip."

With Alex Stepney moving on to play in Dallas after 539 United games, Roche recovered from his injury and started 1978/79 as United's first-choice 'keeper under Dave Sexton. He would make 16 appearances that season.

"The jeering starting again," he recalls. "It wasn't so much during the game, but my name would be booed when it was read out. It wasn't everyone and it was probably a minority, but it was enough to make a difference to my confidence. United were linked with the Coventry goalkeeper Jim Blythe and I think he actually signed, though we also had Gary Bailey. We lost one game against Birmingham 5-1 and the criticism started again."

Gary Bailey remembers the farcical manoeuverings which followed.

"I had been at Old Trafford a year and still hadn't had my break in the first team. I'd actually packed my bags to go back to South Africa. I was prepared to go home. Then Alex Stepney got injured. Paddy Roche was still ahead of me and I was third choice, but after Paddy played in a 5-1 defeat at Birmingham and was roasted by the manager I thought I was in with a shout for the next game against Ipswich."

Bailey was expecting good news when he was called into Dave Sexton's office on the Thursday before the Ipswich game. "I thought, 'This is it, I'm getting the call up', he remembers. "But he actually said, 'I'd like to introduce you to our new 'keeper, Jim Blythe.' I couldn't believe it; he'd gone and signed a new goal-keeper."

Despondent, Bailey called his father and revealed that he was now Manchester United's fourth-choice goalkeeper, as a £440,000 fee was agreed for Blythe. "We agreed that I would go back to South Africa where I would finish my studies," he says. "I had given United my best crack and it was time to leave."

But Sexton wanted to see Bailey again the following morning. "We've got a major problem," said the United manager. "Jim Blythe has failed his medical and you're playing tomorrow. The press want a few pictures of you."

Bailey played and did well. But not every player got on with him.

"I did, though," says Roche, "He had a big ego or maybe it was just a lot of confidence which every goalkeeper needs, but I liked him. He had a book called something like, 'How to speak English properly' which he took to matches and which he got a lot of stick for."

Roche would never be United's number one again – though he was man of the match against Wolves in 1980/81 – and looks back with regret.

"People say that the only way is down once you leave Manchester United. That might be true for most, but I should have left years before. I was a good goalkeeper and could have been number one at a First Division club for years. I spent the best years of my career playing reserve-team football. I would have been sharper playing in the first team somewhere else."

Roche eventually moved to Third Division Brentford in 1981.

"Ron Atkinson let me go on a free transfer. I could never look at him the same way after he lent me his training top one day at The Cliff. It smelt of aftershave and hair spray."

Roche lived in west London during the week.

"Brentford paid me the same as Manchester United, £270 a week. I found out that Dave Sexton had recommended me. I'd drive down from Manchester on Monday morning and stay in digs in London in the week. My family stayed in Manchester and I had a room at a house of a lady who was friends with my wife. I used to drive back to Manchester after a game on a Saturday, have Sunday in Manchester and drive south on Monday. It wasn't ideal."

Team-mates at Griffin Park included Stan Bowles.

"He was coming to the end of his career and could hardly run, but he was still a star and the crowd loved him. He lived next to the ground and didn't always train. He was always in the bookies or the pub. He was forever up to something. He reminded me of a drinking, smoking Macari. I liked him."

And Ron 'Chopper' Harris.

"I stayed at his place for three or four months. He had a smashing house in Epsom with stables and everything. He was very down to earth."

Chris Kamara was also at Brentford.

"We went to Spain on a little tour and got pissed on the beach one day. Chris fell asleep. One of the other players put his dick in his mouth. And then pissed in it. Chris woke up spluttering with all the other lads laughing around him. I can't get that image out of my head whenever I see him on television."

Despite the awkward living arrangements, Roche was happy.

"I really started enjoying my football again at Brentford because I felt appreciated. That makes a big difference."

Not every away fan appreciated him, however.

"Millwall was the worst," he says. "One man, with a small child in his arms, stood behind my goal and spent 90 minutes calling me a 'fucking Irish bastard'. I told him that he was an awful father. He replied by calling me a fucking Irish bastard one more time."

Roche stayed at Brentford for two years.

"The travelling became too much in the end," he says. "I couldn't be away from my family for that long and driving down the M6 and M1 so much started to wear me down."

After 71 games for the Bees, Roche moved to Halifax Town in 1984, where he would make a further 189 Football League appearances.

"Players looked up to me because I'd been at United," he remembers. "They rated me and couldn't believe the stick I'd had. They were in the Fourth Division and always struggled, but it was closer to my family in Manchester. I played for five years until I was 39 and then stayed for another decade as the Football in the Community officer. I used to share a car over the Pennines with Billy Ayres who became manager. Billy died in his 40s of cancer. David Longhurst also played for Halifax, the lad who died on the pitch while playing for York City."

Roche was named either Player of the Year or Players' Player of the Year in each of his first three seasons.

"We played Spurs away in the League Cup. We went down there the day before the game which was a big treat. The coach broke down just outside Halifax on the way. The whole team were thumbing lifts back into Halifax at 2am."

Despite their difficulties, the Shaymen boasted plenty of spirit.

"There were jokes aplenty," recalls Roche. "Most of them too rude to be printed. I was sat in the team bath one day and noticed my team-mates jump out one by one. Some dirty bugger had dropped a shit and it was floating around."

The Halifax phantom shitter didn't just operate in the bath.

"He'd do it in a cup on the team coach and leave it under a seat nearby so that part of the coach stank. I knew who it was. He did very well in football and he was a bright lad with a good university degree too."

Roche left Halifax in 1989 and then received a call from Chester City manager Harry McNally.

"He wanted a back-up 'keeper. I played about seven or eight

reserve games. Harry was a big hero with Chester fans, but a nutcase who used to come in the dressing room pissed before a match. He couldn't remember anyone's names. He wanted me to play in the first team, but I got a knee injury. That finished off my playing career. I've got arthritis in that knee now and it all stemmed from that injury."

Bill Ayres called from Halifax.

"Jim McCalliog had been doing the Football in the Community job in conjunction with the PFA. When he was promoted to manager I got asked to replace him. I shouldn't have done it. The wages were £100 a week and it was costing me £35 a week in petrol."

But he ended up staying in the job for five years, thanks to a perk which Halifax gave him.

"They gave me a little shop on match days," he explains. "I turned into a shopkeeper with a little stall at the back of the stand. I sold anything that I thought would sell: soup, Bovril, crisps. I'd sell the Bovril for 50p but it would only cost me 5p. That's how I made my money at Halifax. It kept me going for a few years. I got to know all the fans and liked chatting to them. Leeds United reserves started playing at the Shay so that was another boost. Their first game was against Man United reserves and there was a big crowd – far more than Halifax ever got. I was happy to sell them drinks. I started selling buns and everything." Fortunately, Lou Macari wasn't around to steal Roche's food.

Roche's life in football ended after Halifax.

"I joined an agency to get some driving work while I figured out what I wanted to do. I'd always liked driving and was used to it with my different clubs."

So, he returned to driving full-time a decade ago, working nights and covering up to 300 miles per shift around the North West.

"I love it," he says. "I meet a lot of people, especially old people who don't come into contact with many others. They really appreciate a chat because they don't see anyone apart from their carers. People know my name but I never get recognised through work.

That happens more in Manchester. People are nice with me, but I still get the odd person at the bar saying, 'Don't drop it,' when I pick up my pint. I tell them that I'll drop it on their heads if they don't shut up."

In 2005, gale force winds blew his lorry off the Southport coast road in the early hours. It rolled over and ended up 50 yards from the road in a ditch. "I was lucky to survive," says Roche. "My glasses came off and I was upside down in my cabin. I felt blood pouring down my face. I'd hit the roof of my cabin and the windscreen. I was trying to get out of the cabin and managed to get a window open.

"A car travelling behind had seen what happened and they called the police and an ambulance. They told me that they thought I would be dead. And I would have been had I not worn my seatbelt."

Roche couldn't work for six months but then made a full recovery and was able to go back to driving.

Roche doesn't go to United games now, despite living just five miles from Old Trafford.

"I hate asking for tickets," he explains. "I used to get people asking me from Dublin so I'd ring Old Trafford. I wasn't comfortable doing that."

He doesn't see so much of his former team-mates either, despite living so close to many in Sale.

"I used to play in the golf days but I have trouble with my legs and struggle to walk distances," he explains. "The golf days were the only time that I really saw them. I am mates with Alex Forsyth but he lives in Scotland now."

Occasionally, he has bumped into some people.

"I deliver things to disabled people," he recalls. "A few years ago I had a delivery in Liverpool. I knocked on this house and John Gidman answered. 'Rocky!' he shouted (that was my nickname at United, nothing to do with the boxer). It was mad. He was visiting a mate and it was his first time at that house, the first time he'd ever opened the door."

"My daughter Sinead is a big United fan, though. She went to Barcelona by herself to see the European Cup final."

That's more than her dad.

"I'll watch United a bit on television, but I couldn't tell you who the game is against this weekend," he says. "The kids keep me up to date. I'm just not that interested in the football and prefer to watch Munster and Leinster in the Heineken Cup."

It's not Manchester United that keeps him in Sale either. He goes to Dublin to see family "three or four times a year" though they haven't contemplated moving because, "our three kids are English and they all live within five minutes of us. I'm a granddad now, as well."

7

JIMMY GREENHOFF
THE YORKSHIRE CANTONA

JIMMY GREENHOFF

Jimmy Greenhoff is not one for interviews. Initially reluctant to be involved in this book because he felt that he "had nothing to say", he became a touch pensive when the recorder was switched on.

But he's now chatting comfortably about his life of ups and downs, sitting in his front room in Alsager, the large village between Crewe and Stoke which the Barnsley-born former striker has called home for most of his adult life. Of growing up in a Barnsley so working-class that you were considered posh if you had a toilet inside your house, of playing for that great Leeds United side under Don Revie. Of spells at Birmingham, his beloved Stoke City and his time as a fans' favourite at Old Trafford.

Greenhoff looked pained when he explained that he's not spoken to his brother Brian for nearly two decades. Sad when he describes how a fraudulent former business partner ended up costing him "everything". And then he's asked about a goal in the

1979 FA Cup semi-final replay against Liverpool at Goodison Park. He bursts into the biggest smile since he started over two hours and two cups of tea ago.

"That was the best goal I ever scored for United," he says. "It was the most important, and it really meant a lot to the supporters."

United had drawn 2-2 at Maine Road in the first semi-final.

"Everyone thought that we'd blown our chance to beat Liverpool. The papers did, and I'm convinced that some of the players did. We'd been dead on our feet and nobody gave us a chance."

United had to pick themselves up for the midweek return match.

"Our legs were dead, but when that whistle went we all ran our bollocks off," he explains. "We got stuck into them and we got under their feet. Mickey Thomas got the ball on the left with 12 minutes to go. He crossed it towards me. I had a quick look to see that Emlyn Hughes was out of position; he was probably frightened to death of Steve Coppell. The ball came over. It seemed to take an age. It bounced. I swear I had time to think, 'Do I head it? Do I bring it down on my chest? Do I volley it?' One eye was on the ball, one on their 'keeper Ray Clemence. Ray moved forward, so I lunged forward and headed past him. Ray coming out had made my mind up for me."

The United fans in the Park End went wild.

"I ran to them to celebrate, and I carried on celebrating. I ended up by one of the television cameras near the half-way line [this was in a pre-Sky age when there were just two, not 22, cameras in the ground]. I had the most stupid face in front of that camera. The referee ran over and said, 'Calm down, calm down'. I couldn't. Joe Jordan came over and gave me the biggest kiss on the lips. He had that big hole where his two front teeth should be. The things you do when you are happy, eh? I'm sure that every United fan at Goodison that day has thanked me since."

United had to hang on for 12 minutes.

"It seemed so much longer," says Greenhoff. "I was convinced that the clock had stopped. It seemed to stay at two minutes to nine for ages. I was looking at it three or four times a minute urging it to change. We survived."

Greenhoff was born in Barnsley in 1946 and has nothing but happy memories of his early years.

"Barnsley is lovely," he says. "I just wish I could turn the clock back and live my life again and again and again. Growing up was lovely. I'd come home from school and play football on the rec until it was dark. We'd have games between the gable ends of terraced streets not far from the centre of Barnsley. It was all terraced houses with outside toilets. Mother was a housewife and father was a steelworker at Stocksbridge Steel Works near Sheffield, then he became a bookies' runner. You were either a miner or a steelworker in Barnsley. I grew up seeing miners walking home with blackened faces. I just thought that was normal life, I thought that every town had mountains of coal surrounding it."

Barnsley is still famous for being a close knit place. "Barnsley folk are very proud of their town," says Greenhoff. "They know that people laugh at it and that it is the brunt of jokes but that doesn't stop them being proud. It's Barnsley first and Yorkshire second. Listen to Michael Parkinson, he talks about Barnsley with great affection."

The Greenhoffs took their annual holiday in Blackpool.

"A fleet of coaches would leave Barnsley at the same time – it was known as Barnsley week in Blackpool. Everyone I knew went, including the three children in our family. We thought Blackpool was the bright lights, a really special place.

"I didn't go without," he recalls. "If I needed a new pair of football boots then I got a new pair. I'd get a football for Christmas and I thought I was king of the town. But every day was like Christmas in Barnsley. I had everything I needed."

Greenhoff naturally followed his local team.

"I was the first one inside Oakwell from the minute I was allowed to go on my own when I was nine or ten. The turnstiles would open at 12 and I'd be straight in, heading for a couple of bricks by the home dugout. I'd pop my head around into the dugout just to make sure that everything was okay in there. I'd smell the liniment, then wait and wait. It was my dream to play for Barnsley in the old Second Division, a dream to play football in front of 13,000 Barnsley folk."

Tommy Taylor had been the town's most famous football export when he moved to Manchester United in 1953 for £29,999.

"He was a big star in Barnsley, everyone knew his name," says Greenhoff. "My heroes came a few years later and only Barnsley folk would have heard of them, but Tommy Taylor was a big, big name and I started liking United because of him."

Taylor's life would be cut tragically short at Munich.

"I remember hearing about the Munich Air Disaster," says Greenhoff. "I was walking home from school and everyone kept their doors open in those days. I was a mile from home when I heard news of the air crash on a radio through an open door. I started to cry and then sprinted all the way home. I wanted my mum to tell me that everything was alright, but it wasn't. I cried again."

Greenhoff was 11. Even at that age, he claims that he knew he was going to be a professional footballer.

"I just knew," he says confidently. "I passed my 11-plus and went to Barnsley Grammar School. Most grammar schools played rugby, but ours played football. At the end of the first year you were put into sets according to academic ability. 'A' and 'B' were for the brightest, 'C', 'D' and 'E' for those below that level. I was put into 'C' which I was quite happy with seeing as it was a grammar school.

"In those days you had to do five years in a grammar school, unless you were bought out of school after the fourth year. I knew at the age of 11 that a club would need me at 15 and asked my dad if he could buy me out of my last year."

Greenhoff's confidence came in part from his starring role for an all-conquering Barnsley Schoolboys team.

"We won the schools equivalent of the FA Cup and beat

Liverpool in the final over two legs at Anfield and Oakwell," he recalls. "There were 13,000 watching at Oakwell and my brother Brian was a ball-boy. I played at right-half."

£10, reasonably serious money then, was the price of leaving school early.

"My dad asked me if I was sure about being a footballer. He knew deep down that I'd make it, and so he paid the money. Clubs were not allowed to tap up players like now, but a phone call from someone associated with Leeds United gave my father the assurances that he wanted. I was worried that we were doing something illegal and that I'd go to prison. I didn't want it to go against me in my future career."

Greenhoff duly left school at 15 to join Leeds.

"I travelled to Leeds and back each day. I'd leave Barnsley at 6.30am and it took 55 minutes each way every day. The train stopped at every station and then I took a bus from Leeds Central to Elland Road. After training and doing my duties as an apprentice, like cleaning the boots and the stands, I would set off back to Barnsley at 4.30pm. It was a long day and hard work.

"Don Revie told us that jobs such as sweeping the terraces should be done with a positive attitude because then we'd take that onto the pitch when we played. He said that if we went about our jobs in a slovenly manner then that's how we'd play. I believed him, even if the toilets in the Lowfields Road stank on a Monday morning. All those men, all that Tetley's Bitter. I used to hold my breath for as long as possible as I attempted to clean the toilets. It stood me in good stead, but I missed my stop at Barnsley many times because I'd fallen asleep on the way home."

Revie was the undisputed main man at Elland Road.

"He was a players' manager who wanted to be with his players all the time," says Greenhoff. "If he had had his way he would have never sent them home. They would have gone from training to a hotel, played bingo with him and then carpet bowls."

Greenhoff was determined to make his mark and was not short of confidence.

"I showed him what a good player I was, and by the time I was 16 I was knocking on his door and telling him that I should be in the team."

He made his Leeds first-team debut at 16 in a 5-0 home win against Swansea in 1963.

"I knew I was good enough," he says. "That wasn't me being big headed, I just knew that I was better than some of the players who were 10 years older than me. Eventually, Don did what Fergie did in the Nineties – he played a lot of youngsters all at once, the likes of me, Paul Reaney, Terry Cooper and Gary Sprake. He also bought Peter Lorimer, Eddie Gray, Paul Madeley and Johnny Giles. Leeds had a great side, a great, great side. Liverpool and United were our main rivals."

United pipped Leeds to the title on goal difference in 1965, but despite playing nearly 100 games in five years, Greenhoff wasn't satisfied.

"I never felt happy at Leeds," he says. "I never felt that I was going to be on the team sheet every week. I also felt that I always had something to prove, and I didn't enjoy playing at Elland Road either. I was the type of player who needed a pat on the back, but the crowd were too harsh, especially on their own. It wasn't the things they'd say, but you could feel the mood if they were against you. They never changed at Leeds. David O'Leary once took his side on a big winning streak. He drew one home game and they booed them off. I was at the game and thought, 'They never change these Leeds folk'."

Greenhoff had already met his future wife, Joan, a Leeds girl.

"We were both going for the bus in Leeds. I'd seen her around. We agreed a date . . ."

Greenhoff smiles at the memory. "Oh, come on," he says, clearly surprised at being asked to talk about the love of his life. Then he pauses and says, "Meeting Joan was the best thing that ever happened to me. We married at 22 and bought a house in Leeds. Her father had done it all up, and we had it how we wanted it. We were sad to leave, but I had to get out of Leeds."

In 1968, after five years in West Yorkshire, Greenhoff instigated a move away shortly after playing in the first leg of the Fairs Cup final against Ferencvaros.

"I was the only player to be transferred in the middle of a cup final," he recalls. "I was sad at leaving such a great side, but relieved to escape the Leeds crowd. I went to see Don Revie and told him that I wanted out. I think he was sick of me going to see him and telling him that I should be playing more so he agreed. I'd seen in the paper that clubs like Arsenal were after me. I later found out that he wouldn't let me go to Arsenal. I also found out that Shankly told Revie, 'I didn't know Greenhoff was for sale. I would have gone for him.' But Don Revie was happy to shove me down into the Second Division."

Leeds sold Greenhoff to Birmingham City for £70,000 in August 1968.

"I went there and signed that day. I shouldn't have done it so quickly, but I was desperate to get away from Leeds. The money was the same, £60 a week, so I signed."

It was not a good move.

"I scored 12 goals in the first nine games. The manager, Stan Cullis, got me in his office and told me that I should be scoring more. I thought it was a joke. He was known as a hard manager from his Wolves days [Cullis, along with Busby, was one of the greatest post-war managers, but very different in his approach]. That was his way of getting more goals out of me. I told him there and then that I wasn't happy and that I couldn't possibly score more goals."

Indeed, Greenhoff scored just two more goals in the next 22 games and didn't manage a full season at St Andrews.

"Stoke City's Tony Waddington came in with an offer. Birmingham made a profit on me," he says of his £100,000 transfer to First Division Stoke in 1969.

"Signing for Stoke was one of the best things I did in football," he says. "I stayed there for seven years. Joan was pregnant with our first child so I paid a family an extra £250 to move out of the house they were selling more quickly so that we could be settled.

"We reached the FA Cup semi-finals twice in 1971 and '72 – and were robbed on both occasions. We played Arsenal twice and lost to them twice," he explains. The Arsenal curse would never go away, as Greenhoff later found out in the 1979 FA Cup final.

Stoke fared better in the League Cup.

"We won it in 1972. The fans still talk about that era here, and I'm not surprised. We played good football and had a fine side. I wish I'd had a pound for every time they chanted my name back then."

Greenhoff is still revered in the Potteries.

"I loved them to death, I really did. They supported me all the time. Stoke supporters made me as a player. I went 18 games without scoring in my first season there and they never ever had a go at me. They knew I was giving 100 per cent. Then the goals started coming.

"The manager said, 'Go out and entertain them.' He bought lads like Alan Hudson, the best player I've ever played with. I had a telepathic relationship with the guy. We played in front of 40,000 all the time. I loved it, I loved training every day, I loved hearing the fans chant my name. It really lifted me."

His performances won him international recognition of sorts – five caps for England under-23s.

"Don Revie was the full England manager, and maybe he held a grudge for what happened at Leeds. Playing for England was never big on my agenda, and it was lovely to be known as the best uncapped player for a long, long time. Then Steve Bruce came along and took that claim off me, the bugger."

Greenhoff still lives close to Stoke and watches them play when he's not watching United at Old Trafford. His departure from the Victoria Ground could be put down to an act of God when the roof of the Butler Street Stand blew down in 1976.

"The stand wasn't insured," he explains. "I found out on a

Friday afternoon when I went for a meal with the other players at the social club in the Boothen End as normal. I got a message saying that Tony Waddington wanted to see me. I walked into the ground and saw him waiting at the top of the tunnel. I followed him into his office and he started talking about the stand blowing down and how it wasn't insured, not about football as he would normally have done because I was captain."

"We've got to sell someone to pay for it," said the agitated Stoke manager.

"You're joking," replied his captain.

"And I've been told to say that it's you."

"'Forget it!' I said, before storming off effing and jeffing, back to the other players who were having their lunch. I sat down, and the phone went again with another message that the manager wanted to see me. The lads were asking me what was going on."

Once again, Waddington was waiting for Greenhoff by the tunnel.

"He was a bit shaken," recalls Greenhoff. "His adam's apple was going up and down.

"'I'm sorry,' said Waddington, 'but I have something else to tell you . . .'

"'I don't care, I'm not going anywhere,' I said.

"'Everton are on the way down the motorway. Someone must have tipped them off. But I've spoken to Manchester United too and they want you. I called Tommy Docherty and he said, "Get Greenhoff down here straight away."'"

Docherty remembers the call from Waddington, who told him that he had to sell players as they were getting no leeway from the bank and the stand hadn't been insured.

"Waddington said, 'I have one who is a snip at £120,000'," recalls Docherty. "When he told me it was Jimmy Greenhoff I said I'd buy him without hesitation. I also told him that I'd take Peter Shilton off his hands." Shilton agreed to move to United, where he would have replaced Alex Stepney, but the United board had reservations about the £275,000 fee and Shilton's £210 a week wage demands – £50 more than United's highest earner.

"Matt Busby finally told me that United couldn't justify Shilton's terms," said Docherty. Shilton would move to Nottingham Forest, where he would win the league and lift two European Cups.

The Doc wanted a second Greenhoff – even if he was 30.

"Jimmy was a class act as a striker; he was extremely skilful, he had a good football brain and a keen eye for goal, was a super team player and a committed professional."

Greenhoff was in shock.

"I didn't want to leave Stoke, but the United news softened the blow. I kept repeating, 'Man United, Man United.' My brother was playing there too, yet it was still the hardest decision I've made. Some of the other players could not understand why I was so reluctant to leave Stoke, but me and the Stoke fans understood it."

Those fans reacted angrily to the news that their star striker was leaving. Windows were put through at the Victoria Ground and 'Greenhoff Must Stay' graffiti sprayed around the ground.

Stoke fan Anthony Bunn was eight at the time.

"United were at the top of the hate list for many Stoke fans because they took our hero away," he explains. "Where were you when JFK got shot? Who gives a toss? Where were you when Jimmy Greenhoff was sold?

"The city was stunned and it was no surprise that Stoke's star started to wane just as United's rose – the Greenhoff effect, we call it. For an eight-year-old it was almost impossible to reason with."

Greenhoff's move went through – eventually.

"I travelled to Manchester three times in five days, but each time Tommy Docherty sent me back and asked me to think about it. He knew that I didn't want to leave Stoke. I called a Board meeting at Stoke and asked, 'Why me?' Finally, one of the directors stood up and said, 'We think you're past it.' That was the push I needed to leave."

Greenhoff continued to live in Alsager.

"I told my daughter that Daddy was going to Manchester. I

explained as best I could that we needed to move and she started crying. She didn't want to leave school because she was happy there. My wife and I agreed that we had to be fair to her too, and we stayed. I told the Doc that I would be driving from Alsager each day. He said that wasn't a problem as long as I wasn't late for training. I made sure I wasn't."

Greenhoff's Rover was soon cruising north up a largely empty M6 each morning to The Cliff.

"I used to drive up and down each day thinking, 'How lucky am I getting paid to do what I love?' My first impressions of United were how big the club was. You think you know how big it is from a distance, then you get there and realise that it's even bigger. The training facilities were fantastic, with luxury baths. I'd trained at the club's home ground with my previous clubs, whereas United had a training complex."

Greenhoff's first day in training brought a pleasant surprise.

"Two players had to pick teams. Gerry Daly was one of the pickers and I was his first choice. I didn't play long with Gerry, but he's always been alright in my book for choosing me first in training on my first day at United."

United fans took to the second Greenhoff brother straightaway.

"I had the same chant as my brother and it was strange at first. I didn't want to take Brian's thunder and he was a bit of a hero so I let him take the chant. Eventually you got to know when they meant you or your brother."

Brian Greenhoff had joined United in 1968 as a youth player and established himself in the side that won the Second Division in 1974/75.

"Good player," says Jimmy of his brother, who won 18 England caps. "He was a defender who could play centre-half, right-back or midfield. He was a 100 per cent man who would die for the cause. I would think that he was the first name on Tommy Docherty's team sheet. He was quality on and off the ball. If you wanted someone in the trenches then you'd choose my brother."

Jimmy was one of those who got on with Docherty.

"He had a lot of enemies and a lot of people disliked him, but I wasn't one of them. He was always alright with me."

The Doc certainly had his work cut out.

"I sat in the dressing room before my first game at Old Trafford, a 2-0 defeat by West Ham in November 1976, and saw that United were fourth from bottom. But there were no thoughts of being relegated and we finally finished sixth."

Greenhoff's first return to a struggling Stoke in a United shirt should have come in May 1977.

"I drove to the ground to meet the team there, and Tommy Docherty pulled me to one side to explain that I wasn't playing. I thought I'd been dropped for not playing well.

"'You're not sending them down,' explained the Doc. That was one of the nicest things ever done to me. Gone was the question of what would I do if I scored, likely because I'd scored the week before and I scored a week later against Arsenal."

So he watched the game in the directors' box alongside Docherty.

"I felt shielded next to Tom," he says, his Potteries hero status undiminished.

"Stoke manager Tony Pulis invited me to Stoke recently with another former player, Gordon Banks. I was introduced to Ryan Shawcross, and he said, 'I feel like I know you already because my girlfriend's dad never shuts up about you.'"

After all the trials and tribulations of his season, Greenhoff's first term at United finished with a series of massive highs.

"We won an FA Cup semi-final so that was a first for me," recalls Greenhoff. "It was against Leeds at Hillsborough. My legs had gone in the last five minutes and I was just trying to hold on to the ball. I passed one ball to Stewart Houston and it went through Tony Currie's legs. He said to me afterwards, 'I can't believe that you nutmegged someone five minutes before the end of an FA Cup semi-final.' He thought it was class. I assured him that it had not been intentional."

The Leeds fans were not an issue either.

"It was nearly ten years since I'd left Leeds so there were no problems. I'd scored for Stoke against them and celebrated by doing cartwheels. We stopped them breaking an unbeaten record. I didn't give a monkey's about Leeds fans."

The United coach stopped on the way back from Hillsborough.

"We got some good Yorkshire beers in, none of this gassy stuff you get in Stoke or Manchester. We brought them on the bus in old wooden crates. I liked that side of being a player. Don Revie used to stop the coach for fish and chips as a reward if we'd won at Leeds."

United were in the FA Cup final for the second successive year, but it was Greenhoff senior's first FA Cup final.

"I walked up the Wembley tunnel before the game and saw the top of the stands and the blue sky. There were 100,000 red-and-white scarves. I thought they were all United fans but half were supporting Liverpool. I know it's a cliché, but the hairs really were standing up on the back on my neck. I looked around the stand to try and find my wife and kids but didn't have any joy.

"The game was over in a flash. You're so desperate to win that sometimes you don't play your true game. Liverpool were a great side going for the treble. They were the top dogs for most of my football career, but they weren't top dogs in a one on one against United."

Greenhoff's impact on the game was significant.

"There were three goals in five minutes, two great goals and a fluke. The fluke turned out to be the winner. Lou Macari hit it and I tried my damnedest to get out of the way, but the ball hit me and I redirected it into the net. I felt like I'd scored the best goal in the world. And so did Lou. We both went up to the television studio after the game, and Brian Moore showed us the replay. I said, 'If Lou's shot was on target before it hit me then it's Lou's. If it was off target before it hit me then it's mine. It showed that Lou had mis-hit it and it was going wide. So the goal was mine. Did it matter? Not really. What mattered was that we stopped Liverpool winning the treble and we won the FA Cup."

Ownership of that goal is still disputed by the pair.

"Lou has tried to claim it loads of times! He doesn't really go on about it in front of me, but he does to other people."

The United players went back to the Royal Lancaster hotel for the post-match party.

"My brother came into our suite with his wife and a bottle of champagne. The four of us had a glass of champagne each and it was lovely. Moments like that are nice aren't they?"

Some players celebrated longer than others. Brian Greenhoff, Steve Coppell and manager Tommy Docherty sipped champagne as they crossed the lawns of Hyde Park, their garish cup final suits absorbing the warmth of the early morning sun. It was 7am.

"It was the greatest moment of my career," recalled Brian Greenhoff in an interview with the author in 2005, "and we deserved to celebrate through the night."

Why?

". . . Because it was Liverpool, because of what had happened in '76 and because of our performance."

At 7.30am, the older Greenhoff finally went to bed in the nearby Royal Lancaster. Three hours later he was a guest on national television, enthusing to presenter Martin Tyler about the victory.

"I didn't look my best," admits the former England international, "but it didn't matter. We'd won the cup."

Greenhoff had been in a worse state one year earlier when he lay disconsolate on the Wembley turf, shedding tears following Southampton's surprise 1976 cup final victory over United.

"That hurt," he remembers, "I was so disappointed that I didn't shake hands with any Southampton player. I don't regret it because that's how I felt. I couldn't even watch them receive the cup. After the match, I returned to the Russell Hotel and threw my losers' medal across the room. I said to my wife, 'You can have that. I'll wait for a winners' medal next year.' It was the end to a bad day. I'd not even been able to say sorry to the fans because we'd been given orders not to."

After the 1977 victory over Liverpool, both Greenhoff brothers had to come to terms with Docherty's departure.

"I wasn't happy when the Doc went," says Jimmy. "I didn't want him sacked, but I can understand why he was. From a personal point of view, when a manager buys you then you don't want to see him leave. I quite fancied Lawrie McMenemy taking over, and his name was being bandied about, but Dave Sexton got the job."

The new regime didn't suit him.

"Change for the worse," says Greenhoff. "The Doc used to walk into the dressing room in the morning with a laugh and a joke. When Dave walked in it went quiet.

"Look at the type of players at Old Trafford when Dave took over. The Doc had off-the-cuff attackers. He'd tell us, 'I wouldn't swap any of you 12 for any other players – go and entertain the crowd, pass to red shirts.' And that was about it. It was simple and understood by the young players.

"Dave was a lovely man, but there had to be a move behind every free-kick, a plan for everything. The players didn't want that. Sammy Mac would be on free-kicks. He wanted to get the game moving quickly and get a goal, but now he had to go through over-complicated rituals in the hope of getting the perfect goal. You could see the shoulders of the young players drop. He'd done that at QPR and Chelsea and it worked for him because he had older, more experienced players like Frank McLintock, Gerry Francis and Stan Bowles."

Ever in the background was Sir Matt Busby.

"I liked him a lot," said Greenhoff. "He was a lovely fella who had the time of day for you. In later years he would come down to Alsager and play golf with me once a year. There was a big hill on the course, but he always refused a buggy."

Louis Edwards was chairman, with his son Martin

"I got on fine with both of them," says Greenhoff. "We knew

that old Louis liked a drink. He would always be at the bar and would buy us a drink if we were on tour. And we had some huge tours to places like Hawaii on holiday and played some games in America. Martin would come on the tours too, and I liked him. Maybe because he was of a similar age I felt that I could always speak to him.

"I liked those tours and the pranks they got up to. I stayed out of the pranks, which usually involved Macari winding up Gordon Hill. I can remember them having a game of table tennis at Mottram Hall in the reception. Except there was no table or bats or ball. They would dispute points. Gordon Hill would slice the imaginary bat and ball for effect. I couldn't believe what I was seeing. They were like kids. People will say that Gordon Hill was a headbanger or whatever, but if you wanted a winger who would get you 20 goals a season then he was your man. He and Steve Coppell were the best two wingers that I ever played with – and I played with some good ones.

"The Doc would laugh at the pranks over a cigar and a glass of red wine. Dave Sexton would try the Havana cigars but it just wasn't him. Maybe he was trying too hard."

Greenhoff has fond recollections of his other United team-mates.

"Sammy McIlroy was a great player, one of the best engines that I've ever known in football," he says. "He had a love for the game that was second to none.

"Alex Stepney was the best back-four player ever. That's because he was a goalkeeper who never stopped talking. He was forever putting people right in front of him. I've never seen a goalkeeper with better distribution. Paddy Roche was the best outfield goal-keeper I knew. Him and Alex Stepney were brilliant in eight-a-side and Alex was the team's top scorer for a long time.

"Jimmy Nicholl was a great overlapping full-back, while Lou Macari was a box-to-box midfielder, a fitness fanatic who didn't smoke or drink. He wouldn't even have a sherry trifle."

Arthur Albiston played as the other full-back. "Chippy could chip a ball onto a sixpence," is Greenhoff's judgement. "I would trust in him every time. Wherever I went I knew that ball would be there. Stewart Houston was the same. I'd trust them absolutely.

"Arthur played alongside Gordon McQueen – or 'Bambi' as we called him. I would loved to have played against him every week. I was sharp and he was gangly. I'd come off quick and would have left him after 15 yards, but then after that he would have caught up with me with four giant strides. He was dynamite in the air, the best header of the ball I played with."

Greenhoff also has praise for some of the lesser lights.

"Ashley Grimes was a world-beater in training. If you watched him you'd think he should be the first name on the team sheet. He'd work his way into the first team, but after half a dozen games he'd start doing silly things in the game and be dropped again.

"David McCreery was super sub. He was really quick and should have started more games at United, maybe in front of me at times. While Andy Ritchie – along with Peter Lorimer – had the hardest shot of anyone I ever played with."

United didn't come close to winning the league under Sexton, and the arrival of Joe Jordan in 1978 added a different dynamic to United's front line.

"It had been me and Stuart Pearson up front," explains Greenhoff. "Stuart was a very similar player to myself. I was a target man, always available for people to knock it up to, even when marked. We were sharp and would combine well for one-twos, but Stuart was a better goalscorer than me."

Sexton wasn't convinced by the combination.

"I don't think Dave fancied the pair of us," admits Greenhoff. "I never thought that Dave rated me. You get word if a manager rates you or not, you hear on the grapevine from other players and you have a good idea of who likes you in football, but I never got that from Dave.

"Dave brought Joe in from Leeds and told me that he was playing Stuart with Joe. He changed the three of us around quite a lot. "

Jordan and Pearson finished the 1977/78 season together, but United only managed 10th place – mainly because of a poor start to the season which saw just six wins in the first 19 games.

Greenhoff had played in Europe for the first time with United that season, though he didn't play in the 4-0 defeat by Porto in the Cup Winners' Cup.

"I took ill in Portugal," he says. "I was pouring with sweat on the way home with the team. I've never felt so rough in all my life. I remember looking out of my bedroom window not knowing what to do. We called an ambulance."

Greenhoff was hospitalised with a virus. His first visitor surprised him.

"The boss," he says. "I still call the Doc 'boss' to this day. He was manager of Derby County then. He came straight in and said, 'Hello, Jimbo, I bet you're glad I signed you aren't you? If you ever want to move then I'll have you at Derby.'

"I could listen to the boss all day. He makes me laugh. I feel at ease with him. I remember Lou Macari asking him who the funniest man in the after-dinner circuit was. 'Me,' replied the boss. And he was right. He was the funniest man and he probably still is."

A knee injury to Pearson meant that United would start with Greenhoff and Jordan together in 1978/79.

"We finally hit it off," recalls Greenhoff, who was voted United's Player of the Year in 1979. Fans particularly appreciated his ability to hold the ball up and play people in. His intelligent reading of the game was invaluable. With typical modesty, Greenhoff lays the credit elsewhere.

"Joe was an old-fashioned centre-forward. He really worked on his game at United. He felt that the ball wasn't sticking when it came up front. He worked on that part of his game and became a really great centre-forward. That was all down to him working. He was a joy to play with. He was a big factor in why I got Player of the Year."

Whoever played up front relied on service from winger Steve

Coppell as Gordon Hill had left at the end of the 1977/78 season.

"Coppell was a great player who worked his socks off. They all did, though. I loved them to death. All those United lads loved the game. There was no mither in the dressing room, no talk behind people's back. The Doc had got rid of the old guard, which he needed to do, and built a young team. We all felt as though we were in it together – one for all and all for one. Dave Sexton inherited that spirit."

Sadly, Greenhoff's days at Old Trafford were numbered. A bad pelvic injury sidelined him for most of the 1979/80 season and he only started the 1980/81 season before making way for new signing Garry Birtles in the autumn of 1980.

"Garry was a lovely lad but didn't exactly set the world alight," recalls Greenhoff, with considerable understatement. United's £1.25 million record signing from Nottingham Forest didn't score a single goal.

"There was only one sub in those days, and I did the honourable thing and offered to move on. I felt that some of the younger players coming through deserved a chance."

Greenhoff still had two and a half years to run on his United contract at £350 a week. In December 1980, aged 34, he quit United after 36 goals in 123 appearances and moved to Crewe, safe in the knowledge that he had a good contract lined up in Canada playing for Toronto Blizzard.

"I would never have left United if the Doc was there, but I didn't have the same inclination to stay. I played a few games for Crewe Alexandra near my house to keep my match fitness before going over to Canada for their season."

But the move across the Atlantic didn't work out.

"Toronto was probably a good city, but I was living there by myself and the football was crap. I missed my family, and that's when I knew I'd had enough."

Greenhoff returned home and turned out for another local club, Port Vale.

"I did the chairman a favour and we got promotion, but the

manager felt I was after his job when I wasn't. He tried to embarrass me by playing me at left wing. He'd try and ridicule me by making me mark the fastest player in training, but I just got on with it."

Being a Stoke legend, a move to cross-city rivals Vale was perhaps not the wisest career choice.

"I realised that and maybe it was a mistake, but the rivalry wasn't like United v City or Villa v Birmingham. I was just trying to do a little bit for another local team, just like I'd done with Crewe, but it was hard. At the top level you'd get the ball passed to you even if you were marked, because you knew how to keep hold of it. At the lower level you wouldn't get the ball if you were marked or the ball would be hit 50 yards in front of you. It was difficult. The top players of today will never have to ply their trade at a lower level because they are financially set up for life. I wasn't. I'm deeply envious of the money in the game today, but I don't begrudge the players. I just wish that I'd had a year of their money."

In 1983, the Greenhoff brothers were reunited at Rochdale.

"That was another rick in my life," he says. "My brother persuaded me to go there as player-manager, with him as player-coach, but Rochdale was a mess. We had no physio or training pitch, nobody to wash the kit. We'd have to ask a school to use their gravel pitch to train. The board promised us an increased budget if we kept them out of the bottom four and possible re-election. I tapped a few players up for the following year because I thought we'd been promised a few more quid, but it never increased. Rochdale's entire budget for the year was 90 grand."

After over 650 Football League games Greenhoff called it a day in December 1983.

"I should have known not to trust people, but I didn't learn," he says cryptically of the Rochdale board.

Greenhoff needed to keep working. He'd earned far more than the man on the street, but financially there was no question of him stopping work.

"People would come up, especially when they'd had a drink,

and say, 'What are you doing? You must have made a fortune as a footballer.' We hadn't. Comments like that really get under the skin of some older players."

For the first year after Greenhoff hung up his boots he coached kids around the country at holiday camps. But the constant travelling led him to look for something different. Greenhoff went into the insurance industry.

"I went into a business with my so-called best mate and lost everything, including my house, in the early Nineties," he explains. "I was never rich, just comfortable with a lovely house with a mere and landing stage and my own rowing boat behind it.

"It was an insurance company, but my partner was fraudulent. I had the money to pay the debts off, he didn't have a penny – or supposedly not. He was jailed for three years, and I was told by the police that he was lucky not to get four times that. The judge at the sentencing said that I was totally blameless, but I still lost everything.

"The beautiful house went and we moved into this box," he says, pointing around the front room of his three-bed suburban semi. "It hurts me that we could be in a house with a garden going down to the water where my grandkids could have grown up."

Help came from an old team-mate.

"Stuart Pearson was there for me and my family in the bad times. He was wonderful in those difficult days."

Greenhoff had to find work in a warehouse.

"There were a lot of Stokies there and they were good with me," he says. "They knew that I had fallen on hard times because it had been in the papers. Some people probably had a chuckle at my situation, but I wasn't ashamed. I put my overalls on and did my work. I then moved to a pharmaceutical company that made respiratory products for people with hay fever. The company have been marvellous with me. They didn't put me in a goldfish bowl. They understood what my life has been about. Understood that I had been idolised. They never pestered me, never said, 'Will you just come and do this for us, just come to meet this guy, just get some tickets for this, just get someone to sign that?' They just treated me normally and let me do my job."

Brian and Jimmy Greenhoff haven't spoken for nearly two decades.

"I don't like the situation," he says. "Family arguments. I wish it wasn't like this. He's still my kid brother and I still love him to bits. My sister keeps me informed a little bit of what he's doing. He was living in Menorca for five years, but he's back now. She doesn't take sides. It just hurts her that we don't speak."

Despite the set backs and the fall outs, Jimmy Greenhoff is still enjoying life.

"I do the hospitality lounges at Old Trafford for every home game and I absolutely love it," he says. "I put my suit on and drive up to Manchester. I see all the old players, and the banter is lovely. There is always a story with the old players. The fans thank me for goals that I scored 30-odd years ago."

Which ones?

"The semi-final against Liverpool at Goodison Park . . ." he says, bursting into that smile again.

8

GERRY DALY
THE DUBLINER

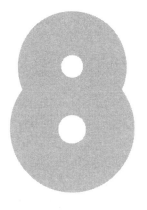

GERRY DALY

It was pre-season in Belgrade in the mid-Seventies and two players were missing from the coach waiting to take the squad to a club dinner. Alex Stepney explained to Tommy Docherty that the absentees had been locked in their room by he and Lou Macari. Docherty's response was to burst out laughing and to join in gleefully with the joke, boarding the coach and telling the driver to set off. Gerry Daly, United's former Republic of Ireland midfielder, one of the victims, shakes his head in disbelief as he recounts how it all started.

"I was in the toilet, and Paddy Roche was lying on the bed smoking and reading a book. Paddy was very relaxed, and that was him to a tee. He never knew what day it was."

But a pre-season tour with Manchester United in the Seventies was no place to drop your guard. Hidden dangers lurked round every hotel corridor corner, an impish Scotsman by the name of Luigi Macari the biggest threat.

"Lou and Alex came into our hotel room. I heard them, but didn't see them. By the time I had left the toilet they had gone."

Daly was almost as laid back as his usual room-mate Roche. He retired back to his bed, passing the time away by reading and sleeping. Not for these Dubliners a view of the ancient fort which commands fine views of the Danube, nor the giant white orthodox cathedral in what was then the capital of Yugoslavia.

"I did have a feeling that something was not right." says Daly, nearly four decades later, occupying his favourite corner of a golf club on the outskirts of Derby, which has a picture of him playing for Derby County discreetly placed above the bar. But he didn't bother to find out what that something might be, and the pair left it as late as possible to go down to the coach.

"It was only then that I realised that we couldn't get out of the door," says Daly, smiling. "I told Paddy the door was locked."

An unruffled Roche offered to ring reception to explain the problem door.

"Only problem was the phone had gone," recalls Daly. "Macari had taken it. I stared at Paddy and said, 'Not only did you not see them take your room key or hear them lock the door from the outside, you didn't see them take the phone from the table between our two beds. It was right beside you."

Stuck in their room, powerless and hungry, they soon found themselves back on their beds smoking, having discounted shouting through an open window as these were clamped shut.

Meanwhile, the United coach sped off into the night, and eventually the Dubliners went to sleep on empty stomachs.

"What could I do?" asks Daly. "Nothing. Though I don't think Paddy was too concerned throughout the whole encounter."

Others might have called it an ordeal, given that it lasted well into the next day. While the duo dozed, United's players went to a restaurant, had a night out, slept, woke for breakfast and went through a full training session the follow day. Finally, someone – nobody knows who – informed reception and a minion was dispatched to open the door.

"We went straight to the hotel restaurant," Daly goes on. "And the food was lovely. There were no complaints about the food from us, yet the rest of the players did nothing but complain about the meal they'd been served the night before."

The freed prisoners still had to face their manager.

"He was in on the joke, but he still gave us a bollocking and asked us how we could not have noticed someone taking a great big phone from between our two beds," recalls Daly. "But it was Paddy who didn't notice them taking it, not me.

Daly is now 57, jovial yet jaded by the unfortunate cards life has dealt him in the last year. He was born in Dublin's east side in 1954, one of ten children – eight boys and two girls.

"I was brought up in Cabra West, about two miles from the city centre," he explains. "It's a lovely area, very close-knit, but if you or the family are not well known you might have problems.

"My mother was busy producing kids, and my dad worked on the docks on the River Liffey. He went around on a little boat repairing the dock walls.

"I always supported Manchester United because it was my mother's team. We used to have photographs of United all over the house, photos of players like George Best and Brian Kidd."

But Daly was only allowed to play hurling and Gaelic football in school.

"I used to dribble a lot with my feet in Gaelic, and one of the teachers said to me, 'Who do you think you are? George Best? You need to pick the ball up with your hands. You can kick it further from your hands.'"

Association football was his game after school.

"I was good at it, but I packed the soccer in for a year or two to go back to playing Gaelic football. Then I packed that in – it was a bit too rough for me, that game – and I took up soccer again."

Daly had an enjoyable childhood.

"But you had to get out and go to work once your school days were over," he says. "I was lucky because I got an apprenticeship as a coach painter. I would spray cars, and then I would go off to college to do sign writing. I was also playing for Bohemians at Dalymount Park."

Daly's career as a semi-professional player, performing in front of crowds of 6,000, took off quickly, but the day job was hazardous.

"You should use a mask to stop you from breathing the fumes in, but none of us did," explains Daly. "I trained twice a week, and in the evenings I'd spit out whatever colour I'd been spraying in the day. I'd have red days, blue days and green ones. It wasn't good for my health and I found the job hard work. I looked to football as an easy way out, but I didn't have a contract."

Daly, 18, hatched a plan to ensure that he was taken on full time.

"I went to see the manager and told him that I had to pack the football in as it wasn't doing me any good coughing all the spray up for £4 a week. Of course, I knew that they rated me and that I'd been playing well.

"The Bohemians manager told me to pack the job in and offered me £25 a week to play football. It was a lot of money because the average wage in Ireland at this time was about £8. I didn't just *think* I was rich, I *was* rich!"

Bohemians understandably wanted their prize youngster to sign a contract.

"They knew there was interest in me," he explains. "I signed, but told them that I wanted 30 per cent of any future transfer fee. Me and my brother decided to do that."

In a time before agents, Daly's move would be a shrewd one, but first he had football to play.

"We had a European match against Cologne. We lost 2-1 away and I scored. They had one player, a German international, who tore us apart at Dalymount. We lost 3-0 and we were out, but I remember things taking off for me soon after.

"I found things rather easy in the League of Ireland," he says without a hint of false modesty. And it wasn't only in the domestic league that Daly found himself comfortable.

"Man United came to play us in 1972, and once again I found it rather easy," he says of a mid-season friendly game which United won 3-1 in front of 38,000. "In fact it was a doddle playing against Martin Buchan and Alex Forsyth. I scored, too. United had Mick Martin, who had just signed from Bohemians for £25,000. I was pleased for Mick – he was a good player – but I was a bit disappointed because I thought I'd missed my chance for United to sign me too, but they came back for me a few months later in the summer of 1973."

Daly was sold for £20,000 and pocketed over £6,000 from the transfer – a healthy profit for both the Dublin club and the player.

"United put me on a flight to Manchester with my brother, and I was enjoying a cigarette as I walked through arrivals at Manchester Airport," he explains. "Paddy Crerand was waiting for me. He tried to get me to stop smoking several times, first on the way from the airport and then on the way to my first training session. He pointed out of the window and said, 'There's some great players on that building site over there, but they didn't make it because they smoked.' That didn't put me off in the slightest. In fact, I used to smoke on the team coach. Bobby Charlton did not approve of Alex Stepney and I smoking on the team bus, but what could he do?"

Then there was the small matter of Daly signing his United contract.

"I went to see Tommy Docherty," he remembers. "He asked me if I wanted my brother in the room and I told him that I'd be okay by myself. The Doc told me that I was to be given a two-year contract on £60 a week. I said, 'Done.'

"Docherty looked up, astonished, asking, 'Are you not going to haggle?'

'I'm over here to play football, I'm not interested in money,' I replied.

'Well, if you are not arguing then I'll give you £80 a week,' the Doc said."

The United manager then explained to Daly that £80 a week

UNITED! UNITED!

would put him on the same wage as established, but still young, first-team regulars like Sammy McIlroy and Brian Greenhoff. Daly was 19.

"There were bonuses too," recalls Daly. "It was good money. The bonuses were for a win, and Manchester United were expected to win – not that that happened much when I first arrived."

Daly moved to digs in Chorlton, then to Wythenshawe.

"I lived with Ray O'Brien, who had come over from Shelbourne. We lodged with a hairdresser. Then I moved to Warwick Road North, near Old Trafford."

The Dubliner made his debut against Bari in the Anglo-Italian Cup in April 1973 in front of 14,303 at Old Trafford. His league debut followed at Highbury in the first game of the 1973/74 season.

"I was thrown into the lion's den. We lost 3-0 and the game was over before it had started. I was taken off at half-time, and I was relieved. We weren't a good side and Arsenal were. They took us apart, but I remember thinking on the way back to Manchester that Arsenal were playing at the level we were trying to get to."

United's season had started badly and, as Daly indicated, would seldom get better. One win in the first eight games and just two victories before Christmas would set the template for relegation.

"Docherty resigned himself to relegation," opines Daly. "He wanted to start over again with young players, which turned out to be the right thing to do. The players who had won the European Cup were not the future of Manchester United. We were."

Daly wasn't distraught at the relegation like some players.

"It was no big thing, and it wasn't such a blow to younger players like me because it wasn't our fault. I played 14 games that season, and some of the other lads were playing 45 matches. I turned out more for the reserves, which was still important to my development and we'd sometimes play in front of 7-8,000 if it was a voucher game."

United issued special vouchers at selected reserve- and youth-team games until the early 1990s to reward fans who attended such matches. These could be used, along with a full token sheet, to apply for tickets should United reach a cup final. Special vouchers were necessary because token sheets could be filled up with tokens from match-day programmes, purchased at Old Trafford on the day of the game. The system was open to abuse – there was nothing to stop a fan buying five match programmes for absent friends. If 35,000 fans had full token sheets and there were only 25,000 tickets allocated for a cup final, of which just 5,000 went to non-season ticket holders with full token sheets, then the full token sheet was of no real advantage. If, however, you also had a special voucher which was only issued as you clicked through the turnstile before one of these special games, then that as good as guaranteed you a ticket. Of course, this system only came into play if United reached a cup final.

In 1973/74, they didn't even come close.

Docherty's men were knocked out of the League Cup in the first round by Second Division Middlesbrough and the FA Cup at the fourth-round stage by Ipswich Town, yet Daly still saw the positives in what was a dire season which led all the way down to the Second Division.

"Personally, it was a learning curve for me. I was still settling in as a player and into my life in Manchester. I was still a kid. I liked the idea of starting afresh the next season – the new United with fresh young players."

Daly played 45 games in United's promotion campaign and scored 11 goals.

"We weren't playing the best teams in the world but Second Division sides, but we still had to go out and perform and we still had to win games. We did that. We took the league by storm and winning against inferior sides boosted the confidence of a young team at the right time. I know that my own confidence was really lifted and a lot of that came from the crowd. I don't know why, but I had an exceptional rapport with the United fans. They used to sing, 'Five foot eight, underweight . . .'"

Daly is reluctant to finish his own song off. "Five foot eight, underweight, Gerry Daly's fucking great."

"I was actually five nine and ten stone one, which was perfectly healthy . . ." he smiles. Not that he looked it. Pallid and skinny as a rake, with his smoker's complexion, he was a surprisingly elegant player who seemed to float across the pitch, earning the tag 'the grey ghost'.

"We were an entertaining team with a lot of good players and no inhibitions. Stadiums were full home and away. The Doc had made great signings, players like Pancho [Stuart Pearson] and Steve Coppell. We played with two wingers at United because we could.

I was lucky to play on the right-hand side of midfield next to Coppell. He was a pleasure to play with. He had a great foot-balling brain and he was quick. He would track back. The reason I scored so many goals was because Steve would let me get forward and then cover for me. He was an intelligent player and person. That wouldn't have happened on the left-hand side of the field with Gordon Hill.

"I didn't suffer the kind frustrations Lou did playing on the left alongside Hill. No disrespect to Merlin [Hill], but his idea of playing was to stand on the left and wait for the ball. He felt that players should get him the ball so that he could do the tricks."

Daly's adaptation to English football was complete.

"I found it a doddle," he says, again without arrogance.

Given Daly's composure and quiet self-confidence, he seemed an obvious choice to take spot kicks, but he hadn't always fancied the job.

"I was known as the penalty king," he says of his record of just one miss in 17 for United's first team. "But I'd never taken penalties until I played with United in an under-19s tournament in Switzerland. We reached the final against Juventus. We drew and penalties were needed after extra-time. I took – and missed – a penalty. We lost."

While in Switzerland, Daly received a phone call.

"It was a message to get over to Oslo. I was to be capped by the Republic of Ireland for the first time. After that game, I had to get back to Zurich to play in another tournament with United. Again, we got to the final, and again it went to extra-time and penalties."

This time, Daly refused to take a penalty. A younger player took one and missed. United lost again.

"We sat back in the dressing room but I had a smug look on my face," recalls Daly. "It was as if I was saying, 'We lost but at least I didn't miss a penalty.' Bill Foulkes, who was our manager, saw me. He came over and tore me apart."

Foulkes, a United legend with more appearances than any player apart from Sir Bobby Charlton, didn't mince his words.

"You," Foulkes pointed at Daly, "you little Irish shit. You've let that young lad take that penalty. Look at him, he's distraught. You've just come back from winning your first cap with your country and you haven't had the balls to take a penalty. I hope you feel happy for yourself, you smug bastard."

"I felt about one inch high," remembers Daly.

Foulkes wasn't finished with him.

"We went out that night as a treat and he made me buy everyone a drink," recalls Daly. "Zurich is not cheap. It cost me a bloody fortune. Bill was a bit tight, so he was doubly happy as he got a free drink. I made up my mind that night that I would never shirk from the responsibility of taking penalties."

There would be more controversy before Daly cemented his place as United's penalty taker. The regular penalty taker was actually goalkeeper Alex Stepney. There is no better measure of the problems at Old Trafford by Christmas 1973, than the fact that Stepney was joint leading scorer with just two goals, both scored from penalties.

"Imagine the goalkeeper being the leading scorer?" Daly says. "Well Alex was."

Then Stepney missed one penalty at Old Trafford and had to sprint back to his goal before he was stranded. It was decided to change penalty takers.

"I looked around and saw established players like Martin Buchan and Willie Morgan. None of them wanted to take a penalty. Someone had to be prepared to look a twat if they missed, so I decided that it may as well be me."

Daly would become United's most prolific penalty scorer since Charlie Mitten in the late 1940s. But while Mitten decided where he would put the penalty before his run up began, Daly's technique was different.

"I had no idea where the ball was going until that split second when I actually struck the ball," he explains. "I put them in left or right. I'd never hammer the ball, but always side-footed it. It's all to do with confidence. It's about being able to do that in front of 60,000. I would just get up and side-foot it home. Simple."

Simple?

"Okay, it's simple to take a penalty when you are two or three up, but it's different when it's 0-0. But I could handle it. I never missed a penalty playing for Ireland, including one against England at Wembley, and I only missed once for United."

Daly would later enter football folklore when he scored a penalty for Derby in a 4-0 drubbing of Manchester City. The penalty spot had disappeared in the mud and Daly needed all his sangfroid as several officials and ground staff used a tape measure and bucket of whitewash in front of the *Match of the Day* cameras to paint a new one.

Daly enjoyed playing for Ireland, where he earned 48 caps.

"Playing for your country for the first time at home is the best moment for a footballer, especially if your parents can see you. When that national anthem is played it's very emotional.

"Myself, Johnny Giles and Liam Brady were Ireland's midfield three for a decade. None of us were the best defenders in the world. I was a midfielder who liked to get forward and score goals. I couldn't tackle a fish supper and I wasn't the best header of a ball. I knew where the net was and where other players were. I could run all day and knew how to track people, to fill in space. That was me."

His talents were appreciated at Old Trafford, but United could be a complex club.

"Jimmy Murphy always maintained that it was he who'd spotted me in Dublin. He used to like a pint in the Trafford pub at the top of my road, and he said to me when he caught me on the street one day near my digs, 'When you go out to play, don't listen to a word of advice from your manager. You go out and do your own thing, that's the reason we signed you here.' At the time I thought, 'What's all that about, does he not like the Doc?'

It was only later that I realised that there were severe personality clashes at Old Trafford."

Daly's life was a good one. He got married in Dublin in 1976 and moved to Flixton.

"My wife Sheila [who passed away in 2010, a few months before this interview] was a Mancunian from Miles Platting," he recalls. "I met her in Slack Alice, Bestie's club. Wonderful place."

Daly got on with Best.

"George was good as gold, and I have nothing but compliments for the player. He came back to Manchester after being away in Spain with one of the Miss Worlds. There was a controversy about him, he'd put on a bit of weight and obviously wasn't fit. He asked me to do a bit of training with him."

Training entailed Daly standing in goal and kicking balls to Best on the halfway line.

"George would then come towards me at pace and try and slot the ball by me. I wasn't a goalkeeper, merely an obstacle, but I found it a great privilege that George asked me.

George told me that he owned a greyhound called 'Parkhead Best'. It was a big black dog. Lou Macari, Mick Martin and myself were all interested in greyhounds and had agreed to buy a dog between us."

The three went to White City, the dog track near Old Trafford which closed in 1982 but whose white neo-classical entrance with its graceful columns and arches, a listed relic of its past as a Royal Botanical Gardens, still stands on Chester Road, to see the dog perform in trials. Daly and other United players could mingle comfortably with the punters on its shabby concrete terraces.

"We didn't want it to do well because that would have pushed the price up," explains Daly. "So we thought we'd do a bit of cheating to slow the dog down. We hatched a plan at The Cliff. Bestie was sat at another table talking to journalists and must have known what we were talking about."

Daly and the other players thought that they would be buying a fast greyhound, but Best tried to convince them otherwise. United's famous number seven shouted over.

"That dog you're interested in," said the Belfast Boy, "The last time it ran it was slow away and then faded."

Daly suspected a ruse and that Best was lying to stop them from buying the dog, but the next day he received a call from one of his brothers in Dublin.

"What's this about you owning a greyhound?" asked his brother.

"How do you know that I own a greyhound?"

"Because it's on the back page of the *Evening Herald*. It says your dog was slow away and then faded."

One throwaway comment from George Best was enough to make back page news in Dublin.

"We didn't need to cheat with the dog," explains Daly. "We could see from watching it that it couldn't run. We didn't buy it."

He counted Best as a friend.

"I'd been told off in school because the teacher thought I was trying to be George Best. And I never was close to being Best, but not many people could say that they were paid to play with him either. And after I joined United, I did pop back into school to remind the school teacher who had cursed me for thinking I was George Best that I now played with him."

Daly found the reaction interesting when he returned to Dublin as a United player.

"Kids would come to my parents' house and ask for my autograph, but many longstanding friends changed towards me. They were never the same. They didn't want to be seen with me because they felt they would be seen as hangers-on. It's a psychological thing. People like to know someone who has had a bit of success, but they don't like to be seen by other people to know them. They don't like to be accused of being arse lickers."

Many of his friends and family came to London to see the 1976 FA Cup final.

"We had the reception at the Russell Hotel in London. Everyone was really sad after we lost. I had all my family over from Dublin, but they were not allowed in the main room with the team. A band was playing, and Stewart Houston called me to get up on the stage with them and we sang *The Boxer* by Simon and Garfunkel. The mood lifted. I then went down to another bar because I wanted to get away from it all and to see some of my family too. This bar was almost empty, so I asked Martin Buchan to get his guitar. We started a singsong, and within ten minutes the place was absolutely packed.

"Martin Buchan wasn't everyone's cup of tea," adds Daly. "He wouldn't talk to people if he felt they weren't as intelligent as him, but maybe he wasn't as clever as he thought. That said, he was a very good club captain. He was always absolutely immaculate, something for which Jim Holton would take the mickey out of him. A loose button was a big issue to Martin. I respected Martin for challenging the manager if he thought he was wrong. He would also challenge stupid rules – like the club keeping hold of your passport. Martin quite rightly said that he was perfectly capable of looking after his own passport, and that's how he was. But other players would have looked at that and said, 'What difference does it make? Just give them your passport.'

"Willie Morgan – who was a decent lad by the way and not as aloof and opinionated as some made out – was a good snooker player, but he wasn't as good as me. I used to play a lot with Alex Higgins and John Virgo at the Potters Club in Salford. They were both on the Manchester scene. Stuart Pearson and I took the TV cameras there before the '76 cup final."

That final was the closest Daly came to winning a major honour with United.

"We did everything differently to every other game that we'd played," explains Daly. "We stayed at a hotel we'd not been at before. There were cameras following us all week. We had a masseur, which we'd never had. What a load of shit. We made a bloody record. We were offered £100 each, but whoever was in charge offered us a chance to take royalties instead and hinted that it could go to number one. We took the £100 because we thought the record was crap.

"The build-up got out of control, and we had more attention than Southampton because we were knock-down certainties to win the game . . ."

Daly has never forgotten the scramble for tickets.

"We were allowed to buy 120 tickets each," he recalls. "And I needed that many because of the size of my family. Half of Dublin came over." Several players passed their cup final tickets on at a profit.

"If you wanted to knock them out to touts, you could knock them out.

"Tommy Docherty pulled up alongside me in his car when I was walking along Warwick Road. He wound his window down and asked me what I was doing with my cup final tickets. I told him that I needed them all as I had a lot of family coming over. The window went back up."

The money going into the players' pool was the subject of some controversy. Newspapers who wanted access to players before the cup final were told to contribute £250 towards the kitty. The players thought the newspapers made money from their sales, so why not? The press did not respond well, with the *News of the World* describing United players as 'scroungers.'

But generally Docherty's United had won a great many friends. In his newspaper column Brian Clough wrote, "I don't want to see Manchester United walking single file from the Wembley tunnel. I want them parading proudly, marching 12 abreast, with manager Tommy Docherty applauding them from behind. They deserve the distinction."

Summing up United's attacking style, Clough continued: "The wonderful young men he's produced have remade a great club. They have had us talking all season. They have dragged people from their armchairs who abandoned my game years ago. They have done more in three weeks for *Match of the Day* than Jimmy Hill could do in 20 years.

"I can't remember another Wembley final where one team could look at the other and say truthfully that they wouldn't swap a single player.

"I can't see Southampton touching them. They could carry a banner reading: 'Well, anything can happen in football.' That's their only hope."

Southampton won 1–0.

Despite the defeat, a civic reception was held back in Manchester the day after the final.

"I went to the toilet and saw that Paddy Crerand had the Doc by the throat up against a wall," Daly recalls. "Players shouldn't have been seeing stuff like that and yet it didn't seem out of the ordinary. Fallouts seemed normal. Alex Stepney fell out with Tommy Cavanagh because he felt that he didn't respect him and tried to belittle him. I agreed with Stepney there. I tried to ignore Cavanagh – his continual foaming at the mouth wasn't to my liking."

Daly played just 16 times for United in the following season, '76/77.

"Docherty had his favourites like Brian Greenhoff and Sammy Mac," says Daly. "Obviously I wasn't one of them because he sold me, but until I left United I got on fine with them. Ian Storey-Moore and Stuart Pearson were probably the only players I socialised with, went for a pint with. Ian was a great player who had been bought by Frank O'Farrell, but he had to retire with injury not long after the Doc took charge."

"The Doc was great with young lads because he would give them a strong belief in themselves. If he thought you deserved a chance then he'd give you a chance. He was never afraid to throw a young player into the team. He struggled more with older and more established players, who could see through him more."

Daly has a theory about Docherty and his arguments.

"If you look at all the people he fell out with, it was almost always with an older player who had come to a certain stage in his career. Maybe someone had to break the bad news to them, and the Doc was never going to be thanked for that, but I knew that I could have carried on playing to a high level – and I would prove that. As for me and the Doc, after I left United we became known as the Tom and Gerry Show because we always argued."

That arguing continued at Derby, the club to which Docherty had sold Daly in early 1977, not knowing that he would be managing at the Baseball Ground later that year.

"We had a major disagreement when he arrived at Derby because he had wanted to sell me at United and I didn't want to be sold," explains Daly in a surprisingly matter-of-fact manner.

Docherty had told Daly that if he didn't leave then he would be put in the reserves.

"It was bullying," says Daly. "He told me that no matter how well I played in the reserves I would never leave the reserves. He said that I would never play football for United's first team again."

Daly was in two minds as to how to react.

"On one hand I was a pretty street-smart kid from Dublin and wasn't prepared to be treated like that. On the other I was a young lad who just wanted to play football. No footballer wants to be stuck in the reserves."

Daly was approached one day by Matt Busby.

"He knew that something was going on at the club," explains Daly. "Whether it was the Doc's affair with Mary Brown, the physio's wife, or not, I don't know. But Matt said to me, 'Don't leave. We want you at this club.'"

Daly repeated Docherty's threat about putting him in the reserves.

"There are things going on here at the club. All I am saying is don't leave, we don't want you to go," added Busby. But Daly felt the balance had shifted away from Busby.

"The Doc had power because things were going right with the team," explains Daly, who felt that his options were limited.

After 137 starts and 32 goals for United, aged only 22, Daly went to Derby. Docherty later admitted it had been a mistake to sell him. United fans were mystified by Daly's departure, and rumours flew around about the reasons for it.

"As far as I was concerned, Derby were the only club that came in for me and United accepted it," he explains.

He heard of Docherty's sacking a few months later.

"I don't think it is the right thing to do, to mess about with the physio's wife when you have the responsibility of telling that man when he has to be in work. He could tell the physio that he wanted him working with the players in the afternoon while he crept round to his house. It's not very nice and it was right that he was sacked."

Daly had time for the physio, Laurie Brown.

"Laurie was known as 'After Eight Man' because he bought so many packs, either for himself or his missus. He was a quiet, unassuming man, but you had to be careful what you said to him when you were injured stuck on his bed. You knew the conversation would get back [to the manager] – and that's the same with physios all over the country. Injured players tend to be discontented players. That's where the bad talk goes on, and it's part of a physio's job to report back."

Daly considered United a Catholic club.

"Sir Matt and his son Sandy and Paddy Crerand all used to go to that church in Chorlton. I'd go the odd time to show my face, but when I didn't people would say, 'We didn't see you at Mass on Sunday.'"

Events back in Manchester initially had little bearing on Daly, now settled at Derby. He had been playing well, he was earning more money than he'd been on at Old Trafford following his £175,000 transfer and Jock Stein of Leeds United tried to sign him. Then Docherty was appointed manager of Derby County.

"He came up and shook my hand," recalls Daly. "I told him that he'd got me out of Old Trafford, but that he wouldn't get me out of the Baseball Ground. It was me saying, 'You won't be selling me this time!' I was playing well for Derby. He just looked at me."

Docherty took his first training session at Derby later that day.

"Doc being Doc, he invited the television cameras down to film him introducing himself to all the players."

Docherty told the assembled players – many of whom had played in the Derby team that had won the league in 1972 and 1975 – that if they wanted to know what he was like, they just had to ask Gerry Daly. As he did it, the camera, spun around to see Daly's look of surprised indignation.

"I didn't trust him and didn't believe a word that came out of his mouth. People used to say when he walked in at Old Trafford that if he said 'good morning' you'd have to go outside and check."

Daly had been happy at Derby, but just as United had been when Daly joined them, Derby were a team full of ageing internationals. Docherty was unfazed by such reputations as he started another rebuilding project in his own inimitable, breakneck style.

"He got straight into the task," explains Daly, "but the Doc's usual tricks started too. Snippets started appearing in papers that linked Derby players with a move away when they had been completely settled. There was a feeling that the Doc didn't like the Welsh and he never liked Leighton James. I told Leighton that he might as well put his house up for sale when the Doc arrived.

"I can remember what he'd told us while at United when we played Derby in the '76 FA Cup semi-final. He'd instructed Alex Forsyth to 'kick Leighton James up the arse and then you won't see him for the rest of the game'. Alex heeded his words and, actually, the Doc was right because he did nothing in the match after that."

Leighton James was concerned enough to go and see the Doc about his future at the Baseball Ground. Docherty told him that he intended to build his team around him, adding, 'And don't listen to those bad thoughts that Gerry Daly tells you.'

James was briefly satisfied with Docherty's explanation, but kept seeing his name being linked to transfers in the paper. And there was no evidence of the team being built around him. He went to see Docherty again . . . who told him that he could leave.

Daly outstayed Docherty at Derby by 14 months after the former United manager, who was embroiled in court proceedings at the time, resigned and moved to Queens Park Rangers in 1970. Daly, meanwhile, moved to Coventry for £300,000 in 1980.

"I had a smashing time at Coventry and worked under the best manager of my career, Gordon Milne. He was studious and would go into detail about whoever we were playing against. He was the opposite of Docherty, who would not know about individual opponents unless they were big names. His attitude had been 'go out and play'."

Daly went on the transfer list at Coventry.

"In those days, you would befriend the person in reception," he says. "They would be the ones who took the phone calls from any interested clubs. I would ask the receptionist each day after training if anyone had enquired about me."

Each day Daly was met by a depressing, 'No, no and no.'

"One day the girl signalled to me as she was on the phone. She put the call through to the manager's office and then told me that it was Tommy Docherty from Wolves. The manager confirmed later that he had been asking about me. I told her to tell Docherty to 'fuck off'."

Tom and Gerry have made their peace now. "I hadn't seen him for 20 years and I was at a sportsmen's dinner he attended. I didn't know that he was going to be there and I said, 'Hello, boss'. I wouldn't dare call him Tommy. He looked at me and took a second to realise it was me. 'Oh Jesus – Gerry,' he said. 'Hang on a minute I'm going to the toilet.' He came back and we sat together and talked for half an hour. We had both mellowed with age."

Daly then played at Birmingham City, Stoke and Leicester City alongside a young Gary Lineker – "nice lad" – again under Gordon Milne. He also had spells at Shrewsbury Town and Doncaster Rovers.

"I never had to move very far," he says. "There was always a club nearby which wanted me and I only had to move house three times in my whole career."

One transfer that definitely needed new accommodation was a move to the Boston Teamen in the North American Soccer League for three consecutive summers. Daly enjoyed his time in Massachusetts, and the Teamen were managed by the former United players Noel Cantwell and Dennis Viollet.

"Bestie was out there playing for San Jose, and they came to play us," he recalls. "Dennis Viollet, who was a great friend, told me after the game that we were going to have a meal – just the former Manchester United players including Bestie. There were be to be no women, though all George had to do with women was smile.

"The one regret I have was that I was abroad on holiday when they brought his ashes back to be spread at Old Trafford. Dennis's wife Helen invited myself and Noel Cantwell."

In 1989, Daly was briefly involved in management at Telford United.

"Sammy McIlroy, my former team-mate, was at Macclesfield at the time, and Martin O'Neill, a former rival, was at Wycombe, who were both managing in the same league. It was difficult because as soon as you had a decent player you had to sell him. There was no ambition. I felt like I was banging my head against a brick wall."

At 37 Daly retired and lived in Derby, where his wife Sheila was a solicitor specialising in family law.

"My wife was a very intelligent lady, and I also had enough to live off from a private pension. While Sheila was doing all the studying for her law degree, I looked after the kids. We had three, but one died aged six months when I was at Shrewsbury. That was horrific."

Daly had offers to stay in football, but had little interest in doing so.

"I did a bit of TV and radio work in the early 1990s, but I couldn't be bothered pushing that. I used to watch Derby County every home game because I was friendly with the owner Lionel Pickering. Unfortunately he died, and I stopped going. I still get invites to go back to my former clubs, but I'm not so bothered. I watch a little bit of football on television, but only the big games."

Daly also goes back to Dublin less frequently.

"It's usually for funerals or weddings these days," he says. "And I've also got all sorts of back and vascular problems which is not very nice."

Looking back at his time at Old Trafford, Gerry says, "The one thing that sticks in my mind from that time is celebrating goals and going towards the old Stretford End. One game stands out – Wolverhampton Wanderers in the FA Cup sixth round in 1976. It was a full house, with almost 60,000 there. We were the better team, but Wolves took the lead. The crowd were desperate for an equaliser and I got it, one of the best goals I scored.

"It was under floodlights and it was lashing down. I liked night games when it rained. I struck the ball cleanly and it flew into the top corner. I ran towards the crowd and they surged towards me, thousands of them. It was love, pure love. They loved me and I loved them."

One paper reported, "Full marks to Daly because the glory could not have gone to a better performer. His touches had been magical and United should have made more of them."

"We won the replay 3-2 at Molineux," the Irishman concludes with a smile as he remembers. "My goal had helped us win the semi-final."

9

JOE JORDAN
JAWS

JOE JORDAN

A month after our meeting in a café close to Liverpool Street station in London, Joe Jordan hit the headlines following a touchline confrontation with AC Milan captain Gennaro Gattuso. Gattuso grabbed Jordan by the throat and later headbutted him in the tunnel, claiming that Harry Redknapp's assistant was "busting his balls" from the touchline throughout Milan's Champions League defeat by Tottenham Hotspur. Jordan's refusal to be intimidated divided opinion.

The majority, led by venerable ex-hardman Graeme Souness, could see only one likely winner, despite the difference in age between him and his assailant and Jordan's two titanium hips, should the pair square up to sort it out, "Gattuso is a little dog. I wish he had five minutes with Joe Jordan in a room on his own," he said. Spurs' manager Redknapp concurred, "Joe was ready. He'd taken his glasses off at the end of the game." But former

Red Andrew Cole begged to differ, calling Jordan an "old school ranter", and describing him as a dinosaur in a game which had moved on since Jordan's playing days.

When Jordan joined Manchester United in 1978, his signing similarly divided fans. A few muttered that Jordan, schooled in the ways of 'dirty Leeds', was not a United player. They pointed out that he had racked up more bookings than goals at Elland Road. But for the bulk of United's support, Jordan's reputation and combativeness were a bonus. The hope was that he would give United's front line some much needed aggression and height.

Jordan was Dave Sexton's first signing, and at £350,000 he was United's new record fee. Again, for most fans this was welcomed as the beginning of the end for United's famed parsimony in the transfer market which had seen the club regularly miss out on big names. Sexton was to break United's transfer record four times in all.

In person, Joe Jordan is diffident, bespectacled and reflective – as far as it's possible to get from his image as a player. As assistant to Harry Redknapp at Tottenham Hotspur, just as he was at Portsmouth, he doesn't have the same leisure time as most of the other interviewees to talk – he's got to prepare Spurs for the visit of Manchester United in two days. At first he seems like he'd rather be anywhere but talking to a journalist. But his long-time best mate Gordon McQueen had insisted, "Persevere with Joe and get him to talk. He's a very interesting man."

Jordan had been at Old Trafford for 15 months when he got his first chance of a trophy with United in the 1979 FA Cup final. Unlike many of those who played in red in the Seventies, he already had a cupboard full of medals. In an eight-year spell at Leeds, he'd been a European Cup and Cup Winners' Cup runner-up and a league champion in 1974 as Leeds briefly shed their 'always the bridesmaid' tag after finishing runners up in '71 and '72. But he claims it is the memory of missing out on the 1979 FA Cup which makes him grimace most of all.

"All these years later and I still can't bear to look at that game again," says Jordan over coffee. "We let Dave Sexton down with that one by taking our eyes off the ball for a split second, celebrating when we should have been concentrating. Victory might have also won him the time to continue what he was doing at Old Trafford. The next season we were in contention for the First Division title, but the Board wouldn't give Sexton the time he needed."

Jordan was born near Motherwell, Lanarkshire, in 1951, a historically rich picking ground for Manchester United. Brian McClair, Jimmy Delaney, Arthur Graham, Jack Picken, Tom Reid, David Herd, Charlie Rennox, Jim Holton, Harry McShane and Francis Burns all came from within ten miles of Motherwell.

"Jimmy Delaney was from Cleland, my village," says Jordan. "That was my first contact with Manchester United because my father was a friend of his. Jimmy played for Celtic, but he was one of Sir Matt's first signings and played in the United side which won the FA Cup in 1948. When I was six, my father went to watch Jimmy play in Manchester and came back with a Manchester United shirt for me. I have treasured it ever since."

Cleland was a mining village.

"Like many of them were in that area," Jordan continues. "Matt Busby was from three or four miles away in Bellshill. The area had a history of producing footballers, not just for Manchester United. Everyone was obliged to play football and the other requirement was that you did it well, with confidence and panache. There's not so many footballers now, but football was a way of life for that part of Scotland and nearby Glasgow."

Jordan supported United and Celtic as a boy.

"The direct contact with Jimmy and my dad meant I was a Celtic supporter," he says. "Jimmy was a Celtic man before he played for United, but he came back to live in the village and I went to school with his sons. I also delivered newspapers around the village for his eldest son, Patsy, who ran the local paper shop."

Jordan was one of three siblings.

"My dad, who worked at the Ravenscraig steel works, would take me to watch Motherwell because he wanted me to get a feel for football," he says.

"It was closer to home than Celtic and a wee bit less congested, but I started to watch Celtic when I got a bit older. Jimmy Johnstone was my idol and I watched the Celtic team which won the European Cup. They were exceptional. I would go on a supporters' bus which left for Parkhead from my village, but I admired other Scottish players like Jim Baxter of Rangers and Denis Law."

Jordan wanted to become a footballer from an early age.

"I wasn't one of these lads who had it stamped all over me that I was going to go right to the top," he explains. "I didn't play for Scotland at 15, 16 or 17 like some lads, but I thought I could be a football player."

Jordan was offered the chance to train at Celtic, but it was too informal an offer for his liking. Greenock Morton were more serious about their interest.

"I played for North Motherwell against Morton's youth team and was approached after that to have a trial playing for Morton's reserve team.

"The game was against Partick Thistle against a background of shipyard cranes on the River Clyde."

Jordan, then a midfielder, did well and signed for Morton. He quickly progressed.

"I trained on Monday, Tuesday and Thursday nights. I spent mornings working in an architects' office in Glasgow. I was a draughtsman's cubicle having studied that at college and I wanted to keep my options open."

But at 18 Jordan had to make a choice between football and work.

"My mother didn't want me to pack in my profession," he recalls. "She worried that I would have nothing to fall back on if I was injured or failed to make the grade. My parents wanted more security for me."

But it was one or the other.

"A draughtsman who wore a collar and tie and commuted every day or a footballer?" smiles Jordan.

The rising star from Cleland signed a deal worth £7 a week, with £5 extra if he played in the first team. He would play just six first-team games before making such a big impression it would lead to a much bigger club showing interest.

An injury to a team-mate meant Jordan was picked for an Anglo-Scottish Cup tie at West Bromwich Albion in 1970. At centre-half.

"I told my manager that I had never played centre-half before," he recalls. His manager Eric Smith, a former Celtic and Leeds player, told him that he'd be fine.

Unbeknown to Jordan, the Leeds manager, Don Revie, had been tipped off by Bobby Collins, a great Scottish footballer who was enjoying his last days at Morton after a spell at Leeds. Revie had asked Collins if he'd seen any boys north of the border and Collins had named Jordan as a 'kid who played like a man'. Jordan was stunned by the interest.

"I'd been to see Leeds play at Celtic in the 1970 European Cup semi-final a few months earlier," he says. "They were one of the best teams in Europe. And now Bobby Collins was telling me that they had put a bid in for me. I hadn't had any recognition in Scotland, yet one of the greatest managers in the world put a price on me – £15,000 plus £5,000 if I played 20 first-team games. I was very excited."

Jordan signed with no hesitation, was taken to Glasgow Central and took the train south to Leeds. He wore an oilskin coat which his mother had bought for him, together with a sweater she had knitted from the finest Aran wool.

These practical, warm garments were not appreciated when he arrived at Elland Road.

"The first words Billy Bremner said to me were, 'Jesus Christ, where did you find that? He said the sweater made me look like Val Doonican [a folksy Irish singer with a penchant for bright woollies]."

But Jordan was in Yorkshire to be judged as a footballer and not as a clothes horse. There was no shortage of opinions about his potential.

"When Jordan arrived at Elland Road," Johnny Giles, the former United star who had become an even bigger star at Leeds, wrote later in a tribute to his former colleague, "He was a half-formed professional footballer, 18 years old, quiet, intense, as nervous as a colt. You could see that he had a lot to do. Physically and mentally, he had to toughen up to make his way in an environment that gave few favours. He was by no means a certainty."

Giles was always on hand to dispense advice.

"He told us to look out for the best examples in the game and particularly admire the artistry and timing of Johnny Haynes at Fulham," recalls Jordan. "He also told me that football was a simple game, but a hell of a lot of work has to go into making it so."

The new recruit settled, though his four front teeth were early victims of the Revie regime.

"Two of them were kicked out of my head after colliding with an opponent's boot, another two were loosened and were subsequently lost in one of my first appearances for Leeds, a reserve game against Coventry." Dentures were made to replace them, but for safety reasons he left them out when he was on the pitch. It transformed his appearance and defined his image, leading to him being predictably dubbed 'Jaws', though, as he once commented, there was more to him as a footballer than just his front teeth, or lack of them.

The Scot's first-team debut was in the Fairs' Cup trophy play-off in 1971 against Barcelona away.

"What an occasion in a wonderful stadium. I scored but we got beat 2-1."

Jordan then got on with being a Leeds player, earning his £35 a week wage.

"I couldn't have chosen a better club. The squad was full of good pros and there was a professionalism about them and a desire to be successful. Don Revie was the best manager that I ever played under. He gave me confidence, good discipline and the solid habits which he instilled into his other players."

Leeds were runners-up three seasons in succession at the start of the Seventies and then won the league in '74.

"We were always there or thereabouts. And although we didn't win the things that we should have won, we always came back the next year and challenged. That was a great strength."

Jordan played in two European finals and lost both.

"There's ill-feeling about both," he says. "They weren't right. You'll have to ask the referees. We felt they were against us."

Jordan considered Liverpool rather than United to be Leeds' main rivals, but the 20th-century War of the Roses between Manchester and Leeds was about more than just football and could be traced back to the Industrial Revolution. Cotton became king in Manchester when cheap coal transported down the Bridgewater canal fuelled its factories. The success of cotton ruined England's traditional woollen cloth industry partly based in Yorkshire, because wool was costlier and not as suitable for the new machines.

The Yorkshire weavers loathed the new wealth pouring into industrial Manchester in a century when civic pride was all. A rivalry had begun, but it took many years before football became an outlet to vent it.

Football came late to Leeds, and in 1904 it was the biggest city in England without a senior club. Leeds City were then formed and admitted to the newly formed Second Division alongside another upstart, Chelsea. United's first game against Leeds was a 3-0 home defeat in 1906, watched by the lowest gate of that season, 6,000. United won the return at Elland Road but Leeds City never provided opposition again and the club was wound up in 1919 after being found guilty of financial irregularities. They re-emerged as Leeds United, opponents for the first time in 1922/23, but thereafter only sporadically as both relatively unsuccessful clubs switched divisions.

It was only after the Second World War that Manchester United emerged as a football power, but it was 1961 before Leeds impressed when a new manager, Revie, set about assembling a tough young side. At the same time, Matt Busby was building his second great team at Old Trafford and two fine teams emerged – United with Bobby Charlton, Best and Law; Leeds with Bobby's brother Jack, Bremner and Norman 'bites yer legs' Hunter.

When United's dexterous young Irish winger Johnny Giles fell out with Matt Busby and moved to Elland Road in 1963, there was some ill feeling, but it wasn't until 1965, when United reached their fourth consecutive FA Cup semi-final, that the previous largely friendly rivalry took on a new edge. United's opponents were Leeds, now in Real Madrid inspired all-white, and both clubs were battling for success in the League and Cup. In front of 65,000 at Hillsborough, Jack Charlton and Denis Law wrestled like two schoolboys in a playground as players swapped punches and did neither side credit. The game finished 0-0, with the referee, both managers and players all being criticised for their conduct.

The replay was in Nottingham four days later where, unfortunately, players fought again. Fans from both sides joined in, with one running on the pitch and knocking the referee to the ground, and there were disturbances on the terraces, with some fans being thrown into the River Trent. Leeds won the tie 1-0 with a last-minute goal, but in the league United finished champions for the first time in eight years – on goal difference from Leeds.

Busby's third side hit their zenith with the 1968 European Cup success, but thereafter Leeds became the stronger force, consistently challenging for honours and winning the European Fairs' Cup twice in four years, the league title in '69 and the FA Cup in '72. In 1970, an ageing United team drew Leeds in the FA Cup semi-final. The tie went to three games, played at Hillsborough, Villa and Burnden Park, and watched by an astonishing 173,500 people. The first and only goal was scored in the final game – by Leeds.

As United's post-Busby decline became apparent, so Leeds grew into a major force at home and abroad. United fans don't need reminding that on 19th February 1972, Leeds hammered the side 5-1 at Elland Road. Leeds fans greeted the United team upon their return from relegation a year later with the song, "Where were you in '74?"

"United were always a special club and going to Old Trafford was special as a player," says Jordan. "Gordon McQueen and I would drive over to watch United play if Leeds didn't have a game, but Leeds were a better side, no doubt about it."

McQueen and Jordan, two rising stars at Leeds, have been best mates since they met.

"We are completely different characters – exact opposites in some ways – but we hit it off as mates. I trust Gordon and he has a great sense of humour. We also had the same targets in life and we were from a similar part of the world. We wanted to be the best we could be, we had the same objectives." Much to the suspicion of Revie, McQueen and Jordan moved out of their digs to share a flat. Freed from the constraints of living in lodgings, Revie imagined the worst.

McQueen was a joker and, despite their friendship, Jordan was often one of his targets, but he wasn't responsible for one of Jordan's greatest embarrassments.

By 1975, Jordan had made such an impression that he was linked to Bayern Munich.

"Bayern's manager had spoken well of me in the media before we met them in the final," says Jordan with a rare smile. "We went to Marbella after, where there was an interesting phone call."

McQueen takes up the story.

"Joe had done well that season, especially in the final and there was a phone call at our hotel. The waiter came down to the pool and said, 'Telephone call for Mr Joe Jordan from Mr Dietmar

Cramer in Germany.' He was Bayern Munich's manager. Joe looked around and when he didn't see Billy Bremner and Johnny Giles – the club's two most notorious wind-up merchants – he assumed that it was one of them ringing reception from their room. Joe gave me a nudge and said, 'Go and deal with it, Gordon.' I went to the phone and pretended to be Joe.

"The man said, 'We want you to join Bayern Munich, we've been really impressed by you and would like you to join this great club of ours.'

'Yes, no problem but you have to sign McQueen too,' I said.

'McQueen is a good central defender, but we have Beckenbauer and Schwarzenbeck who play all the time.'

'They couldn't lace McQueen's boots. They are not in the same class. You don't know what you are talking about.'

'Okay, maybe we speak later but I'm not so sure.'

"Later on, just as we were all dressed up to go out to Puerto Banus, there was another phone call, claiming to be from Dietmar Cramer. I answered it and realised that really had been him earlier. Joe was mortified."

Bayern's interest was serious and their offer would have been a record for German club.

"I told Jimmy Armfield, who had by then replaced Revie, that I wanted to go," says Jordan. "Leeds wouldn't accept the bid and demanded I stay. I wasn't too happy about it. I wanted to join the best team in Europe in the new Olympic Stadium and wanted to play in Europe. I wanted the adventure."

Bayern imposed a deadline which came and went.

"Jimmy Armfield looked at me, puffing on his pipe, and told me that was just the way things were." Jordan stayed in what was a Leeds team on the slide.

"Leeds began to decline after '75," he says. "Sir Alex sees decline coming. He brings players in who ignite the others. He let Hughes, Kanchelskis and Ince go and fans were not happy, but he'd thought everything through. It can be precarious when you are making changes and it's difficult to get it right, but you have to get it right if you are looking for a continuity of that success. Sir Alex has been unbelievable because he's produced team after team. Sir Matt did it as well. It's a sign of a great manager."

But there was no such process of renewal at Elland Road.

"Leeds were fantastic in '74," he says, "but we had a turbulent year domestically in '75 because Brian Clough came and we got a terrible start."

Clough's brief 44-day sojourn at the club has become the stuff of fact and best selling fiction.

"I read *The Damned United* but after reading it I didn't want to see the film," says Jordan. "It didn't tally with what I saw when I was there. In Brian Clough, I didn't see someone who was the worse for wear because of drink. He was the wrong man in the wrong place at the wrong time at Leeds, but he later proved himself to be a great manager.

"Jimmy Armfield replaced Clough and he stabilised things, but the squad wasn't what it had been. It wasn't an easy thing to keep going what Revie had done. And if you are not careful in football, look what can happen. Who would have thought that Liverpool wouldn't win the league for so long after 1990 given the way they played in the Seventies and Eighties?"

Not that Jordan's future was set to be in Yorkshire. He had many suitors, especially in Europe. Ajax Amsterdam made an approach to Leeds and agreed a fee of £300,000.

"I was going to go to Holland in 1977," says Jordan, "Ajax had given the world Cruyff, Neskeens and Krol. I met with them at a hotel near Leeds airport but later decided against it. Dutch tax levels were as punishing as those in Britain and the wage on offer was just a few pounds more than I was on at Leeds."

In 1977, Leeds made it to an FA Cup semi-final, where they lost to Manchester United at Hillsborough. For Manchester United fans packed on the giant banks of terracing at Sheffield Wednesday's ground, the 2-1 victory was cathartic, exorcising the demons of past defeats. For Jordan it was disappointing.

"We had good new players like Tony Currie and Bryan Flynn, but the team refused to catch fire," recalls Jordan.

Armfield called him one afternoon at home.

"Calls about transfers usually came through a third party, not from a manager. He told me he was giving me permission to speak to Manchester United and that Leeds had accepted a bid for me."

Events moved quickly and Jordan met the United contingent in the car park at Elland Road later that night.

"Louis Edwards, Sir Matt, secretary Les Olive and Dave Sexton followed me back to my house," explains Jordan. "My father was there at the time. He'd come down to visit with my mother and was delighted to talk to Matt about Lanarkshire. Delighted too that I was going to join United. I didn't sign, but I sat down in the kitchen and verbally agreed to join United that night. I was impressed that those four individuals from one of the biggest clubs in the world came at short notice. That really showed that they wanted me, despite having Stuart Pearson and Jimmy Greenhoff up front, both of whom were fine players."

Jordan knew United were not renowned as great payers.

"I'd been on £270 a week at Leeds. I was newly married [to Judith, a Leeds girl] and wanted a rise," explains Jordan. For once, United were thinking big.

"We're thinking of paying you £500 a week," said Sexton. "That was in line with their top-paid players, my compatriots Lou Macari and Martin Buchan. I said it would be fine. I was also due a signing on bonus of £17,500, five per cent of the transfer fee – a record between two English teams. The tax man would have taken 82 per cent of that if I hadn't put it immediately into my pension fund."

It wasn't all about money.

"I was very excited," says Jordan. "Dave Sexton had a very good name in the game. And I was so proud that I could tell my father that he now had to come back to Old Trafford all those years after watching Jimmy Delaney to see me, his son."

There was a late development.

"I went to Elland Road to collect my gear and told Jimmy that I was going to sign for Manchester United. He handed me a piece of paper and said Liverpool Football Club had called. Bob Paisley wanted to talk to me."

Liverpool were the reigning European champions.

"I called Liverpool. Paisley knew I'd been talking to United but wanted me to think about the past and probably future achievements of his club. The idea briefly appealed, a chance of sure-fire glory. But I had already promised that I would go to United and I kept my word." Jordan drove back over the Pennines and signed for United, but visits back to Leeds were fraught.

"I went to a game a few months later because I was still living in Leeds," he says. "I was denied access into the official car park. Then I saw the secretary and he was fine with me and gave me a pass. I tried to leave the game early, but the man who had not let me in the car park had decided to park all the other cars around me so that I couldn't get my car out. I was the last to leave the car park and didn't go back to Elland Road after that unless I was playing."

And he wasn't an immediate success at United.

"I didn't score until my sixth game against Newcastle, but I did score in the derby against Manchester City which was a big help in winning over the crowd. They were patient with me, as was Dave who told me not to worry as I was playing well. I bumped into Matt Busby in a corridor at Old Trafford too. I told him that I was anxious to score and he said, 'Don't worry laddie. The goals will come. You're playing fine.'"

Jordan was an aggressive, battling centre-forward who was picked out by opponents for rough treatment. He used his aerial prowess to set up attack partners like Macari and Greenhoff. Both speak well of his style in this book, a style which suffered no fools.

West Brom's John Wile punched him off the ball in one game. Wile would later leave the field with a broken jaw after Jordan protected himself from another reckless challenge.

"And Brian Kidd punched me while he was playing for City in a derby game. It was uncalled for and out of the blue, we hadn't even been involved in anything all match. I didn't square up to him or make a fuss, but let him know how I felt and told him to be on his guard. I'd been taught at Leeds not to forget being punched."

Jordan was cheered by the arrival of McQueen, also from Leeds, a few months after his own. Leeds supporters felt very differently about this second defection across the Pennines.

"I was blamed by Leeds fans for Gordon leaving which wasn't true," he adds. "But it did mean that we could drive together from Leeds each day. We'd stay overnight at Mottram Hall before matches and I started to look for houses in that area so that I could bring my young family closer to Manchester. We settled in the lovely Cheshire village of Prestbury.

"Gordon was my roomie at United and Scotland. We remember those years as among the happiest in all our careers."

Jordan wanted to bring success to United.

"With players like Martin Buchan, Sammy McIlroy and Lou Macari, we went about the business of remaking the greatest club in the history of English football, but it didn't quite happen for us."

Still, he was not disappointed by Old Trafford.

"We knew we were part of something great. United had a smell that was different to other clubs. I don't know whether it was the oils that were used to massage players, you could smell it a mile away – that football smell.

"Some players were keen but could not handle the pressure. I had experience of a big club at Leeds and that helped me handle the pressure at Old Trafford. If you can't then you have no chance at United because it's a challenge playing at home. The crowd were always wonderful, but once the game started they just became background. There could be 100,000 at Hampden Park or 60,000 at Old Trafford, but they became background when the game started."

Jordan relished the challenge.

"I became a better player at Old Trafford. Experience, belief, confidence and expression were all factors. I took more responsibility than I had at Leeds."

Jordan played in his second World Cup finals in 1978 for Scotland. In 1982, he would become the first and only Scotsman to score in three World Cup finals.

"When I was first called up by Tommy Docherty for the 1974 World Cup finals, I never made it my ambition to play in three World Cups. You needed luck and I had that luck. I also played with some great Scottish players as I picked up 52 caps. Great players like Paddy Crerand only picked up 16 caps. Billy McNeill had a mere 30.

"Playing in the World Cup finals gives you the opportunity to pit yourself against the best players in the world," he says. "I was never disappointed, though 1978 could have gone better. That tournament in Argentina was hugely memorable and I didn't take these trips for granted like I did some games. Sometimes you go to a game in Bradford or London. You prepare for the game, you travel, play and then come home. You see nothing of the city you are in."

Scotland were hugely fancied in 1978 – by Scots.

"In one sense, the euphoria was pathetic; there was far too much compensating for the lean years that had gone before, the barren years from 1958 to 1974 which were notable for the odd victory over England. There were tens of thousands waiting to send us off from Hampden Park and thousands more on the route to Prestwick airport. Gordon McQueen turned to me and said, 'Christ, what's going on?' Playing in England, I hadn't really noticed the hype and expectation in Scotland. The manager Ally MacLeod had added to the expectation by saying that Scotland were going to win the World Cup. In South America. He also suggested to me that I was central to his plans to beat the world. Some pressure then!"

Scotland lost their first game 3-1 to Peru.

"I gave us the lead and we could easily have won it," rues Jordan. "We returned to the training camp in a state of shock."

Scotland's next game was against Iran. They needed to win but drew "a dreadful" game 1-1. "A group of Scotland fans demonstrated as we returned to the team bus. They sang: 'You only want the money.' It was based on some TV adverts we had done for Chrysler cars before the competition. That was hurtful."

In the final group game, Scotland needed to beat Holland, potential World Cup winners, by three clear goals to qualify.

"We won 3-2 in a superb game which told you everything you needed to know about the Scottish knack of straddling heaven and hell. Archie Gemmill scored that gem of a goal. We were 3-1 up and needed another goal in the final 22 minutes."

A Johnny Rep shot from distance three minutes later killed those hopes. Scotland were out.

"I trailed back to Manchester and took a holiday in Cornwall where it rained every day."

After the 1979 final defeat, United made an unexpected challenge for the League title the following season. Under Docherty and Sexton they had reached three FA Cup finals in four years, but were not credited with the stamina or sticking power to maintain a league challenge when the pitches got heavy. Jordan was injured at the start of the season and in his absence and that of Jimmy Greenhoff, United took the field with its infamous 'midget line' attack.

"It was so frustrating. I picked up a really bad injury, a pulled muscle in my thigh. It just wouldn't clear up and I aggravated it by trying to keep playing. Dave Sexton kept reassuring me and refused to put me under any pressure to recover more quickly."

Sexton switched Lou Macari from midfield and he played alongside Ashley Grimes with Steve Coppell in the middle. Despite its collective lack of inches, the improvised formation coped, though the goals hardly flowed. Jordan returned to fitness in mid-November and showed what United had been missing in a home game against Crystal Palace, scoring the late equaliser as well as causing Gerry Francis to limp off the pitch and leaving goalie John Burridge with a sore and bloody head.

United followed this up by trouncing Norwich 5-0, Jordan scoring twice. Sexton enthused:

"It was great to see Joe score his goals because he so thoroughly deserves them. If he never scored another goal in his life I would still have him in the team because he plays so well for the rest of the team. When he scores as well it is a bonus."

It was to be Jordan's best season at Old Trafford. He doubled his League goals tally, scoring 13 despite missing much of the first three months. Seasoned observers felt that he was becoming a more complete footballer rather than someone who created mayhem in opposing defences with his strength and the fans voted him their Player of the Year. David Meek believed that Jordan's improvement was down to the fact that, as the team's most booked player, he adopted a more prudent and less aggressive approach in January when he reached 18 disciplinary points to avoid being suspended. After one game, Sexton said of Jordan's performance, that he thought 'it was Pele out there'. Not that Jordan had mellowed completely. United made an early exit from the FA Cup after a replay with Tottenham in which Spurs' goal-keeper Milija Aleksic was taken to hospital after a clash with United's striker and had to be replaced in goal by Glenn Hoddle.

Despite only conceding four goals at home, beating eventual champions Liverpool 2-1 as the campaign drew to a close, and winning the last home game of the season 2-1 against Coventry to draw level on points with the leaders, United were given scant credit for their second place. Patrick Barclay described their season as one of 'barren success'.

Until Alex Ferguson, Sexton was the only post-Busby manager to finish in the top two of the English League. But he failed to make any sort of connection with United's fans, whose barracking of the team from the terraces was a common motif in newspaper reports. David Meek complained about the constant moaning about the lack of flair evident as Sexton concentrated on defence from sections of the support. Off the field, damaging revelations were made about Louis Edwards on Granada's *World in Action* programme. Edwards had a fatal heart-attack in 1980, which his son Martin attributed to the stress brought on by the programme.

Jordan had a lot of time for Sexton. "Sexton was good company with a quick sense of humour. You could sit down and talk to him. He was always relaxed – except when in front of a television camera. But imagine being the Manchester United manager on television? You have to represent the club with your voice and words – that can't be easy because you cannae slip up.

"I was happy at United and my family were settled. But when United didn't replicate their league challenge the following season, 1980/81, the climate began to alter.

"They lost patience with Sexton. We won our last seven league games but it made no difference, Sexton was dismissed.

"He lived near me and phoned me to tell me he been sacked. He asked me to collect some prints by the Manchester artist Harold Riley, which he had bought to give the players, and hand them out for him."

The picture was of Old Trafford and a game between United and Spurs. It still has a place at Jordan's home in Bristol, where he would settle years later after managing Bristol City.

Martin Edwards, who had taken over as chairman from his father in March 1980, later explained the thinking behind Sexton's dismissal and disagrees with Jordan's positive assessment of United's prospects under him.

"The second position in 1980 flattered us," he said. "We finished eighth the following year. I felt that Dave had had four years in charge and that United were not progressing. We were no nearer to winning the league. I also felt that the supporters were a little bit disgruntled with the style of football we were playing. We had some very poor attendances that season [attendances dropped from 54,394 on the opening day of the season to 40,165 on the final day]. So I decided to dismiss Dave, my first major decision. I know that some players were not happy, but I felt it was right. The Board saw me act decisively and I felt stronger in the position from then on."

Edwards' first choice as Sexton's replacement was Lawrie McMenemy, the Southampton manager who had excelled at The Dell and led the Second Division side to surprise FA Cup success over Manchester United in 1976.

"I'd spoken to him and he indicated that he would come to United," says Edwards. "McMenemy then rang me and told me that his wife didn't want to move to Manchester and that he would not be coming. That left me in the lurch. My second choice was Bobby Robson. I spoke to him and he said that while he was very flattered, he had unfinished business at Ipswich. He explained that he had a young squad with players he had brought in and he didn't want to leave them."

Inconceivably, United were struggling to find a manager.

"So I was really in the lurch wasn't I? The next choice was Ron Saunders. He'd been successful and led Villa to the championship, but he wasn't interested and turned us down flat.

"United were different then," says Edwards, explaining Saunders' reluctance even to discuss the job. "While it was a big club, success was lacking. Between 1968 and '83, the club won just one trophy, the FA Cup in 1977. It was a bleak period. United didn't have enough money in the kitty either. Managers asked me how much money there would be. I was honest. They weighed up what I said and turned us down."

The solution was provided when journalist John Maddock approached Edwards and informed him that the West Bromwich Albion manager Ron Atkinson would take the United job.

Jordan had been in the process of negotiating a new contract with Sexton and he went to see Atkinson to continue the talks,

"I'd told Sexton that I wanted £1,000 a week," recalls Jordan. "He was keen to do it but United didn't tie me down and had let the contract run out. Atkinson asked me how much I wanted and got the same response. He reported back that the directors were agreeable. That was a rise of 100 per cent. But before Atkinson made his offer I'd gone to watch Liverpool in the semi-final of the European Cup against Bayern Munich. There, I was approached by Tony Damascelli, a journalist from the Italian daily *Il Giornale* of Milan."

Damascelli asked Jordan if he had ever thought of playing in Italy and that if he did, there would be interest from AC Milan and Bologna.

"Milan were a giant of the game who had just been promoted back to Serie A after being relegated following a bribery scandal. I was told that I was on a shortlist of strikers with the Belgian Jan Ceulemans and the Brazilian Zico.

"Crucially, my lawyer had established that under Common Market regulations, with my contract up at Old Trafford I was effectively a free agent. Milan would have to pay United compensation but not as much as United had paid Leeds for me."

Milan were soon on the phone with an offer of wages far higher than Old Trafford. A few days later, Jordan met a Milan official at an Italian restaurant in Leeds.

"My wife liked the idea, and the following day I told Ron Atkinson."

United fans were stunned, while Jordan flew to Milan where he was met by scores of journalists and hundreds of fans at Linate airport.

"I was the only foreign player in the team so there was a lot of pressure. I was used to pressure in my career. It's how you handled it that mattered."

Jordan learned Italian.

"It was still difficult to adjust. There were huge demands on every Milan player. You represent Milan at all times. You wear a club blazer and a badge and you are proud to represent Milan. That wasn't a problem to me and it was also a better way of living. The other players were from a completely different background to me and I was learning all the time."

The fans warmed to their toothless Scottish centre-forward and, adding their own twist, called him *Lo Squalo* (The Shark).

"I have never regretted moving. I loved Italian culture, loved the country and Judith was prepared to do everything to help me settle,"

Being a footballer in Italy was very different to England.

"It was a better way of living," recalls Jordan. "I'd come from a working class background in Scotland and I was playing in a dressing room of Italians who all seemed well educated and cultured. There was so much to enjoy – the cafés, the museums. But there was no free time in Milan – your time is the club's time."

Jordan played in a side with internationals who would go onto win the World Cup in 1982.

"Franco Baresi was a young lad at Milan and he told me that he could get me tickets for the World Cup final in Madrid," he recalls. "I arrived in Madrid wearing a t-shirt and flip flops with Gordon McQueen. We started the World Cup playing for Scotland and finished it celebrating with the victorious Italian players in Madrid."

Baresi and Jordan played for Milan during a time of serious upheavals following the bribery scandal which had rocked Italian football a year before he arrived. Players were imprisoned, the club president lost his job and Milan were relegated to Serie B though they were promoted by the time of Jordan's arrival.

"I scored against hated rivals Internazionale in one of my first games which saw me mobbed by fans. I thought that would continue, but results were not good for us.

"I lay flat on the team bus with my team-mates when bricks were coming through the windows after a game after which the referee had to disguise himself as a policeman to leave because his decisions had so inflamed the crowd," he explains. But he grew to understand the Italian mentality. "Italy's a great country. I have a daughter who lives in Milan. The Italians have their ways, but as long as you know what they are like you are fine."

Jordan was playing in a struggling side.

"The coach Radice was sacked midway through the season when things were not going well. The directors called all the players to a hotel and asked them what they thought of the coach. Something like that was unimaginable in Britain. With my limited Italian I was almost a bystander but I knew the coach had no chance."

Radice was replaced by Italo Galbiatti, an experienced professional who had worked with a fast-rising coach called Fabio Capello. Galbiatti was later installed as assistant England coach to Capello.

Milan may have had Baresi, but there was too much ground to make up and they were relegated.

Jordan survived the cut that summer and enjoyed a season in Serie B, scoring 15 goals as Milan pipped Lazio to the title.

"Average crowds were above 60,000 and I felt that I had rescued my situation in Milan after the struggles of the relegation season," says Jordan. However, Milan let him go that summer with a year left on his contract.

"I was 31 when I was told 'you can leave' for the first time in my career," he recalls. "I'm not being big headed, but prior to that it was always my decision."

Jordan turned down a move to Southampton to stay in northern Italy, where he joined Verona.

"I liked the sound of it straight away, a good team playing in a beautiful old city. It was the right move and Hellas Verona were a good team. We reached the Italian cup final after I'd scored against Bari in the semi. We lost against Roma in the Olimpico and that was my last-ever game in Italian football, not a bad place to bow out."

Milan, meanwhile, were sold to the TV magnate Silvio Berlusconi, a move which cemented his role as a national figure.

"He installed the brilliant coach Arrigo Sacchi," explains Jordan. "The Dutchmen Frank Rijkaard, Ruud Gullit and Marco van Basten were signed and suddenly Milan were the team who had it all. Soon enough, Paulo Maldini emerged. He was a player in the youth team when I was in Milan, but whenever I went back to Milan after I finished playing I've met up with Paulo and he was always a distinguished gentleman."

Jordan now had a choice between Southampton and Celtic, the team he'd supported as a boy.

"I would have gone to Celtic had I been younger, but I had a good feeling about Southampton under Lawrie McMenemy and they were a very well-run football club. He had also signed Kevin Keegan, Peter Shilton and Mick Mills. Celtic and Lawrie offered me roughly the same money, but the clinching factor was the offer of a three-year contract at Southampton."

Southampton paid Verona £150,000 and the move worked out very well, with Jordan scoring 17 goals in his first season at the Dell, 1983/84. A torn cartilage hampered his second season and during his third he was selected to play in a game with the youth team.

"I felt frustrated, but I was determined to give a good account of myself. A boy was brought on to play alongside me. I liked the look of the kid immediately. He was tough and smart and very confident. He did everything with hard purpose. I thought, 'This boy could go to the top of the game.'

His name was Alan Shearer."

An offer from cash-strapped, Third Division Bristol City through ex-team-mate Terry Cooper came next.

"I didn't jump at the offer," he said. "I'd not played in the Second Division, let alone Third. But I had to expel a few demons and accept where I was rather than where I wanted to be."

He drove to Bristol with Judith.

"It was a fine city," he says. "And Ashton Gate was a fine football ground."

Jordan played 57 times for Bristol City, the last few as player-manager. He was in charge when City were promoted to the Second Division in 1990 – after finishing second behind local rivals Bristol Rovers.

During this time he forged a friendship with the United manager and would often call him for advice on football matters.

"I was given an excellent piece of advice by Alex Ferguson," says Jordan. "He had said to me, 'Remember Joe, when you send a team out you always have to give them a cause to fight for.'"

Jordan was doing well.

"My name was being linked with the big clubs," he says. "I was listed as one of the up-and-coming managers of the game."

He was offered the Aston Villa job but, knowing the reputation of chairman 'Deadly' Doug Ellis, turned it down. Instead, he went back to Scotland to become manager of Hearts.

"That was where my management journey went awry," attests Jordan. "Hearts had to pay Bristol City £80,000 compensation for me. I was told that I would have to sell a player to make up for that."

Still, Jordan guided Hearts to second in the Premier Division and to two Scottish Cup semi-finals.

"In my third season I told a press conference that if Hearts wanted to develop, if they were to qualify for Europe regularly and truly compete with Rangers and Celtic, then there had to be more serious investment. We had to be honest with our following, I thought, but apparently that was something to think and tell the chairman privately, not to say in public."

Jordan was dismissed at the end of his third season.

"The secretary of Hearts gave me the news, reading from a fax sent from Monte Carlo, where the chairman was a tax exile," Jordan muses.

He spent a brief period at Celtic as assistant manager to Liam Brady, who resigned four months after he arrived. Jordan felt obliged to do the same.

"I took the Stoke job for a year, then went to Bristol City for a second spell between 1994 and 1997."

This time, he was dismissed from Ashton Gate – "another blow to my profile" he says. He served as assistant manager to Lawrie McMenemy at Northern Ireland and assistant to his former team-mate Lou Macari at Huddersfield Town. A change of chairman meant a change of manager.

"I was told of my sacking by a reporter while on holiday," he says. "When I called home my son told me that the news was running on Sky Sports. When I told Judith I saw the anger in her eyes. I felt numb. Football had given me so much of what I had wanted in life, but as it gave, it also took away. Loving it was one thing, making sense of it quite another."

Jordan spent a few years out of football, living in Bristol and doing television commentary for Channel 4's Italian football coverage.

"I had a call from Harry Redknapp one morning. He asked what I was doing. I didn't give him a sob story. I simply told him how it is when your name is out of fashion. I wasn't telling him anything he didn't know."

Redknapp asked him to go to Fratton Park to talk about helping coach Portsmouth against the likes of United.

"I've been with Harry ever since at Portsmouth and then Tottenham," says Jordan. "Been involved in the company of top-flight players. However many times football knocks you down, it always has the potential to lift you up."

JIMMY NICHOLL
THE OTHER BELFAST BOY

JIMMY NICHOLL

J immy Nicholl, United's former flame-haired Irish full-back, is down in Manchester from Scotland for the weekend for a family visit. Nicholl is one of the three ex-players featured in this book who has had a long-term career in football management. When interviewed he was manager of Cowdenbeath, newly relegated to the First Division of the Scottish Football League. At the time of writing he has just had a "surprise" return to the Scottish Premier League, beginning a second spell as assistant manager at Kilmarnock.

Nicholl is remembering growing up in Belfast. Although actually born in Canada, in Hamilton, Ontario, he moved back to Ireland to live in Rathcoole, a large council estate in Belfast with over 10,000 residents, built in the 1950s as housing for those displaced by the demolition of slums in Belfast's inner city.

"That's where I grew up, that place was the making of me. All

I needed was a bit of education and a bit of grass to play football. And that's what I had. My dad was born in Belfast, and he was going to see his brother who lived in Canada. He met my mother, who was from Greenock just outside Glasgow. She was in Canada for her sister's wedding. The two of them met at a dance in Toronto, a chance meeting. Me and my two younger brothers were born there. When I was three, my dad decided that the family would go back to Belfast."

Nicholl's dad was a goalkeeper.

"He played for Ontario All Stars. Dad played against Spurs when they visited for a pre-season game in '57/58. Danny Blanchflower told manager Bill Nicholson to sign him for the rest of the tour with the view to taking him on permanently. But my mum wouldn't let him."

When Nicholl was three, his father brought the family back to Rathcoole. "It was a mixed estate with both Catholics and Protestants. There were no problems at all, it was brilliant. It didn't matter which religion you were. I had a paper round delivering the *Belfast Evening Telegraph*. I had 173 papers and the estate was evenly split.

"Then it changed. The Troubles kicked off in the late Sixties and the Catholics had to get out of Rathcoole. It made me really sad seeing people I liked such as our neighbours moving out, people I'd grown up with. They'd get a threatening letter saying, 'That's it, you'd better be out in two days.' You'd see their furniture in the street. I didn't even know where they were going, but they were replaced by similarly displaced Protestants. After that, things really started to deteriorate."

Nicholl was a boyhood Linfield fan.

"When I was 11, I represented Linfield in a half-time penalty competition at Cliftonville," he says with a cheeky smile.

Linfield have a reputation for being a predominantly Protestant club and Cliftonville a predominantly Catholic one (the only one in the top division since Belfast Celtic folded and Derry City started playing games south of the border) and encounters between the pair have a history of being problematic. Cliftonville/ Linfield clashes have always had religious connotations and been viewed as a microcosm of sectarian strife in the province. During the Troubles, the police refused to police a Cliftonville v Linfield match in what is a largely nationalist North Belfast. So between 1970 and 1998, it was not deemed safe for Linfield to make the journey to the wonderfully named Solitude, the home of Cliftonville. Known by various epithets including 'murder mile' and 'the killing fields', more lives were lost in the area around Solitude during the troubles than in any other part of Northern Ireland.

For 28 years, therefore, Windsor Park, the venue for Northern Ireland internationals, was the only stadium considered safe enough territory for Cliftonville/Linfield matches. It was also adjacent to a motorway which aided pre- and post-match segregation. But Nicholl was taking penalties at Solitude before the move, which explains the smile.

"The fans hated each other," he recalls. "As I was running up to take penalties, I saw the fans throwing bricks at each other behind the goal. But I didn't miss."

Sectarianism was a facet of his life every day.

"We used to get chased all the time by Catholics," he says. "Because I played football I often left the safety of Rathcoole. One day in 1970, I went into Belfast with Bobby Campbell, who went on to play for Aston Villa. We were 14 and playing for Northern Ireland schoolboys. A lot of bombs were going off in Belfast that day. The buses were stopped and all the passengers were thrown off the bus in a Catholic area. The locals knew we were not from there, they just knew. A group of lads near a pub started to chase us and we grabbed a couple of bricks to protect ourselves, but we dropped the bricks as we were getting chased. The lads were catching up with us, and all we had to protect ourselves was our boots. We swung our boots at the lads and somehow got away. It was scary, yet I look back at growing up in Rathcoole with great memories. We played football every day, sometimes in matches of up to 60-a-side. I would never ever change the upbringing I had."

It was against such a backdrop that Nicholl's career was taking off.

"I played for the school and for 7th Newton Abbey Boys Brigade on a Saturday morning and in the afternoon at a boys' club run by the Mitchell Brothers, two Liverpool supporters. People on our estate supported Manchester United, Rangers, Linfield or Liverpool. The brothers would organise trips to Anfield. We'd get the overnight boat from Belfast to Liverpool and play football in Stanley Park before the match on Saturday morning. Sometimes the boat was full of United fans and there would be a lot of trouble. The brothers tried to get me to support Liverpool, but I wasn't for turning. I'd made my mind up after watching Georgie Best and the 1968 European Cup final."

Nicholl got his break when he was spotted by a legendary United scout.

"An injury to an older boy meant that I had to change teams one week and fill in for a lad at the Boys Brigade club. I was approached at half-time by Bob Bishop, the man who spotted George Best."

Bishop asked him if he had signed for anyone.

"He wanted to know if I'd signed the pink form which in those days linked you to a club, and I told him that I hadn't. Bishop was a real character. He wore a wee cloth cap above a hearing aid and a tweed coat. He asked for my address and said that he wanted me to have a trial for Man United. I told my parents as soon as I got home."

Bishop was United's scout in Northern Ireland, charged with recruiting the finest talents from Belfast to Derry, Newry to Portrush. And it was with Bishop that Nicholl made his first trip to Manchester alongside six other boys – also the first trip on a plane he could remember.

"We stayed in digs on Chester Road near Old Trafford. Bob treated us to a fish supper at the chippy nearest the ground. Then two men came out of the Trafford Pub and into the chippy. One had orange, steel-capped boots on. Bob let on to him in a Belfast accent. He would talk to anyone and commented that it was a nice night."

The friendliness wasn't reciprocated.

"I saw the man say something to his friend, and a minute later I saw a group of men leave the pub and come towards us. I knew there would be trouble and told Bob to run away. I watched as his little legs scurried off. Apart from him being an old man, he had all the money. Within seconds we were getting a hiding – probably because we had Belfast accents. Our fish suppers went everywhere. We made it back to the digs, battered and bruised and the police arrived soon after. I was taken into The Trafford pub to identify the culprits. I saw the man with the orange boots and pointed him out."

It wasn't the best preparation for his trial the following morning.

"Six of us were picked up in a mini-bus and taken to The Cliff in Salford. I was the only one who made it through the trials. Another player was going to sign until his medical, when it was discovered that one of his legs was an inch longer than the other."

Not that any of the aspiring youngsters knew whether United wanted them or not when they returned to Belfast.

"I received a letter in the post asking me to come back to Old Trafford in the summer. I had to show that to the careers officer at school. I wasn't bad academically, but my standards slipped after Manchester United showed interest."

Nicholl had other diversions as well.

"I loved Rod Stewart and The Faces, but the first record I ever bought was *Hi Ho, Silver Lining* by Jeff Beck. We had a piano in our living room – don't ask me why. But sometimes it became a focal point for all the parties which my parents used to hold. I can remember hearing them and the music of Patsy Cline or the Four Tops. It was a very happy household with us five kids. I was the eldest, with two brothers and two sisters.

"Dad worked on the buses and my mum worked in the shops opposite the house. Because I was the eldest I had to look after the others. I was given five shillings a day and always bought the same thing – a quarter pound of luncheon meat and a long Vienna roll. One day one of my sisters asked me for a cream cookie. I asked her why. She said that she was sick of eating the same thing every day. She's still known as 'Cookie' now!"

Nicholl's recall to Old Trafford was actually only the first step; he had several further trials at United.

"The final trials were a process of elimination," he explains. "Some of the lads only lasted a day or two, but I kept being asked to stay on. I wasn't a full-back then but a central midfielder who used to get about the pitch and fly into tackles. I wasn't a good tackler, but I only learned that later. By the final day I remember Frank O'Farrell [then first-team manager] watching with Paddy Crerand and several other first-team members."

The news was delivered afterwards in the changing room.

"Arthur Albiston was in the same group as me, and we were the only ones who would make it at United," recalls Nicholl.

He moved to digs with Mrs Laffy in Park Road, Stretford, in the summer of 1971.

"Her mother was there and her daughter too. There were three generations of women in the same house. And me. Mrs Laffy was a golfer. She'd give me cereal each morning and then disappear to play golf. She put on a lock on the phone so that I couldn't use it. After training, I'd go to the other lads' digs or we'd meet up in the city centre or play snooker at Potters in Salford.

"George Best used to play there with his best-mate-cum-agent Malcolm Wagner or professional players like Alex Higgins and John Spencer. People would play for money, all kinds of people from villains to footballers.

"Malcolm told me that he and Bestie had been followed one day in Bestie's new car. After three miles, they pulled over and this fella got out of the car behind and came up. Bestie pressed the button on the electric windows. His car was one of six in the

UK and one of the very few with electric windows. The man said, 'I'm opening a new hairdressers. Will you open it for me?'

'How much?' said Best.

'I'll give you £300,' said the fella.

'Three grand,' said Best, who was just 19 at the time.

"The fella thought about it and eventually agreed.

'No thanks,' said Bestie, and put the window up.

'Are you crazy?' asked Wagner, who would have made about £700 commission, a vast amount in those days.

'He should have offered me three grand in the first place,' said Bestie, before driving off."

Such figures were incomprehensible to Nicholl, who spent the next four years learning to be a footballer starting on £6 a week, but he had other issues to deal with, ones which he shared with George Best – tormented by fears for the safety of families in Belfast as the Troubles worsened.

"I was allowed back from Manchester on the final weekend of every month. I'd play football on a Saturday morning and get a train to Liverpool. Then I'd catch the boat to Belfast, which would travel overnight. I'd arrive on Sunday morning and go straight to Rathcoole. I'd return back to Liverpool on Monday night. I was 15.

"One day, one of the coaches pulled me to one side and said, 'You're not to go home this weekend.' The Troubles were getting out of hand in Belfast. The order not to go home had the opposite effect on me. I had to get back to see what the problem was."

By 1972, pressure was being exerted on individuals to sign up to loyalist paramilitary groups. Nicholl's family were vulnerable.

"I'm glad that I went home," says Nicholl. "I stayed longer than I should have done and called the club to explain why. United told me to bring my whole family over to Manchester straightaway and that they would sort out a house. We all flew over to England and were put up in Bill Foulkes' old home in Sale which the club owned. It was a three-bedroom house in a cul-de-sac in a nice part of Manchester."

It was far calmer than Belfast.

"United's groundsman used to come and cut the grass," explains Nicholl. "My family still live in the area. We weren't happy to leave Belfast, but it wasn't safe. I was pleased about what United did, but I was worried about the rent in Sale. I was 16 by then, still an apprentice hoping to earn a professional contract."

Nicholl went to see the club secretary, Les Olive, and told him that he intended to get a part-time job to help pay the rent.

"Les told me not to do that, but to pay a little bit of rent until I earned more money. At 17, you sign a pro form or you are released, it's as simple as that. I was offered forms and signed under Tommy Docherty for £7 a week. I was happy to sign, but I was actually worse off than I had been as a second-year apprentice because the club stopped helping with the rent."

After playing with the reserves, Nicholl's first-team chance came in a testimonial game for the Chelsea full-back Eddie McCreadie at Stamford Bridge in May 1974, watched by just 6,437.

"Tommy Docherty told me that I was going to be in the squad. We travelled down to London on the train. It was magnificent, they served us a meal on the train and everything.

"Before the game, Eddie McCreadie came in with brown envelopes for all the lads. The other players just put theirs in their pockets, but I opened mine to find £50. That was seven weeks' wages!"

Nicholl came on for Jim McCalliog.

"The game was only ten minutes old when the Doc said, 'Jimmy, get your bottoms off, McCalliog doesn't fancy it'. But I couldn't get my tracksuit bottoms off. They were the type with stirrups on the bottom and I'd not worn them before. But I'd put them on wrong and could get them off. I'd put them inside my boots and not outside. I was getting dog's abuse from fans.

"I did okay in the game and I was getting changed afterwards when McCreadie came to thank the United players. Martin Buchan felt sorry for him because the crowd had been so low and suggested that we should return the envelopes to Eddie. I was gutted!"

The players went out in London that night.

"I didn't have any money," said Nicholl. "I wasn't old enough to drink and just sat in the hotel reception. McCalliog, a Scouser, said, 'Come on, son, you're out with us, we'll take care of you'.

"We went to the Playboy club and were surrounded by Bunny girls. We ate steak sandwiches. I thought, 'This is the life.' McCalliog paid for everything with a gold card. I didn't even know what a cheque book was, let alone a gold card. It was almost magic to me."

It was almost another year before Nicholl made his competitive debut away as a sub against Southampton in a Second Division game.

"My position was sweeper and I'd been doing well in the reserves in that spot, but I couldn't get in the first team because of Martin Buchan," he explains. "Assistant manager Frank Blunstone told me that I would have to change my style and I switched to full-back. I played nothing but full-back for two weeks in training. The plan was for me to replace Alex Forsyth at right-back. I remember my first start better than that Southampton game. That was when I was picked ahead of Alex. It was against Tottenham at Old Trafford in September 1975. I gave away a free kick with a clumsy, rash tackle and Glenn Hoddle scored from it. I was a reckless tackler. We won 3-2. Gerry Daly got two and Spurs helped us with an own goal. I didn't enjoy it."

Nicholl, 18, kept his place in the team for the next 15 games at the expense of the older Forsyth, who was 23.

"Alex was a great player who was two-footed and would shoot from distance. The other lads called him Bruce, but I always called him Alex. He cost £100,000, but I was chosen over him. He runs a pub called the Auld Hoose in Hamilton these days. I popped in to see him one day, gave him the fright of his life."

United fans were not convinced that Nicholl should be starting ahead of the popular Forsyth.

"They let their feelings be known," recalls Nicholl, who went on to play 248 games for United. "I went to get the ball for a throw in on the half-way line and someone squeezed through the bars as if he was trying to get at me. He called me an Irish so and so. It was clear that he did not like me. And he was one of our own fans. What could I do? I knew I could do better, I knew I was clumsy in the tackle, but I was getting abuse for playing in a position I was not used to.

"I remember one player saying, 'It's great being cheered by 50,000 people, but can you handle being booed by 50,000?

"That's the character you need to make it as a player. You need more than ability."

But it only took one special moment for the situation to change. "Things weren't going well, but then I crossed the ball for Stuart Pearson to score in a 3-1 win against Arsenal. I heard the deafening roar which followed. A weight was lifted that day. I knew I could contribute to the team. The following Monday in training, the manager said, 'That's you son, you're alright now. You were making a lot of mistakes, but I kept picking you because you always showed for the ball. You never hid.' I was fine after that and never worried about a game of football again in my whole career."

Nicholl became 'Jimmy Nic' to fans who came to appreciate his wholehearted effort during every game, as he ran up and down the pitch. He developed into a strong player physically, though he wasn't initially.

Tommy Docherty took him out of the firing line at the end of November.

"I was looking at the pitch before Middlesbrough away when he said, 'Come here, son. I'm going to leave you out tonight. You've done well but you're still young and the pitches are getting heavy'. Alex Forsyth was put back in and I was fine with that."

In demonstration of Docherty's confidence in him, Nicholl was awarded a new contract, which took his weekly wage up to £45, plus a £20 per match appearance bonus. George Best had been United's top earner in 1974 on £175 a week, but his contract had been cancelled. That left Lou Macari, Willie Morgan and Martin Buchan as the top earners on £160 a week.

Life was good for Nicholl.

"I'd met Sue, a Stretford girl, in the Sands nightclub in Stretford. She was from a family of eight kids – seven boys and her. The brothers were all United mad. Still are. And Sue and I are still together."

Nicholl had gone to the Sands, in the less-than-glamorous environs of the car park at the Arndale shopping centre, with another reserve player, Peter Sutcliffe.

"No, not the Yorkshire Ripper," he confirms. "We went twice a week on a Saturday and Monday. Sutty was a dancer, I wasn't. We stood at the bar and saw a couple of birds. He wanted to ask them to dance. The song playing at the time was *Kung Fu Fighting* [by Carl Douglas]. Sutty started dancing by himself, kicking his legs in the air and all that. I didn't know whether to laugh or cry. I asked the girls if they wanted a drink."

Monday was a big night in the Sands for United players.

"We'd get a lock-in and Martin Buchan would get his guitar out. He was really good and played Elvis songs as we sang along. Tuesday was always tough in training, but we'd be playing golf at Davyhulme or the Mere by Wednesday afternoon."

Buchan was captain on and off the field.

"I got on really well with him. I respected him as club captain. He used to come to training dressed in a shirt and tie. He was always clean shaven and immaculate, like a Manchester United captain should be. He looked and acted like a captain. Some of the players used to wind him up – or try to. Maybe he did take some things to an extreme, throwing people out of the players' lounge if they didn't have a ticket for instance, but he was hands on in everything he did. I respected Martin as a footballer too, because he was one hell of a player."

Nicholl was great friends with three of the Dublin-born players in the squad. He'd promised wife Sue that he'd decorate the bedroom at their house in Davyhulme ahead of the impending arrival of the first of their three daughters. Then he went to training at The Cliff, where his Dubliner team-mates tried to persuade him to play golf that afternoon at Davyhulme, the club in west Manchester where the United team used to meet for their pre-match meal in 1960s and early Seventies. Nicholl declined, explaining that decorating came first.

Paddy Roche, Ashley Grimes and Kevin Moran hatched a plan to help the Ulsterman.

"Right," said Grimes in his Dublin accent. "We're all coming to help you wallpaper. One wall each. We'll do it in no time and then play golf."

The four of them agreed that this was a fine idea and were soon at the Nicholl residence on the opposite side of the M60 to where the Trafford Centre now stands.

"Ashley suggested we each pick a corner, and we were done in no time," recalls Nicholl. "And though the strips didn't quite match up, we went off to play golf happy with our work. In fact, we praised each other that three Dubliners and a Belfast Boy could co-operate so well."

After returning from work in nearby Trafford Park, Sue Nicholl didn't quite share the appreciation of their handiwork.

"It was Mr Men wallpaper. My wife correctly pointed out that some of their boots were upside down," says Nicholl. "And that there were gaps in the paper. She also suggested that it was as if four different people had done the job, such was the difference in style. Some of the paste had been laid on a bit thick, in other parts a bit sparse. The wallpaper was soon on the floor."

Nicholl was re-introduced to the United team at the start of the following season and was a virtual ever-present in the first team in 1976/77 and 1977/78.

"I have a lot to thank Tommy Docherty for," he says. "I've heard all the criticisms, but he was great for young players like me coming through. I used to love going up to the noticeboard at The Cliff to see the teams on a Friday. At 15 you expected to be in the B team, at 16 the A team. If you signed pro then you went into the reserve team at 17 and into the first team if you were a first teamer. What I loved about the Doc is that he was prepared to shake all that up. If you weren't playing well then you were dropped down, no matter how big your reputation was. Or, if you were young like me, he'd give you a chance. He gave youngsters a chance."

Nicholl's talents were appreciated by his team-mates.

"Jimmy offered solid support at full-back," said Lou Macari. "He did what all good defenders do – defend properly. He wasn't eye-catching in the way Tommy Gemmell was for Celtic or Patrice Evra for Manchester United, but when the chance came he would get forward and cross the ball. The Doc encouraged that."

Nicholl had an ungainly style. He ran like the back of a pantomime horse, but nobody was laughing when he scored one the best goals of his life in a 7-2 League Cup victory against Newcastle United at Old Trafford.

"One of the biggest disappointments of my life," says Nicholl. "My first United goal and it was an absolute screamer. I went back in the players' lounge where I spoke to Gordon Burns, the BBC presenter who also came from Northern Ireland. I told him that I couldn't wait to watch the goal on the highlights show the following night. He told me that the heavy rain had got into the camera and stopped it working – no footage existed."

Nicholl's first full season as a United regular would end on a happy note with FA Cup success.

"We beat Leeds in the semi-final at Hillsborough. They were a top side with players like Eddie Gray and Paul Madeley. Allan Clarke was the centre-forward who had all the tricks, a nasty player when he wanted to be. He once helped me up from a tackle by grabbing and twisting my armpits. It looked like he was helping me, but I felt like he was killing me and I started lashing out. So I was the one who looked in the wrong.

"That was a big game for us. Losing a semi-final is the worst thing in football, and I should know as I've lost a few. You don't get the trip to Wembley, so we were well up for it at Hillsborough."

Victory meant United were through to the FA Cup final against treble-chasing Liverpool.

"The focus was on me and Arthur [Albiston] because we were young full-backs. We were seen as the weak points of the United team who were already underdogs. I read that that Stevie Heighway was going to take advantage of me and thought, 'Come on then.' Such comments spurred me on. I respected that Liverpool team because they had everything. They were good passers and had an aggressive streak. Souness was clever, but nasty, so was Terry McDermott. They proved their quality by winning a number of trophies that we could only dream of at United, and Liverpool had depth too. They won the reserve league almost every year.

"*Match of the Day* came to the hotel before the game. All my mates were watching on TV. We had a great night after celebrating, but then it turned out to be the night that the Doc told the chairman that he was seeing the physio's wife."

Nicholl was stunned when he found out.

"None of us knew that the Doc was having an affair with Mary Brown. Was it right for him to be sacked? In those days it was morally right for him to be sacked. The mindset has changed. I was sad to see the Doc go. I enjoyed playing for him. I had a cup-winners' medal in my pocket and I was earning £150 a week [the average wage in 1977 was £68]. Suddenly I was worried about the future and life under a new manager."

Dave Sexton was appointed that summer.

"A lovely man who was the opposite of the Doc," says Nicholl. "Everything about him couldn't have been more different to the Doc. Training and tactics, the atmosphere, it all changed. Dave had us thinking about tactics a lot more. The pre-match warm-up for me was usually a stretch and a kickabout. Dave wanted me to sit in the dressing room and envisage the game ahead, my opponent and likely scenarios. He wanted me to imagine myself running down the wing, talking and scoring. I'd try and do that and Dave would come over and ask, 'How are you going on?' I'd tell him that I'd just crossed a couple of balls and that the 'keeper caught one while the other went over the bar. 'I'm having a bit of a 'mare in fact,' I'd reply.

"Dave probably felt that I needed that, but I didn't."

Nicholl didn't feel that Sexton was totally convinced by his talents.

"Although I played most games, he'd try Brian Greenhoff at right-back now and then. I felt that I had to prove myself all over again, which is not a bad thing, but I liked to be loved."

The cup win meant United were back in Europe the following season.

"We played at Saint Etienne and there was trouble in the ground. There was trouble in the guts of the Greenhoff brothers too. They went out after the game. They thought they were being all cosmopolitan by eating French food. They tried snails and all that. They were both sick the next day and were never out of the toilet."

Porto were United's next opponents.

"They hammered us 4-0 in Portugal," recalls Nicholl. "Most English teams played 4-4-2, but Porto were so superior to us. Their players kept switching positions and pulling us everywhere. I wanted to say to the lad I was marking, 'Don't go there, I'm not allowed to go there'."

United did better back at Old Trafford.

"I scored from distance just before half-time to make it 2-0. We went 3-0 up and the roar was incredible. The atmosphere was always best on European nights. It was 3-1 and then 4-1. We thought we had a chance, then big Alex Stepney misjudged a ball and it went in 4-2. We were running out of time. We won 5-2, an epic match but it was not enough to go through."

There was more heartache a season later when United were defeated in the 1979 FA Cup final by Arsenal.

"That was my lowest point in football," he recalls. "They called it the eight-minute cup final because all the drama came at the end."

Arsenal had surged into a 2-0 lead thanks to first-half goals from Brian Talbot and Frank Stapleton. Gordon McQueen netted for United in the 86th minute then Sammy McIlroy levelled the scores two minutes later.

"I was so pumped up that I charged forward from right-back

because I thought we'd get a winner. But I should have kept my position. Had I kept my position, I don't think they would have been able to cross for Alan Sunderland to get the winner in the last minute. I only have myself to blame. The final whistle went and I was stood next to Liam Brady. We swapped shirts and he said, 'You would have won that in extra-time.' I got a message asking if I wanted to sell it back to him last year. Sell it? Surely the message should have been, 'Do you want to swap it back?' Where's my shirt?"

That would be the last time Nicholl came close to another trophy at United.

"Dave Sexton offered me a very good three-year contract which would have meant that I would get a testimonial. Then he got the sack and was replaced by big Ron Atkinson. I went to see Les Olive to ask him what was happening. He told me to go and see the manager in his office around the corner. I told Big Ron about the three-year contract and the testimonial. He said, 'I know all about it, I've put the block on it'. I asked him why. He told me that I wasn't fast enough. I told him that I needed to give myself a couple of yards against Tony Morley of Aston Villa, but other than that I was okay. He wasn't having it. He then told me that I couldn't head the ball, tackle or defend properly. He also said he was going to swap Mickey Thomas for John Gidman.

"'That's it then, put me on the transfer list,' I said. My head was spinning, I'd only been in his office two minutes.

"'No, no, no,' said Ron.

"'Why?' I said. 'You don't rate me. You don't even think I can play.'

"'I've seen you play sweeper,' added Ron. 'I think there's a chance you can play sweeper. There's five games pre-season. You will play two, Buchan will play two. If you do what you are capable of doing, you'll start as sweeper in the fifth.'

"'Can I tell you something,' I said. 'I admired your honesty five minutes ago. But how can you play me as sweeper if I'm slow, can't head or tackle? I've weighed you up in five minutes. Get me out of here.'"

Nicholl's last performance for United was as a substitute for Buchan in a 3-1 defeat at Tottenham in November 1981 before he went on loan to Sunderland.

"I loved it at Roker Park because I was playing, but the loan only last two or three months. Sunderland wanted to sign me, but United wanted £250,000 which they didn't have. I had to go back to Old Trafford and train with the kids."

Salvation came because of Nicholl's birthplace.

"Toronto Blizzard paid the £250,000," he explains. "They played in the NASL and were only allowed four foreign players. I was classed as Canadian because I'd been born in Hamilton."

Nicholl's career was far from dead. A 73-cap Northern Ireland international who'd won his first cap in 1976, he was integral to his country's plans for the 1982 World Cup finals. His spell in Toronto gave him much-needed match practice.

"I'd played under the great Danny Blanchflower who was Northern Ireland manager for a while. He was very relaxed, and there was a brilliant atmosphere, but things really started to change when Billy Bingham took over from him. He was a disciplinarian. No drinking was allowed, and there was an 11 o'clock curfew. We used to order pints of blackcurrant and lemonade instead of Guinness. We were confused by it all at first but, boy, was he effective. Billy got Northern Ireland, a country of just 1.5 million, to two consecutive World Cup finals. He was very astute tactically. He'd study opponents like Bulgaria, and we wondered how he'd done it.

"Beating Spain in Valencia was the highlight – probably of my whole career. When you play for United or Glasgow Rangers, as I did later, you get used to winning matches. That's not the case with Northern Ireland. Even George Best couldn't help Northern Ireland qualify, so to reach the World Cup finals was a huge deal. To beat the hosts in their own country was the greatest result in the history of Northern Irish football, but that was Billy showing what you can achieve if you put your mind to it."

Gerry Armstrong scored in the 47th minute.

"Apart from our couple of thousand fans going deranged in the corner, Gerry thought the goal had been disallowed because there was a silence in the rest of the stadium," recalled Norman Whiteside. "Then he heard me yelling, 'Gerry, Gerry, it's a goal' as I jumped on his back.

"If the match up to then had been the most physically and mentally demanding of my career, the remaining 43 minutes were more like the Alamo than a game of football."

Nicholl agrees.

"We were down to ten men after [future Red] Mal Donaghy was sent off with over half an hour to play. We hadn't expected to win. We didn't even have a hotel booked because we thought we were going home."

Not that the victorious players were thinking about sleep.

"Gerry Armstrong had some Spanish friends over from Mallorca, where he'd played. They told him that they were disappointed that Spain had been beaten, but insisted on a night out. The whole team went to a club where they put our names on whatever bottles we were drinking from. So the words 'Pat Jennings' were on a bottle of red wine for example. Loads of names were spelt wrong, which added to the fun. We went to the same club three nights on the trot before flying to Madrid for the next game."

Nicholl remembers fellow Belfast Protestant Norman Whiteside joining United.

"He was a man at 14," he says. "I remember him moving into digs with his shaven head and Doc Marten boots. A few years later, just a few weeks after he'd made his United debut at Brighton, we went back to Brighton to prepare for the World Cup. We trained at the University of Sussex for ten days. Big Norm was just 16, but I remember Pat Jennings saying to Billy Bingham, 'I don't know who your two forwards are [Northern Ireland were using Bryan Hamilton and Gerry Armstrong], but I'm telling you that the best finisher is the boy Whiteside. With the others I've got time to set myself up, with the young boy the ball has already passed me.'

Bingham later told Whiteside that a goal he'd scored – similar to the one which won the FA Cup for United in 1985 – in those sessions convinced him that he was good enough to be picked as the youngest ever player to start in the World Cup finals a few weeks later."

After the World Cup, Nicholl spent the next three years playing for Toronto in the summer and Sunderland and then Glasgow Rangers in the regular football season.

"Man United, Northern Ireland and Rangers," he says. "That was my dream complete. I had three enjoyable years at Ibrox. Rangers is like United in that you are expected to win every game. You have that intensity at the biggest clubs. I then had a spell at Dunfermline before moving to be player-manager of Raith Rovers in 1990."

Nicholl was a success at Raith, the Kirkcaldy club where he stayed for six years.

"I loved it there. We won the League Cup, reached the Scottish Premier Division and played European football. I played my last game when I was 39 in 1993. We'd already beaten Celtic in the cup that year and our last game was at Partick Thistle, where Hamilton were ground sharing. We got a point there to win the league and go up to the Premier League. It was a great moment for a small club, and I thought it was the perfect time to call it a day."

Raith's players had switched from part-time to full-time in the summer of 1991, with Nicholl in charge.

"I told the players that I wanted them to enjoy their time at the club as much as I'd enjoyed the best time of my career, playing under Tommy Docherty at Old Trafford. Some of my happiest years were at Raith because we had a similar spirit to that which we'd had at United. We had a young team and I didn't overcomplicate things, but told the lads to go out and enjoy themselves. I'd seen how such words of encouragement could lift young players."

Scotland's football writers voted Nicholl their Manager of the Year in 1994/95 and Millwall were sufficiently impressed to offer him the manager's job in 1996.

"That was a disaster," says Nicholl ruefully. "They were in all kinds of financial problems, but I didn't look into that, I just signed."

Nicholl lasted a season and could not prevent Millwall from being relegated to England's third tier. Bizarrely, he then played one game for Bath City in 1997, a game in which he was sent off, and he never returned to Twerton Park.

Nicholl did return to Raith for a second, less-successful spell, then went to Dunfermline as assistant to Jimmy Calderwood. The two Jimmys moved to Aberdeen in 2004, and the management pair spent five years at Pittodrie.

"We took Aberdeen into Europe twice before we were sacked in 2009. I then went Kilmarnock for six months before becoming manager of Cowdenbeath."

The Blue Brazil, who hail from a Fife town of just 11,000, had reached the heights of the Scottish First Division. They have to share their Central Park stadium with stock car racing.

"I went for the interview at eight in the morning. At nine I got a call from the chairman saying: 'Congratulations. The bad news is that you are now the manager of Cowdenbeath.'

"It doesn't matter if there's 1,500 people watching matches like we get at Cowdenbeath or 75,000 at Old Trafford, the game is just as important to those fans. My only ambition is to be successful at the club I'm at." But he couldn't prevent them going straight back down.

In the summer of 2011 Nicholl became assistant manager of Kilmarnock, and his life in football continues.

"I've worked hard but I've been fortunate too," he says. "Which is lucky, as I wasn't cut out to be a painter and decorator."

11

TOMMY DOCHERTY
THE DOC

"I'm travelling up the Amazon for the next month," explains Tommy Docherty on the telephone, "so I won't be able to do the interview until after. Come over and see me when I get back. Get the train to Marple and I'll pick you up at the station. I'll be waiting in the car park in a silver Mercedes."

Docherty is 83 and shows little sign of slowing down. His mind is as a sharp as the suits he once wore, his laugh as infectious as the football his teams played. The journey up the Amazon was on a cruise, and seeing the world by ship is something he and his partner of 35 years, Mary Brown, enjoy. They've made several voyages in recent years, with Docherty's passage paid for by a series of after-dinner speeches to fellow passengers.

"It's not work," he says, "just chatting about football. It's great." On dry land he's still a regular on the after-dinner circuit and delivers man-management speeches for companies.

Four months later, in April 2011 I make a 20-minute rail journey south east from Manchester Piccadilly to Marple in the foothills of the Pennines. Docherty is waiting for the train, standing by his Merc in his slippers, smiling. He is in fine fettle.

Docherty drives the short distance along undulating roads to his house in Compstall, an attractive commuter village, as the conversation swings from his trip up the Panama Canal, Acapulco and the Amazon to "the disgrace of testimonials for multi-million-aire modern-day players". His beautiful home is within view of a village pub ("I haven't been in there for ten years"), a mill pond and a country park. The house backs directly on to fields. He often stands at the bottom of his garden watching the birds and other wildlife.

Mary busies herself in the garden, hiding Easter eggs for the couple's grandchildren while her husband talks. She pops in at regular intervals with tea, biscuits and the type of sandwich Michael Winner would describe as 'beyond historic'. Children and grandchildren come and go. It is domestic bliss encapsulated.

"I had never heard of Manchester United as a kid," says Docherty as he sits down in his favourite chair. "I was just Celtic mad, it was a religious thing in Glasgow. If you were Protestant you were Rangers, if you were Catholic you were a Tim. Celtic Park was only a mile from where I lived, and I'd walk there when they were playing. They would open the gates 20 minutes before the end if they were winning and I'd get in and see the end of the game. Celtic had a very good team in the late Thirties. The first time I paid any attention to Man United was when Jimmy Delaney, who was one of my heroes at Celtic, moved there in 1946."

"Then I started to pay United a lot more attention, not just because of Delaney but because of the man who took him there, Matt Busby."

Docherty, raised in a tenement in Glasgow's Gorbals, is unsentimental about the abject poverty that his family, like many of the area's inhabitants, suffered. When his father died when he was nine, his mother five months pregnant, Docherty had to grow up quickly, leaving school at 14 and delivering bread from a van while playing for Shettlestone Juniors for a pound a week part-time. Junior football was a big deal in Scotland, with the best teams paying their players and the leagues being seen as breeding grounds for future footballing talent. Crowds could rise into five figures. When Docherty was offered £3 to sign for Shettleston and a wage of a pound a week to play part-time, it was like a dream come true.

"I combined football with delivering bread until 1946 when I was called up for national service," he explains. The experience was, he believes, highly beneficial, teaching him self-discipline and responsibility. "The Second World War had finished but I joined the Highland Light Infantry. I could usually get back to Glasgow to play at the weekend, until I was sent to serve in Palestine."

On 26th July 1946, Docherty was on guard by the King David Hotel in Jerusalem, the temporary headquarters for the British Army administration, when it was blown up, killing 91, among them some of his friends.

"Believe me, when you've witnessed what I saw that day," he later wrote, "nothing the game of football can throw at you will upset you."

On the journey back to Glasgow, once his stint in the army had finished in 1948, he decided to write to a number of clubs and ask them for a trial. He didn't need to. Scouts had been tipped off about Docherty's return by an army colleague, and they were waiting for him at the family home in Glasgow. He signed for Celtic part-time, but left for Preston North End in November 1949 because he wasn't getting first-team football at his boyhood club.

He would spend nine years at Deepdale and play over 300 times for one of the best teams in England.

"Tom Finney was the star," he says. "And we had a great rivalry with Blackpool, who had the two Stans – Matthews and Mortensen."

"My first visit to Old Trafford was playing for Preston North End in the early 1950s. We got beat 5-0 at home in 1952/53 and 5-2 away. That may not surprise people, but it should. Preston only lost the league title to Arsenal on goal difference that season, while United finished eighth. If we hadn't conceded ten to United then we would have won the league."

Docherty remembers playing against the Babes.

"The Busby Babes were tremendous," he says. "Awesome. We lost the FA Cup final to West Brom in 1954 and were heartbroken. So I know how Duncan Edwards felt when United lost the 1957 final to Aston Villa. Like me, Edwards felt guilty about returning without the cup when the supporters had been so good to him and his team-mates. Duncan said, 'All the players have vowed to win the cup next year for those supporters. That is what glory is all about.' Tragically, Munich intervened."

United tried to sign Docherty after Munich.

"14th August 1958," says Docherty, remembering the day that he heard from Jimmy Murphy that United wanted him. "Preston wouldn't sell me," he says.

Docherty finally left Preston to join Arsenal in a £28,000 deal. He would be a replacement for Joe Mercer, and he spent three years there between 1958 and 1961. While at Arsenal he was recalled for his country by new Scotland boss Matt Busby and the selectors.

"I loved my time at Highbury and, while we didn't win the league, we had one of the top teams in the country. Towards the end of my time there I took a coaching course at Lilleshall. My fellow students included Bob Paisley, Malcolm Allison, Billy Bingham, Peter Taylor, Dave Sexton, Frank O'Farrell, Tony Barton and Malcolm Musgrove."

All were to play a key role in the development of English football in the Sixties and Seventies.

In February 1961, Docherty was offered the post of player-coach at Chelsea. Less than 12 months later he took over as manager following Ted Drake's departure. Chelsea were relegated in 1961/62, but Docherty was seen as a great motivator with a fine eye for talent.

"I put together a team of players which the press called Doc's Dynamos," he says. That team included players like Terry Venables, Peter Bonetti and Alex Stepney. Docherty built a brilliant Chelsea team in the mid-Sixties. His assistant was Dave Sexton. Some of those leading lights would cause him problems, though, and he ended up walking out after a dispute with senior players led by Terry Venables and George Graham. The dispute arose when, with Chelsea going for the title, Doc sent several players home after they broke a curfew before a key game against Burnley when the team were staying in Blackpool.

"One of my faults is that I have always been quite impatient," he says. "If I got the sack I wouldn't hang around for a good job, I would take the next one that became available, which was wrong.

"That impatience saw me send some players home from Blackpool, but I was a young manager, not an experienced one."

Docherty came close to winning trophies at Stamford Bridge before later he resigned in 1967. "The writing was on the wall after slipping into the bottom half of the table," he recalls. Docherty moved to Rotherham United the following month. "Chelsea to Rotherham may seem strange, but I'm impulsive . . ."

As the famous Docherty quip goes: "I was under instruction to get them out of Division Two," he states. "I did – to Division Three."

Docherty rowed with the board and left the following year. He then became manager of QPR in 1968, but lasted just 29 days. He then travelled north to the Midlands.

Aston Villa were struggling in Division Two when Docherty took over. He was the first appointment of their new chairman Doug Ellis.

"I know he has a bad reputation now, but he had a great sense of honour," recalls Docherty. "I initially enjoyed his support and began revitalising the club, but when results turned the board panicked and fired me." He lasted 13 months.

"My next job was as manager of FC Porto in Portugal," he smiles before reeling off a sentence in passable Portuguese.

"I fancied managing a big foreign club, and the 18-month contract sounded perfect. But while Porto had a big stadium which could hold 80,000, crowds were down to 20,000. They were 14th in the league when I arrived and I got them up to sixth. I spent the following year at the club, enjoyed my time and guided Porto to third in the league and a UEFA Cup spot, but I missed managing in England and we came to an agreement that I would finish at the end of the 1970/71 season."

Docherty returned to England hopeful of work. Once again he acted on impulse and was already joking that he had had more clubs than Jack Nicklaus.

"Terry Neill offered me a job as his assistant at Hull City, so I took it," he says. "I was only there a few months before I was offered the Scotland job on a caretaker basis."

That soon became permanent.

"I had a great time at Scotland," he recalls. "People weren't convinced about me because I'd been at so many clubs," he says. "And the offer to manage Scotland rejuvenated me. It was a huge boost to my morale."

With Scotland Docherty worked with several players who played for Manchester United.

"Martin Buchan, Willie Morgan and Denis Law," he says.

Those influential players would speak highly of him when poor results and a divided dressing room undermined Frank O'Farrell's position at Old Trafford in 1972.

"The [Old Trafford] dressing room was now so riven with splits it resembled the plotline of a sitcom," wrote Jim White in his 2008 biography of Manchester United. "Martin hated Willie, Willie mocked Bobby, Bobby was sunk in depression and everyone had had enough of George. It was the manager's fault, Busby reasoned, and he had to be let go. Not to interfere would be to commit the sin of omission."

Docherty was at Selhurst Park to see United destroyed 5-0 by Crystal Palace in December 1972.

"I was there to watch a Scottish player, Tony Taylor," he says. "But I swear on my daughter's life that I'd not been approached by anyone at United. Frank O'Farrell was a godfather to one of my boys as we'd played together for eight years.

"Tony couldn't really prove his worth in the match because he had little defending to do. United were awful. I went into the boardroom after the game and Matt Busby called me over," recalls Docherty. "He asked me what I thought and I replied honestly, 'Not good.' I also asked him where Denis Law was. Matt told me that he had been in the dressing room. He was supposed to have been on the bench, but Denis hated watching football and had been sitting inside."

Busby had something else to say.

"Do you fancy the job?" he asked Docherty.

"You've got a manager," replied a stunned Docherty.

"Not for long," replied Busby. "And Willie, Denis and Martin always rave about you."

"Then I'd be interested," replied Docherty.

"What do we do if we want to take it any further?" said Busby. Docherty told him that he needed to contact his employers at the Scottish FA.

"I told Frank that I had been offered his job that day at Selhurst Park," says Docherty. "He knew he was going and told me that if I didn't take it then somebody else would. That's football."

United's chairman Louis Edwards duly asked for permission to speak to Docherty. It was reluctantly granted.

"Frank was sacked on the Wednesday night, and I flew from Glasgow to Mottram Hall on the Friday to meet the board."

United offered Docherty £15,000 a year, twice what he was on as Scotland boss. "United were never great payers, but I was happy to sign straight away. I still doubled my wages. More importantly, I was back involved with football on a day-to-day basis at a huge club."

The *People* newspaper also agreed to pay him a further £15,000 for a weekly column.

"All I had to do for that was go for lunch and a glass of wine with a journalist every Friday," he smiles. "United benefited because I said nice things about them.

Docherty also got an agreement that he could bring in Tommy Cavanagh as a coach.

"The board weren't too keen because they'd heard that he was violent with players, but I insisted, and he was the only member of staff I brought in with me."

Docherty got straight to work.

"The club was in turmoil," he says. "I'd inherited the remnants of the '68 European Cup-winning team. Many had been great players, but they were past their sell-by date. Frank O'Farrell had tried to move some of them on, but he'd met fierce resistance from within the club and hadn't been able to do it."

Docherty's first game was at home to Leeds United on 23rd December 1972. United drew 1-1 thanks to a rare goal from Ted MacDougall. Underlining how poor the side was, United would lose their following three games. The starting XI for Docherty's first match was Stepney, O'Neil, Dunne, Young, Sadler, Buchan, Morgan, Charlton, Davies, Storey-Moore and MacDougall. Brian Kidd was substitute.

"I never fancied Ted MacDougall," says Docherty about the line-up. "He and Phil Boyer were great together at Norwich, but Boyer was the player. Ted trapped the ball further than I could kick it.

"After a while, I let Brian Kidd go too," he says. "Nice lad, great pro. But I just felt that I had to move one or two of them on to get some money in and buy the players I wanted."

Docherty wasted no time in bringing in fresh blood – all of them Scots he had worked with for the national team, or whose potential he had spotted in the under-23s. Within a month George Graham, Alex Forsyth, Lou Macari and Jim Holton arrived and were pitched into a full-on relegation struggle.

"I paid £120,000 for George Graham from Arsenal and £100,000 for the Partick Thistle full-back Alex Forsyth. I spent a lot of time travelling up and down the country, calling from hotels and public phone boxes. Jim Holton came from Shrewsbury. He could win the ball in the air or on the ground, but he couldn't pass it to anyone."

Docherty recruited Jimmy Curran to work with the youngsters and appointed one-time 'keeper Gordon Clayton, former United legend Johnny Carey and Norman Scholes as scouts. Jimmy Murphy, once Matt Busby's faithful lieutenant, and Jack Crompton, United's ex-goalkeeper, who were both floating around the club without specific tasks, were re-engaged to help with training and give youngsters the benefit of their vast experience.

"Murphy was like a God," says Docherty, "and he knew exactly what he was doing. I signed Steve Coppell without every having seen him play. Jimmy Murphy had seen him twice. He called me and said, 'Tom, sign him.' It was normal for scouts to send a report in, but Jimmy told me that if he had to write a report on Coppell, another club would sign him in the meantime. I signed him."

MacDougall was sold on to West Ham for £150,000, but the early signs of the Doc's regime were not always encouraging.

"Bobby Charlton spoke to me in February 1973 and told me that he was going to retire at the end of the season. That did me a big favour," says Docherty. Charlton played his 759th and final United game at Stamford Bridge in April 1973. He was generously applauded by Chelsea fans – as was Docherty at the club he had previously managed. The United manager had kept the team up after inheriting a mess.

Of the 21 games in his first season, United won seven, drew seven and lost seven. The Reds had won five from their first 22 games that season before Docherty arrived, and for the first time in a long time the word "relegation" began to be uttered at United. They finished 18th, five points clear of the drop, but Docherty still feared for his job.

"I felt that I would have got the sack had we gone down," he says. "Even though I'd only been at the club a few months, there was a lot of friction because I wanted to do things my way. I could feel the negative vibes.

"Your biggest enemy as a manager is an old pro in the dressing room, poisoning the young minds, spreading the gospel – the wrong gospel I might add. The best thing is to get them on their bikes as quickly as possible."

Docherty wasn't convinced by the club's senior management, either.

"Matt wasn't the type of person you could go to for advice," he says. "He was happy sitting in his office running the club. If he wanted a player then he could buy one because he was carrying the cheque book. If I wanted one then he would talk to the chairman on my behalf, who would hang off his every word. Louis was surrounded by nice, but weak people. One or two of the directors didn't have a clue about football. One of the went into the home dressing room at Stoke City and said, 'Good luck, lads'. He thought that Stoke were United because they were wearing red. We were actually in the away dressing room wearing yellow."

Docherty did get on well with his chairman, though.

"I liked Louis. He was a great socialiser who loved his food and wine, but he didn't know a centre-half from a semi-final," he says. "He was a great chairman for any United manager because he just let you get on with it."

The departure of Denis Law, the original King of the Stretford End, would caused much consternation in the summer 1973.

"I'd been big pals with Denis because we played for Scotland together but our physio, Laurie Brown, told me that he was always injured," explains Docherty. "The Denis I had inherited at Old Trafford was not the great, great player I'd known with Scotland. I don't think he was committed."

O'Farrell had been of a similar opinion and Law made just 12 starts in 1972/73.

"At 33, he should have had another season in him at Old

Trafford, but he was going through the motions in games. There was no room for sentiment. I knew that I would receive a mountain of criticism, but Denis had to go."

Busby disagreed and told Docherty that Law had at least one more season left. Docherty was the manager, though, and called Law into his office and told him that he was giving him a free transfer.

"He was understandably far from happy. He had a year left on his contract and didn't agree with my assessment of him as a player. The atmosphere was very strained between us, but there was no animosity. The directors were good to him too – paying him £5,000 tax free for the remainder of the season and granting him a testimonial match."

Docherty had no compunction in releasing 13 players in the summer of '73, including other big European Cup-winning names like David Sadler and Tony Dunne. It was around this time that George Best returned from a sabbatical in Spain and announced that he would only play for Northern Ireland, not United. Docherty was asked for his opinion by the author.

"I believe George was hoping to come back to United, but after his previous shenanigans I wasn't going to jump to his call. We resolved the issue in the end, and he played a dozen times for me the following season but he had gone. He could still beat people, but he'd lost his zip to get away from them."

Docherty appointed men from within the club to run United's youth team, Bill Foulkes and Paddy Crerand.

"One worked out, one didn't," he sighs.

United were relegated the following season, 1973/74. Best played his final United game in a 3-0 defeat at QPR on New Year's Day 1974.

"We were shocking and George seemed uninterested. I gave the players the following day off and told them to report back on 3rd January. George didn't come, but later told me he'd had a stomach bug. We were playing Plymouth the following Saturday and I included him in the squad. We met at noon, but there was no sign of him by 2.15pm. There was a knock on the changing room door and Tommy Cav told me that the 'Quiet Boy' [Cav and the Doc's nickname for Best] was there.

I went to see George, and he was drunk. He had a girl with him, and she was stunning, with film star looks. George told me that he wanted to play. I told him that he should be breathalysed and that we'd speak the following week. He never showed up then either. The board agreed to suspend him for two weeks and put him on the transfer list. The day before his suspension was up, he announced that he was retiring from football.

"I'd given up on him. It wasn't fair on the other players either because he didn't want to train. George had been the finished article at 23. He was a smashing lad: witty, honest, warm and modest. He was probably badly handled earlier in his career."

Rock bottom in March 1974, United rallied in April. Four wins and a draw pulled Birmingham City and Southampton within catching distance. One reason was the arrival of yet another new Scot, midfielder Jim McCalliog, who was signed from Wolves for £60,000 on deadline day.

"He was a typical dour Scot who wanted to be playing all the time," recalls Doc. "He didn't like it when he was dropped or when Cav told him off." But after a promising start, McCalliog's face didn't fit, and in the end he started just 37 games for United.

Despite a rally in April, the Reds were unable to cheer their fans at the time when they most needed it as the whole population had been forced to work a three-day week to conserve energy supplies.

"Everyone talks about the game in which Denis Law sent United down," says Docherty, "except he didn't. It was dramatic though, a former United hero scoring a backheel for City which many inside the ground thought would relegate us. Denis refused to celebrate his goal against the club he had served so admirably."

United fans ran onto the pitch after Law's goal.

"People called those people fans, but to me they were criminals, hooligans," says Docherty. "They were in a minority, but they encouraged the weak and gullible to fall into line with their antics. Matt Busby made an emotional appeal for the fans on the Old Trafford pitch after the Law goal to go back into the stands. He was wasting his time. They were not lovers of the club or the game."

Docherty makes a distinction between those fans who ran on the pitch and others who followed United around the country.

"I had a great affinity with the true fans," he said. "So did Cav – he'd really get them going. People said they were hooligans, but the media exaggerated a lot of the scuffles. I never felt threatened and welcomed the support which travelled around the country in great numbers.

"There were times when people who latched onto United caused trouble and I had several meetings with supporters. The fans I met were always genuine United followers who were as frustrated with the trouble as the authorities. They didn't know who a lot of the troublemakers were.

"I sat at home the night we were relegated with no enthusiasm for anything," he says. "I felt like an empty shell. Once again, I expected the sack, even though I'd brought a lot of exciting players in like Lou Macari, who came for a huge £200,000 fee and took a little time to settle, and Jim Holton. Some, like George Graham, didn't work out. He wasn't the player I'd managed for Scotland, and maybe the Old Trafford stage was too big for him."

Chairman Louis Edwards and Matt Busby asked to see Docherty following relegation.

"They made it very clear that they didn't like the situation we were in, but also that I had the unanimous support of the board. Matt reminded me that when he first spoke to me about the United job, he'd described the task as like turning an oil tanker around. With that he gave me a case of champagne and, even though I wasn't a drinker, I considered it a marvellous gesture for which I showed real gratitude. Frank O'Farrell also called that weekend to offer his condolences and wish me well for the future. He'd been Cardiff manager for a season but explained that he'd resigned and taken up a new job where he could get on with things in peace, where there was no turmoil or animosity. I asked him where. 'Iran' was the reply."

Docherty's relationship with Busby was initially good.

"I know that Frank felt Matt had interfered in his job," says Docherty. "He didn't interfere with me, but there were a couple of incidents. Before one game, Louis Edwards invited me for a drink with him and the players in his hotel room. It was a one off as I didn't like to socialise with the players. Matt heard of this and asked if I thought it was a good idea to mix with the players. I pointed out that he was playing golf with several of them the next day, but he didn't like it. I felt that he wanted to keep me away from what I called 'The Junior Board'."

Docherty explains.

"We went out for dinner a few times with Matt and Lady Jean, God rest their souls. Matt would go onto the Cromford Club afterwards. I went once or twice. Denis Law, Willie Morgan and Paddy Crerand would turn up with their wives. It wasn't for me, though, and I told Matt that I shouldn't be mixing with players, especially ones I knew I would have to get rid of.

"When results were going well for me, I don't think Matt liked it," says Docherty. "Tommy Cav would say: 'We're winning, we're beating them'." 'Them' would be players considered legends by most United fans.

"I told him that we could never beat them, but that we could only be winning against them," adds Docherty.

Busby suggested that Paddy Crerand was made assistant manager. "I allowed myself to be swayed by Matt," explains Docherty. "But it was a disaster. Paddy wanted to be pally with all the players. I also knew that anything I told him would get straight back to Matt, who he played golf with. I had issues with his timekeeping and organisation too."

Docherty's solution was to send Crerand scouting.

"I found out that he would leave games at half-time so that he could get back to the social whirl of Manchester with the powers that be."

Docherty felt that he never fitted in with 'The Junior Board.'

"The bigger the club, the bigger the politics," he says. "United was riddled with political subterfuge. You get people at every club, businessmen in their 30s or 40s who are not quite rich enough to buy a club so they buy tickets in the posh seats which afford them 'vice president' status. They were allowed to enter the players' lounge and believe they have the ear of the hierarchy because they come into contact with them. They were always a problem to me, as they often preached an 'anti-Doc' agenda and undermined my position."

But the press men couldn't get enough of the Doc.

"I'd give them what they wanted. I told them that they could quote me on whatever they liked. And I liked a lot of them personally."

Docherty admits that he used the media to his own advantage.

"If I wanted to sell a player then I would leak it to the press guys who would play the game with me."

United started the 1974/75 season in the Second Division. The line up on the opening day at Orient was: Stepney, Forsyth, Houston, B Greenhoff, Buchan, Morgan, Macari, Pearson, McCalliog, Daly.

"We would take thousands of fans wherever we went, and not everybody liked it. We played at Hillsborough and drew 4-4. A steward approached Cav at the end of the game and said, 'Get back over the hills and take your crowd of hooligans with you.' Cav replied, 'We will, and you'll be back to 15,000 next week.' The gate that day had been 35,000.

"Buchan was my captain, my Rolls-Royce. He had everything. He was quick and yet you sensed he always had another gear. He was good in the air for his size, a great tackler and great marker. He wasn't a tremendous distributor of the ball, but he kept it nice and simple. If I wanted to make a change to the tactics I would get him to the touchline and we'd make the switch. He was a perfect captain on and off the park, but he was his own man. If you said 'black' he would say 'blue.'

"I used to laugh watching him and Macari because they were so different and yet good friends. If it rained when we were on the team bus, Macari would take bets on which raindrop would reach the bottom on the window first."

Stuart Pearson had signed ahead of the Second Division season.

"Good centre-forward who I knew well from Hull. Hard, but you could never ask him how he was doing because he was a hypochondriac," smiles his former manager.

Stewart Houston was another who had played for Docherty at one of his many former clubs.

"I signed him when he was 15 for Chelsea. Quick, great in the air. Shame he missed the '77 FA Cup final, but I had no qualms about bringing Chips [Arthur Albiston] in. Arthur was a solid pro with a good engine, ultra reliable and never gave me a minute's trouble."

Alex Forsyth was another good signing in Docherty's estimation. "A gambling man. Loved the dogs. Spoke with a Glasgow accent so strong that neither Lou Macari nor I could understand him, but he was consistently good at full-back.

"I never came across a player so particular about his pre-match preparation as Alex. Everything had to be perfect, from the tie-ups around the top of his socks to the way his shirt was tucked into his shorts. He would rub Vaseline on his heels to stop chafing and apply Vicks Vapor Rub to his shirt so that he could inhale it during a game."

That wasn't all.

"He would smother his legs in rub or liniment and place sticky plasters on his shin guards. On Fridays I would tell players what time to report for home games the following day. Often I would say, 'Twelve-thirty, except you Alex, you'd better get here around half-eight in the morning.'

"Brian Greenhoff was a big lad but as soft as putty. He once got knocked out at Anfield. Laurie Brown told me that Brian was concussed and didn't know who he was. I told Laurie to tell him that he was George Best and throw him back on."

TOMMY DOCHERTY

1974/75 would be Willie Morgan's last season for United. Britain's one-time record signing when he was bought by Busby for £117,000 in 1968 had been a terrace favourite who had initially got on well with Docherty, who had selected him for Scotland.

"I played a part in him getting the job," Morgan attests. "I'd been on tour with the Doc when he was Scotland manager, and when Matt asked what I thought of him I said, 'Great'. Matt asked for his phone number, and the Doc became manager. If you met the Doc for the first time he was funny, but obviously there was more to him, a side I didn't like."

Docherty appointed Morgan captain, even describing him as the best winger in the world, but an eye injury and the arrival of Steve Coppell limited his appearances that season. The Docherty *bonhomie* stopped, and the bitterness – which ended up in court when Morgan sued Docherty for libel, and won! – started. One minute Morgan was offered a six-year contract with a testimonial, the next he was sold to Burnley for £30,000, nothing like his true worth.

"I should never have left United," he rues, ". . . should have waited until the Doc had got the sack, but I didn't have much choice."

Morgan's departure meant that only Stepney, Buchan and McIlroy remained of the squad Docherty had inherited from O'Farrell. He had completely transformed the side in little over two years. He explains why McIlroy survived the cull.

"Sammy was a great pro and a terrific player. He was good in the air, could pass and never stopped running."

United returned to the First Division as Second Division champions. Three resounding wins from the first three games saw the *Manchester Evening News* write, "The Glory days are back at Old Trafford once again, with all the glamour and excitement that the world associates with Manchester United."

"I tried to urge caution," states Docherty, "but I honestly thought that we could win the league at the first attempt. But our attacking style of play meant we would concede goals. To be honest I wasn't that bothered if we conceded two so long as we scored three."

Docherty's philosophy was simple: attack.

"It was important that the fans were entertained. I did that at Chelsea when the media labelled my team 'Doc's Dynamos' and I'd played in a side with two wingers at Preston. Entertainment was a priority. I watch the current Barcelona side and they remind me a little of my United side because when they lose the ball they try and get it back as quickly as possible. I loved watching us play and bought players like Coppell and Hill to fit in with our system, which was considered to be 4-4-2 but was more often 4-2-4. All our midfielders were creative players rather than ball winners. We were like Brazil."

One key addition arrived that autumn, Gordon Hill.

"I needed to find a left winger to complement Steve Coppell on the right. Willie had gone and Gordon fitted perfectly for us."

"When we lost the ball the two wingers tucked into the middle of the park. As soon as we got it back they would flank out and pull right on to the touchline. If the full-backs went with them, we could play a ball into one of the forwards. If they didn't we would play the ball to the feet of the wingers, who were very different players.

"Coppell was quick and aggressive. He would go to the by-line and smash his crosses in. Hill was more direct and more inclined to shoot. We scored a lot of goals off him shooting and the goalkeeper spilling the ball into the path of an attacker. Jimmy Murphy loved Hilly – or Merlin as we called him – but he couldn't defend."

The day after Boxing Day, the biggest home crowd of the season so far, 59,726, saw United beat Burnley 2-1, a result that made United joint leaders with Liverpool on 33 points. The *Guardian* joined in the over-excitement, "They can smell the championship around Old Trafford, and the taste is like a drug to United. It drives them on to a peak of performance that keeps going higher and higher."

United drew 0-0 against Liverpool in February in front of another near 60,000 Old Trafford crowd.

"The Liverpool manager Bob Paisley popped into our dressing room after the game and said, 'Your side must be one of the easiest in the league to referee, hardly a foul. As you boys know, football is about winning, but if you can win the way you lads play then it is something special.'"

United lost to Aston Villa a week after the Liverpool game and drew with Derby in the next match. United's only home defeat of the season, against Stoke in April, would prove costly.

"Jimmy Greenhoff was a nuisance for Stoke, and Peter Shilton saved everything we threw at him – that's why I tried to sign him several times."

Liverpool took the lead in the league and held onto top spot. The Reds eventually finished third, four points behind Liverpool and one behind Queens Park Rangers.

United still had another chance of silverware in the FA Cup.

"We had a wonderful run to the final," recalls Docherty. "Exciting victories against Wolves and Derby meant I would have put my house on us beating Second Division Southampton in the final. If I was a gambling man I would have put £100,000 on it.

"I think we began to believe our own publicity in the build-up to the final and Southampton, to their credit, didn't allow us to play our normal game. They had an offside trap which they operated with robot-like efficiency. They had a livewire in Micky Channon, while two former players of mine, Osgood and McCalliog, found their old swagger."

Indeed, it was Jim McCalliog who supplied the killer pass for Bobby Stokes to convert the game's only goal.

"There can be fewer sadder sights and gloomier atmospheres than the losers' dressing room after the FA Cup final," Docherty wrote later. "To a man we were gutted. I remember thinking, 'This must be worse than dying. At least when you die you don't have to get up in the morning and read about it in the papers.'"

The next day, Docherty stood on the balcony of Manchester

Town Hall and told the huge crowd which filled Albert Square that he would bring the cup back to Old Trafford the next season.

"It was wishful thinking," he says. "I had to say something to lift all those people who had come to see us return empty handed."

Time has eased the pain.

"Southampton have a dinner every year to commemorate winning the FA Cup and I get invited. He's a nice man, big McMenemy."

United finished 1975/76, a fine season which had promised to deliver a first major honour since 1968, with little more than the *Daily Mail* 'Fair Play League' winners' trophy.

"The only way to get over the sour end to the previous season's disappointment was by playing games to get it out of our system," explains Docherty.

"I also had my first experience of European football as manager the following season at Old Trafford."

Ajax were United's first opponents.

"Cruyff had gone to Barcelona, but their side was full of quality players like Ruud Krol, Wim Suurbier and Frank Arnesen who had all played in the three European Cup finals that Ajax won in the Seventies.

"We lost 1-0 away, but we attacked them and that shocked Ajax. They weren't used to teams coming at them on their own ground."

United won the return leg 2-0.

"It would have been more had it not been for their goalkeeper, Schrijvers."

On the same night, Juventus ended Manchester City's European hopes.

"Tommy Cav said that Juventus would be the team to beat."

United would find out how right that prediction was soon enough in the next round.

"Their defence was superbly organised in the first leg at Old Trafford," recalls Docherty. "Gordon Hill was the only player who could breach it, and he netted a volley as we won 1-0. But for a team which possessed so much quality it was a shame to see them resort to so many cynical fouls. The victory showed me how far our young team had come though."

Juventus won the return leg 2-0.

"They had too much quality for us, too much skill, too much experience," says Docherty.

United were left to concentrate on domestic honours, but were seldom in contention for the league.

"We picked up too many injuries in the autumn, and I had to promote players from the reserves. I did sign Jimmy Greenhoff from Stoke, who was a class player. I wanted Peter Shilton, and a fee of £275,000 had been agreed with Stoke which would have made Shilton the best-paid player at Old Trafford, but the United board blocked the deal for the sake of £50 a week in wages."

United slipped to mid-table by November 1976, but their league form picked up in the new year as the FA Cup campaign started again.

"We did well and had eight league games and an FA Cup semi-final to play in April alone," he says. "I'd been in five semi-finals and three finals as a manager, but I'd never won the cup. You had to be a good manager with good players, but you needed luck too."

United beat Leeds in the semi-final at Hillsborough.

"A few days before the game, Derby County approached United for permission to talk to me with a view to me succeeding Dave Mackay as their manager. They offered me £28,000 a year, £10,000 more than I was on at United. I told Matt Busby and the United directors that I had no interest in going, and they suggested that we should start negotiations about a new contract at Old Trafford. Attendances were up, the club was financially stable and I was told that things were going exceptionally well. I just wanted to bring a major trophy to the club."

Docherty had another chance to do that in the 1977 FA Cup final against Liverpool, just as he had promised.

"That day was the highlight of my management career," he says. "Having already won the league championship and going for the European Cup, Liverpool were favourites. I had the highest regard for them and their players, but I'd done my homework and spotted one or two weaknesses in their team. I felt my side were good enough to beat them, but we needed what had been absent a year earlier – luck."

Docherty came across as confident on the morning of the game.

"I wanted my players to feel my confidence. Outwardly I was confident, but I was so nervous and distracted that I read a newspaper preview of the match and didn't take a word in."

United wore their normal red shirts, Liverpool their white away shirts.

"I wanted us to take the game to them straightaway, but it wasn't so simple," recalls Docherty. "I had told my players to close them down quickly, especially in midfield so that they couldn't 'boss' the game, as Bob Paisley used to put it. Yet almost all the attacking in the first half was done by Liverpool, and Stepney produced the save of the day from Ray Kennedy just before half-time. A goal for Liverpool then would have been a big blow."

Docherty used his half-time team talk to urge his players to be more positive in the second half.

"I told them that, while we were doing well, we had to do even better if we were to win. I told them to get forward in numbers and put them under pressure."

Jimmy Greenhoff and Stuart Pearson were instructed to be more mobile and pull the Liverpool defenders about. Macari and McIlroy were to exploit those gaps.

"Within ten minutes of the restart the game exploded into action and produced three goals," smiles Docherty as he recalls Pearson's opener, Jimmy Case's equaliser and Jimmy Greenhoff's winner.

"Liverpool were desperate for an equaliser, but they had spurned their best chances in the first half. We had won the FA Cup!"

Docherty offered his commiserations to Paisley, who in turned offered his congratulations.

"In 23 years and seven visits to Wembley I had never been a winner," he recalls. "Life was wonderful as I celebrated with my players on the pitch. I was also delighted to hear the United fans chant 'Good luck Liverpool' to the tune of 'Nice one, Cyril' ahead of their European Cup final.

"We had a champagne reception and everyone who should have been there was there. I had two glasses in my hands for most of the night and I celebrated with Tommy Cav."

Docherty had been offered a four-year contract which he wanted to sign, but he had the small matter of telling his employers about his relationship with Mary Brown, wife of United's physio Laurie.

"It wasn't a case of telling people before I was caught out," he claims, "but I felt that I should tell them that my relationship had ended with my wife and that I was going to live with Mary. It didn't go down well with the powers that be."

"I waited until the end of the season because I didn't want to cause disruption. But I always felt that I would probably get the sack. I'd just won the FA Cup too, and my position was stronger than ever with the fans and media, but I think some people at the club — those I've mentioned — were threatened by that.

"I also knew that if the club kept me on then they were going to get a lot of flak for it, but I decided to come clean and hope that the club would stick with me."

Docherty spoke firstly to Martin Edwards, son of the chairman Louis.

"Martin told me that it was a private matter and nothing to do with the club."

Others didn't share the opinion of Edwards jnr.

Matt Busby called Docherty "a bloody fool". "He told me off for not telling him and suggested that he could have spoken to people . . ."

Docherty sought out club secretary Les Olive, with whom he enjoyed an excellent relationship.

"I want to see the board of directors as soon as possible," said Docherty.

"Do you mind me asking what it's about?" replied Olive.

Docherty told him, and an extraordinary board meeting was arranged at Louis Edwards' house on 4th July 1977.

"The whole board was there, and I told them that I had left my wife, that Mary and I were a partnership and that we were going to live together. I added that I knew it wouldn't be very nice for the club, but that I couldn't carry on with the way we had been living."

Docherty remembers the reactions of those present.

"Matt didn't speak," he recalls. "Louis said, 'Under the circumstances we think it would be in the best interests of everyone concerned if you resign as manager, Tommy'.

"I refused to sign their letter of resignation," recalls Docherty. "I think they had made their decision before I arrived."

"All hell broke lose in the days that followed," says Docherty. "I was disappointed, especially when I see what goes on today. I got sacked for falling in love. The newspapers called it an affair. It wasn't. It was a loving partnership that it still going strong to this day and has produced children who've had grandchildren."

Docherty also feels that the people who axed him were hypocrites.

"When we went away on tour I saw things," he says. "They were hypocrites, but that's how it went and we moved on. Mary has been the best thing that ever happened to me, she's different class."

Docherty had first met Mary Brown in 1973.

"It would be some years before we had an emotional attachment," he says. Her husband Laurie had been taken ill and was in hospital. I paid him a visit, as I would anyone connected with United. On the evening of my visit, of course, Mary was there. When visiting hours were over we left the hospital together and went in the pub over the road and began talking about our lives. I found Mary very easy to talk to, and she felt the same about me, though we hadn't talked about anything personal. I saw her again a week later at Old Trafford. I told her how much I had enjoyed the conversation and she told me the same, so I suggested that we should do it again sometime. That is how it started. On one occasion Mary and I discussed the relationship we had with one another. We also both realised that our marriages were in a rut."

Docherty's relationship with Laurie Brown would obviously change irrevocably.

"I saw him only once or twice after. Once, just a couple of weeks after the cup final, I was in the car outside the house Mary and I briefly lived in. Laurie was living in an adjacent house with his kids. It was surreal. I was about to drive off when Laurie came up and knocked on the window. I wound it down, and he threw a punch which hit me square in the eye. I didn't respond to the punch. I could understand that emotions were running high and I didn't want things to escalate."

His former Chelsea assistant, Dave Sexton, replaced him at Old Trafford.

"I'd got on with the press lads, but Dave struggled a bit," he explains. "They called him the Trappist Monk. He'd say, 'Good morning – but don't quote me.'"

Docherty was offered the Derby job.

"I'd been appointed manager of Derby County, and my side played Manchester United. I shook hands with Dave after the game and he said, 'How's the wife?' I had to laugh because I knew he wasn't happy with the the affair. I haven't seen him since."

There are many other people he hasn't seen since his divorce from his first wife, Agnes, in the late Seventies, either.

"I've got three sons and a daughter from my first marriage. Two of the sons and the daughter haven't spoke to me since my divorce. My other son, Michael, who was a player at Burnley, speaks to me. He's brilliant. Their mother died a few years ago, God bless her soul."

Docherty received countless letters of support from United fans who credited him with making the club great again in the Seventies. Many Reds of a certain vintage maintain that there has never been a more exciting time to be a fan.

Docherty was also criticised for other things – the United board had alleged that he touted FA Cup final tickets. Such practices were common among players and management until the 1990s – even at United.

Docherty insists that he did what he was asked to do – sell tickets on behalf of others at the club.

"Members of the United board received complimentary FA Cup final tickets each season. Louis Edwards had asked me to sell them on his behalf," says Docherty.

That those tickets were eventually sold above face value was an infringement of FA regulations. Fans loathe people on the inside acting as ticket touts.

Still, plenty of United supporters loved the style of the Doc's team and of his ebullient, wisecracking personality, and older fans still recognise him.

"They have great memories of my United team and love to talk to me about it" he says. "And I stayed in Manchester because I love the place and the people, but my relationship with United never recovered. I've rarely been back and never get invited there. Chelsea invite me back every year, Celtic too."

Docherty's relationship with his former club is uneasy at best. He was viewed as a harsh critic of the club in the early years of the Ferguson regime, someone the media could go to for an honest but often damning quote or opinion. He was the opposite of the former pros who only have good things to say about their former employers because quite often they are also their current employers. Former players don't want to rock the boat when they need the income from work in the executive lounges or MUTV. In many cases it's their only source of income.

Alex Ferguson has no time for Docherty because of the criticisms he has aimed at the club. If the main man at Old Trafford has no time for you, then the club has no time for you either.

"He doesn't like me and I don't like him," he explains. "We've met and there's nothing there. He's a great manager, a genius with a great eye for a player. His record would stand up against any manager in football."

But it's not only about Ferguson. In January 1978, Willie

Morgan was interviewed by Gerald Sinstadt on Granada's TV programme *Kick-Off*. Morgan stated that Docherty was the worst manager he had ever played for.

"I didn't see the original programme, but it was pointed out to me that his remarks were defamatory. Criticism didn't usually bother me, and people are entitled to their opinion, but I made the mistake of listening to people who suggested that I should take legal action. Silly me. It was the biggest mistake of my life."

The action would take over three years and wound up in the Old Bailey.

"It cost me £100,000 – most of my savings. Sitting in the witness box and being asked questions was the worst moment of my life."

And yet even when he's talking about proceedings which linger in his mind three decades later, he still raises a smile and a hearty laugh.

"I got in the lift one day at the court and the person next to me said, 'Going down?' I said, 'I hope not!'"

Docherty wasn't sent down, but what began as a libel case against Granada TV and Morgan collapsed and turned into him facing two charges of perjury.

Docherty was manager of Derby County during the court case, one of 16 clubs where he managed. His life there was made more difficult because their local rivals, Nottingham Forest, won the title during his spell – and then two European Cups. Docherty resigned at the end of the 1978/79 season.

"I then took the QPR job for the second time in my career," he says. Three years after finishing second in the First Division, the Rs had been relegated.

Docherty's life continued to be turbulent. Police woke him up one morning while in his temporary home at the Kensington Hilton. He was arrested, but not charged, in relation to financial irregularities at Derby County.

"Never in my career did I get anything out of a transfer deal," he says. "Nor was I offered a bung. The only thing I got out of the police investigation was a £3,000 bill from my solicitor and first-hand experience of the fact that mud sticks, even when you are innocent."

Docherty was still a famous figure, which had its drawbacks. In 1980, while travelling by train between Manchester and Euston with Mary and two of her children, they were verbally abused by a group of youths.

"They sang offensive songs about Mary and me," he recalls. "I was having none of it and tried to reason with them. I asked them in a firm but polite way to stop. They did, but when I left the train at Stockport the same youths jumped me from behind, kicked me in the head and body before running off."

An ambulance arrived to find a semi-conscious Docherty. He was taken to hospital with concussion, badly bruised ribs and ruptured tendons in his right knee. He was in hospital for eight days and advised not to work for two months. He went back to QPR after five weeks, but was sacked that summer, a move which didn't go down well with QPR fans or the players.

"Nine days after sacking me, the chairman, Jim Gregory, called and offered me the job again on the condition that I moved to London permanently and didn't live in a hotel."

Docherty had presided over a decent QPR team, but felt power-less to stop the sale of their star strikers, Clive Allen and Paul Goddard. He was sacked again in 1981.

A stint at Australia's Sydney Olympic followed.

"The contract was for eight months, and we loved life in Sydney," he says. "But I had my work cut out there. There were only three semi-professional players on the books when I arrived."

Docherty did well, and Sydney wanted to keep him on, but then he was offered the job at Preston North End.

"There was no way that I could say no to that request," he says. He started at Preston, the club he'd joined in 1949 as a player, in June 1981.

"The place hadn't changed, and that was part of the problem," he remembers. "The terraces were crumbling and Preston had slipped into decline and were working on a tiny budget."

The perjury case relating to evidence given in the trial against Willie Morgan was still hanging over Docherty's head. But the Old Bailey jury cleared him on two counts of perjury (lying in court while under oath) by unanimous verdicts.

He returned to his job at Preston but was sacked after poor results. The season was only four months old.

The Docherty family returned to Australia in 1982 for a stint at South Melbourne and another with Sydney Olympic. They returned a year later when Docherty was appointed manager of Wolves. He was then sacked within a year as Wolves had suffered three relegations in a row.

"I told Mary that I was managed out," he says. "I'd been in football 38 years – 24 of them as a manager. In all that time I'd never applied for a job. A number of clubs rang me, but I didn't want to go down the same route as I'd done at Preston and Wolves."

Docherty briefly managed Altrincham in 1987 but spent the remainder of the Eighties and Nineties doing media work and after-dinner speaking, which he still does to this day. Of Docherty's style, former United manager Wilf McGuiness said, in a one-liner worthy of the Doc himself, "Some of Tommy's speeches last longer than he spent at some of his clubs." Docherty laughs at that. Football has failed to dent his sense of humour.

ALSO BY ANDY MITTEN...

PLUS:
MAN UTD IN THE '60S: THE PLAYERS' STORIES
AVAILABLE OCTOBER 2013

Available at **www.visionsp.co.uk**